M000195849

THE NEW YORK ACADEMY OF SCIENCES BOOK PROJECT

Science is expanding. Its influence is now global and affects every component of human life. No educated person can afford to be ignorant of this influence and its capacity for creation and destruction. A new world view—a vision of the cosmos—is growing up around science, showing us the nature of the universe into which we have all been born. This view may not always give us comfort, but it has the supreme virtue of being true according to our most effective resources for acquiring knowledge. No philosophy, moral outlook, or religion can be inconsistent with the findings of science and hope to endure among educated people.

A few years ago the Academy, as part of its charge to disseminate scientific information to the public, undertook the sponsorship of a popular science book project. In order to implement this project, the Academy began to facilitate the efforts of scientists and science writers to get their books published for a mass market. As anyone who has attempted to do so knows, writing a book on a complex subject in the sciences that also communicates the excitement and enthusiasm of discovery to the lay reader is not easy. Science books can often either become technically obscure or drift off into superficial discussion that misses the sense of real science. Finding the right balance between scientific exposition and narrative literature is a major challenge. Yet the educated public wants and ought to know what is going on in science.

Ever since the project began, the Academy has been actively soliciting book proposals. We do not try to avoid controversy. We are looking for well-written, scientifically credible books that communicate their author's views. These proposals are then reviewed by a distinguished board of editors and by outside specialists. On the basis of these recommendations, the Academy makes all best efforts to place the book with a major publisher, with whom the decision to publish rests. The Academy thus hopes to promote both the writing of popular science and the development of an audience for popularly written, accessible works on science.

HEINZ R. PAGELS

BOARD OF EDITORS

I. BERNARD COHEN	HORACE FREELAND JUDSON
ROBERT COLES	HEINZ R. PAGELS
FREEMAN DYSON	ROBERT E. POLLACK
GERALD FEINBERG	FREDERICK SEITZ
SAMUEL C. FLORMAN	HARRIET ZUCKERMAN

Messengers of Paradise

OPIATES AND THE BRAIN

The Struggle over Pain, Rage, Uncertainty, and Addiction

CHARLES F. LEVINTHAL

ANCHOR PRESS
Doubleday
NEW YORK
1988

page 197. From "Little Gidding" in *Four Quartets,* by T. S. Eliot, copyright © 1943 by T. S. Eliot; renewed 1971 by Esme Valerie Eliot. Reprinted by permission of Harcourt Brace Jovanovich, Inc.

page 70. Quotation from *Pippin,* "War Is a Science." © 1972 Stephen Schwartz. Exclusively Jobete Music Co. and Belwin-Mills Publishing Corp. All rights reserved, used by permission.

Chapter 1 previously appeared, in modified form, in the Summer 1985 issue of *Perspectives in Biology and Medicine.*

Library of Congress Cataloging-in-Publication Data

Levinthal, Charles F., 1945–
Messengers of paradise.

Bibliography: p. 199
1. Endorphins—Physiological effect.   2. Endorphins—
Receptors.   3. Analgesia.   4. Pain—Physiological
aspects.   5. Narcotic habit—Physiological aspects.
I. Title.
QP552.E53L48   1988   615'.78   87–19557

Copyright © 1988 by Charles F. Levinthal
ISBN 0-385-24067-8
All Rights Reserved
Printed in the United States of America
First Edition

WITH LOVE
TO
MY PARENTS SAM AND MICKEY,
MY WIFE BETH,
AND OUR SONS
DAVID AND BRIAN

Contents

Preface

Messengers of Paradise is a book about endorphins—those brain-produced opiates that serve as analgesics and euphoriants as do opium, morphine, and heroin. It is a chronicling of their discovery and, in particular, the story of an international community of scientists who, having succeeded in identifying them, continue to grapple with the implications of their existence. In the words of Horace Freeland Judson, I have tried to "capture the moments and movements of understanding" by recounting their trials and triumphs. It is also an exploration of the role endorphins have played in the evolution of the brain, from the earliest vertebrate species to the present. The idea will be advanced that the evolutionary development of the brain has depended upon the functioning of endorphins. We have always relied upon these brain chemicals, and we still do so today. It is quite possible that endorphins provide the means for sustaining our creative energies, channeling those ground-breaking behaviors that have gradually freed the human species from the constraints of its biological evolution.

In providing a history of endorphin research, I have been quite fortunate to talk with many of the principal discoverers. In this regard, I thank Huda Akil, John Liebeskind, David Mayer, Candace Pert, Eric Simon, and Solomon Snyder for their generosity and candor in relating their respective stories to me. The ideas expressed here about the role of endorphins in evolution have been inspired by the work of Michael Fanselow, Mortimer Mishkin, Jaak Panksepp, David Pickar, and especially Paul D. MacLean. I am indebted to the help they gave me in providing reprints of their publications as well as accounts of their works in progress. In particular, I would like to acknowledge the help and encouragement Dr. MacLean has given me in the development of an evolutionary overview of endorphin functioning based upon his triune brain model. I hope I have done justice to the major contributions they have all made to the theoretical understanding of endorphins.

I extend my thanks also to John Brockman and Katinka Matson for their masterful handling of the business end of this project, and to Heinz Pagels at the New York Academy of Sciences for having faith in my project and supporting me in my initial foray into trade publishing. I also appreciate the guidance and support extended to me by my editor, Marshall De Bruhl, at Anchor Press/Doubleday. The expertise with which he commanded the editorial process, along with his sensitivity and caring, have been invaluable. I owe a special thanks to my friend and Hofstra colleague Harold Yuker for urging me to pursue the idea of this book when it was at a very early stage of development.

My parents-in-law, Milton and Selma Kuby, have provided me with unending encouragement, support, and love, for which I will always be grateful. In particular, I would like to thank Milton Kuby for serving as the initial catalyst, without whom *Messengers of Paradise* would not have become part of the New York Academy of Sciences Book Project. I also appreciate the understanding and patience my sons, David and Brian, have given me during the long and difficult process of writing this book. Most important of all, I am grateful for the continual love and support that my wife, Beth, has given me, in this and all of my endeavors. She has been my first and best editor. Her steadfast vision of the essential message behind *Messengers of Paradise* has effectively guided my writing throughout, and her instincts and insights have been unerring. Words cannot adequately convey my appreciation for the contributions she has made to the writing of this book and for all that she means to me.

CHARLES F. LEVINTHAL
Huntington, New York

PART ONE

The Endorphin Story

1

Milk of Paradise–Milk of Hell

A HISTORY OF OPIUM

And all who heard should see them there,
And all should cry, Beware! Beware!
His flashing eyes, his floating hair!
Weave a circle round him thrice,
And close your eyes with holy dread,
For he on honey-dew hath fed,
And drunk the milk of Paradise.

SAMUEL TAYLOR COLERIDGE, "Kubla Khan," 1798

At dawn in early May, in the remote villages of India, Pakistan, Turkey, and a dozen other countries where the weather is hot and dry and the labor is cheap, an ancient ritual begins. The petals of the white poppies that cover the fields have just fallen, but the seed capsules of the plants are not yet ripe. Following sunset of the previous day, laborers have made a number of incisions in the capsules, and the milky white juice has oozed out during the night. Now they go from plant to plant, collecting the juice onto large poppy leaves. Oxidized and hardened by contact with the air, the substance has turned a reddish brown and has the consistency of heavy syrup. Later, it will darken further and form small gum-like balls that look like tar, taste bitter, and smell like new-mown hay.[1]

The images evoked by a harvest of raw opium are exotic and full of forbidden mystery. They draw out in us ambivalent feelings toward what seem to be the dark and sinister forces in faraway cultures and times. Who has not looked, with fascination and horror, at photographs of gaunt Chinese addicts, their faces barely visible through the haze of opium smoke? We are at once drawn and repelled by the idea of opium.

Opium has grown into a metaphor for the concepts of heaven and hell. Nature has provided an excellent relief from pain in the by-products of the opium poppy: opium itself and the opiates—morphine, heroin, and codeine—that can be derived from it. The irony is that the freedom from pain and the feelings of euphoria that opiates give us can exact a cost—dependency. It has been long believed that if this process of opium addiction could somehow be understood we might then know something about the reasons the emotions of pain and euphoria seem to rule our lives. But, until recently, we have not understood why the body becomes addicted to opiates, nor even why these opiates reduce pain in the first place.

Now we know why. For the first time, we have an understanding of what the sources of pain and euphoria, the hell and heaven of our existence, really are. This new knowledge is a product of a remarkable series of discoveries, ushering in nothing less than a revolution in biomedical research. The crux of the scientific breakthrough is this one fact: The body makes its own opiates, chemicals that function like opium, and in fact function better.[2]

1. Harvesting raw opium in an Afghan poppy field. (Arthur Bonner/ NYT Pictures)

It is through these new discoveries that we are now able to examine the history of our ambivalent feelings about opium itself. It turns out that opium has been a commonplace and valued commodity by both Western and Eastern civilizations for centuries, with none of the negative imagery accorded it today. During the nineteenth century, in particular, both Americans and Europeans treated opium and alcohol on pretty much the same level. Only since the end of that century has the pendulum swung to what one writer has called the "dark side of Paradise."[3]

Opium was first described in detail in the early third century B.C., but we can be fairly sure that opium was used for at least a thousand years before that. A ceramic opium pipe has been excavated in Cyprus, dating back to the Late Bronze Age, around 1200 B.C. Cypriot vases from this era show detailed depictions of incised capsules of the poppy plant. Egyptians described the medicinal values of the opium poppy in papyri dating as early as 1552 B.C.[4]

Opium played a significant part in the legends and mythology of ancient Greece. In the cult devoted to Demeter, the goddess of agriculture and fertility, there was the legend that in her journey in search for her daughter, Persephone, the goddess came to Siajon, once called Mecone, the city of poppies. In its fields, she gathered a group of poppy flowers. She slit them and a bitter gum oozed out. Tasting it, Demeter forgot her sorrows. Greeks sometimes portrayed her holding a poppy in her hand instead of the more usual sheaf of corn, and the flower often decorated her altars. Opium was used, according to some scholars, in the rites at Eleusis, to symbolize the need to forget the sorrow of the dying year. The Greek word for opium, *mekion,* arose from the Demeter legend.[5]

Helen of Troy, in Homer's *Iliad,* served battle-weary Greek warriors a drug called nepenthe dissolved in wine. The potion could allow both grief and anger to vanish so that the worst afflictions would be forgotten. It is generally interpreted that she served opium. In Greek cities of that time, opium was being sold in the form of opium cakes and candies, as well as beverages of opium mixed with wine.[6]

While opium was prescribed by physicians in ancient Egypt, Greece, and the Arab world for a host of ailments, its medical use could never be separated from its "recreational" use by people without any physical complaint. Its dual attractions made it easy for Arab traders in the eighth and ninth centuries A.D. to introduce opium to Persia, India, and China.[7]

Western Europe was introduced to opium in the eleventh and twelfth centuries from returning crusaders who had learned of it in turn from the Arabs. At first, opium was used by sorcerers as a staple

2. *An ancient Greek cameo showing Nyx, goddess of night, distributing poppy capsules to Hypnos, god of sleep, Morpheus, god of dreams, and Thanatos, god of death. (Courtesy Professor William Emboden, California State University, Northridge)*

in a variety of potions. Later, during the first stirrings of modern medicine, opium began to be used as a therapeutic drug. In 1520 Paracelsus, the foremost medical authority of his day, promoted the use of a drink mixture combining opium, wine, and an assortment of spices. He called the mixture laudanum (derived possibly from a Latin phrase meaning "something to be praised"), referred to it as the "stone of immortality," and began a long medical tradition by advising its use for practically every known disease. The laudanum form of opium proved so popular that, while "opium eater" was the term often applied to one who indulged, for the next four hundred years most Europeans who used opium would actually be opium drinkers, consuming variations of the formula of Paracelsus.[8] There was no awareness recorded during that time in history that opium could be addictive. To this day, laudanum (defined pharmaceutically as alcoholic tincture of opium) remains an official entry in the United States Pharmacopeia (U.S.P.).[9]

OPIUM AND THE CHINA TRADE

Our association of opium with China seems to be so well entrenched that we tend to assume that opium was a part of Chinese life for thousands of years. It is certainly true that sometime between the ninth and eighteenth centuries a new form of opium use was invented that was to become synonymous in the public mind with China itself: opium smoking. Nevertheless, for at least eight hundred years after its introduction to China, opium was used almost exclusively on a medicinal basis (and consumed in its raw state), as a painkiller and remedy for dysentery.[10] Total imports of opium remained quite small and affected a relatively small portion of China, essentially the area around Canton, its southern port city. Pockets of opium addiction existed but were limited to isolated western provinces where the opium was carried through Himalayan passes from Tibet and Burma. In general, what opium there was in China came in from the outside. Considering the immensity of China, the effect of opium use was hardly noticed. As late as 1782 a British trader took a large economic loss in trying to unload a shipment of opium in Canton.[11]

Yet, by the very end of the eighteenth century, the picture started to change dramatically. The English became enamored with the drinking of tea. Domestic demand within England for Chinese tea suddenly grew to tremendous proportions, and in order to trade for the tea, some commodity had to be found for markets in China.[12] Attempts to import English wool proved a dismal failure. Chinese homespun cotton, wrapped in layers, already provided acceptable protection in the winter. From the viewpoint of the English trader, it was quite a problem. Peter Fay, author of *The Opium War,* explains:

> China, it seemed, already possessed everything: "the best food in the
> world, rice; the best drink, tea; and the best clothing, cotton, silk, fur," as

Hart, the Englishman who directed China's customs service later in the nineteenth century, once remarked. To food, drink, and clothing add manufactured articles; for in China, as in India, the industrial arts were so advanced that Europe, before her machine age, could offer almost nothing to compare. What were Birmingham clocks and musical snuff boxes next to the wallpaper, fabrics, lacquer ware, porcelain . . . that poured out of the shops and manufactories of China?[13]

A conquest of Bengal province in India by British forces in 1773 provided a fortuitous solution. Suddenly, a monopoly on selling Indian opium of the finest quality was now under the control of the British East India Company. As historian Jack Beeching has put it, "Into their hands had accidentally fallen abundant supplies of a product which any keen merchant might be forgiven for regarding as the answer to his dreams—an article which sold itself, since any purchaser who has acquired a taste for opium always comes back anxiously for more, cash in hand."[14] Later, when tea became available elsewhere, English traders exchanged Chinese silver for the Indian opium. As a consequence, China paid dearly in a twofold way. The large quantities of opium now flooding the country spread the practice of opium smoking to all of the Chinese empire and extended its use beyond its original medicinal purpose. The prospect of an increasing outflow of Chinese silver was a potential disaster for the imperial economy and a threat to the imperial dynasty itself.[15]

In the meantime, the East India Company managed to carry off the public image of washing its hands of responsibility for opium trade by prohibiting company sailors in their sailing orders from carrying opium, while openly trading the drug at auctions in Bengal and allowing it to be transported to China unofficially in local British and Portuguese ships. In 1799 the first of what would be a series of edicts was issued by the Chinese emperor, banning opium smoking and opium importation. "Foreigners obviously derive the most solid profits and advantages," so stated a decree to the Chinese people, "but that our countrymen should pursue this destructive and ensnaring vice . . . is indeed odious and deplorable."[16]

When it was suggested that a tax on opium might help to reduce its use, the emperor reacted angrily: "It is true I cannot prevent the introduction of the flowing poison; gain-seeking and corrupt men will, for profit and sensuality, defeat my wishes; but nothing will induce me to derive a revenue from the vice and misery of my people."[17] Public opinion in China generally supported the emperor's view, as Confucians believed that opium smoking defiled the body and weakened the link between one's ancestors and one's descendants. Nevertheless, the opium traffic increased rapidly. Canton's opium problem, in the beginning, could be considered in isolation from the concerns of the rest of China: It was a city three months' journey overland from Peking, and mountains separated it from the heartland of China.[18] But the opium-smoking habit could not be so easily contained.

Imperial measures eventually went from decree to action. In 1839 the emperor appointed Lin Tse-hsu to the position of high commissioner, with the specific mandate to deal with the opium menace once and for all. Later that year, in a historic act of defiance against the European powers, particularly England, Commissioner Lin confiscated a huge quantity of opium and burned it publicly in Canton.[19] International tensions quickly mounted, and confrontations between Chinese authorities and the English escalated into what would become known as the First Opium War.

Rarely in the history of warfare have the military concepts of opposing nations been so completely disparate as in the war between England and China. At one point, the Chinese considered throwing monkeys carrying firecrackers into the rigging of anchored British warships, but no one could row close enough to implement this scheme. It is little wonder that, by 1842, British artillery and warships had overwhelmed a nation unprepared to deal with European firepower. An agreement called the Nanking Treaty was signed ending the war.

The victory and the treaty gave England much of what it had wanted and probably a good deal more than it had hoped for. The Chinese island of Hong Kong, with one of the best harbors in the world, was ceded to England as a colony (additional mainland territory was later to be leased to England until the faraway year of 1997); five other cities in China were designated as exclusive ports of entry for British trade, and a large amount of money was paid by the

Chinese government to cover British losses during the war. *The Illustrated London News* in 1842 could boast that the treaty

> secures us a few round millions of dollars and no end of very refreshing tea. It gives an impetus to trade, cedes us one island in perpetuity, and in short puts that sort of climax to the war which satisfies our interests more than our vanity.[20]

The treaty, however, did not end the hostilities. Fighting broke out again between 1858 and 1860, with the British soldiers and sailors now being joined by the French and Americans in what is usually referred to as the Second Opium War. In a treaty of 1860, China was finally forced to legalize opium within its borders. Opium trade continued to grow to represent, in 1872, one seventh of Britain's revenue from India. The Opium Wars had succeeded in opening up the gates of China to the world. It also produced a country that until well into the twentieth century could no longer refuse to serve the economic interests of Western governments.*

OPIUM IN ENGLAND

To the average Englishman, in the mid-nineteenth century, the Opium War was totally a trade issue, of concern to Her Majesty's government but having little or no impact on his daily life. Nevertheless, opium itself was everywhere. It was imported not from India, much less China, but from Turkey and to some extent Holland and France. Enormous quantities of opium, between ten and twenty tons of it in 1820 and four times that amount in 1860, flooded into the country each year.[22] The important difference between China and England with respect to opium was not the extent of its consumption but in the *way* it was consumed. The acceptable form of opium use in Victorian England was opium eating—or, more accurately, opium drinking in the form of laudanum—while the oriental practice of opium smoking was in contrast identified by the English with vice

---

* One of the enduring consequences of this era stems from a personal gift to Queen Victoria in 1870 of a small, funny-looking dog aptly named "Lootie," presented by an English officer serving in Peking. "Lootie" proved so popular in England that similar dogs were soon imported from China. The new breed became known as the Pekingese.[21]

and degradation, a link to the very lowest fringes of society. Opium dens, with all the evil connotations that the phrase has carried with it into modern times, were considered places where opium was smoked; the respectable parlors of the middle-class English family were the places where opium was drunk.

A large measure of the wholesale use of opium in England can be traced to the popularity of a book, *Mysteries of Opium Reveal'd*, written by John Jones in 1700. It is worth noting here because it was the first major work in England to treat opium not merely as a medicine but as a habit. The book's conclusions about opium use were not entirely a whitewash, but unfortunately there was so little mention of the potential hazards of an opium addiction that the reader could easily come away believing that the taking of opium was an acceptable practice when kept within moderate levels. At the same time, a prominent medical authority, Dr. John Brown, educated through his textbooks thousands of medical students in Europe well into the early nineteenth century with the idea that a prescription of opium, particularly laudanum, was the best way to maintain a proper level of internal equilibrium in the body.[23]

With writings of this kind, nineteenth-century England, as well as other European countries of the time, could feel justified in becoming enamored with opium. It so lifted the spirits that the new industrial workers nicknamed it Elevation. Supplies were unlimited and cheap (it was less expensive than gin or beer); medical opinion was at most divided on any potential harm; there was no negative public opinion (an addict was considered no worse than a drunkard); and there was seldom, if ever, trouble with the police. Besides, a host of Turkish or Persian books were being translated into English extolling the virtues of opium. Some of the apothecaries were wary about the trends of enormous opium consumption, but most others were unconcerned.[24] No special qualification was needed for a vendor to sell opium, so it ended up being offered on the retail level along with any other commodity. Records of a "chemist and grocer" shop in London listed entries for ginger beer, paint, turpentine, and laudanum. In that sense, opium was the aspirin of its day.[25]

Nearly all infants and young children in England during this period were given opium. It was given to children on the day they were

3. A nineteenth-century advertising card for "Mrs. Winslow's Soothing Syrup," a popular opium remedy, addressed to mothers and their children. (National Library of Medicine, Bethesda, Maryland)

born, and it was even prepared in readiness for the event itself.[26] Dozens of laudanum-based formulas were sold as patent medicines with appealing names like Godfrey's Cordial, Mrs. Winslow's Soothing Syrup, A Pennysworth of Peace, and McMunn's Elixir of Opium. They were used for teething pain, colic, or merely as a way to keep the children quiet. It was particularly attractive to the new life-style of female workers of the industrial age in the factory towns and cities of England. Historian Peter Fay put it this way:

> They had to leave their infants in the care of old women or very young children when they went off to the mills; there was nothing else they could do; and it was only common prudence to quiet the infants first. One perfectly respectable Manchester druggist regularly supplied seven hundred households for this purpose, mixing his particular brand of "quietness" one hundred drops of laudanum to the ounce, and selling five gallons of it a week.[27]

In the relatively small city of Coventry, the best seller was Godfrey's Cordial, a mixture of opium with sassafras and molasses for flavoring. Ten gallons of it were being sold weekly, approximately twelve thousand doses to be administered to three thousand babies under two years of age.[28]

Out of this climate of acceptance regarding opium sprang up in England a new cultural phenomenon: the opium-addict writer. Opium, it was believed, could be used to aid the creative process, a notion that would prove as erroneous as a similar belief about LSD in the 1960s. The prime mover was Thomas De Quincey, and his book *Confessions of an English Opium-Eater,* first published in 1821, became the movement's bible.[29] At one point, De Quincey declared himself "the Pope of the true church of opium."

It is impossible to say how many English readers started to experiment with opium as a direct result of De Quincey's *Confessions.* A newspaper account in 1823 related a young man's death from an overdose of opium after presumably experimenting with the drug. A physician at the inquest testified of his acquaintance with an alarming increase in such cases, "in consequence of a little book that has been published by a man of literature, which recites many extraordinary cases of taking opium."[30] There is no doubt that De Quincey's book made opium drinking (for despite the title, De Quincey was an opium drinker) fashionable as a way of expanding one's intellectual powers.† The message he conveyed was that opium could unlock a previously unknown realm of imagery for the poet, musician, or artist. To quote Alethea Hayter in her *Opium and the Romantic Imagination:*

> He was like a man who has just explored an almost unknown century and come back to astound his own compatriots with his description of it.[32]

But as with LSD, the advantage that opium seemed to give would eventually be seen as an illusion. Hayter states it well:

> Much of the supposed intellectual impetus from opium is a subjective delusion in the addict—he *feels* that he is having brilliant thoughts and doing difficult intellectual feats with extraordinary ease, but the results

† The particular form of opium drink favored by De Quincey and his literary associates was called Sydenham's laudanum, named for the recipe developed by one of the greatest seventeenth-century English physicians, Thomas Sydenham. It consisted of opium dissolved in sherry and flavored with cinnamon, cloves, and saffron.[31]

are not often shown by achievements objectively measurable. . . . The vast philosophical works which will explain everything do not get written —or if they do, explain nothing.[33]

Nevertheless, a few masterpieces were written. The poet Samuel Taylor Coleridge, an opium addict who tried but could never give up the drug, wrote during the early stages of his habit "The Rime of the Ancient Mariner." His magnificent "Kubla Khan" emerged from images induced by laudanum visions and dreams. Eventually, Coleridge would be consuming over a half gallon of laudanum a week. It is controversial whether Edgar Allan Poe was an opium addict in the same category as De Quincey or Coleridge, but it is generally agreed that he was an occasional opium drinker and that several of his stories and poems emerged from bouts of laudanum.

Perhaps the most direct linkage between an author's opium consumption and a specific literary product is found in Wilkie Collins's *The Moonstone,* published in 1868 and considered by many critics as the first and greatest of modern English detective novels. Through the plot of his novel, Collins appears to have capitalized upon his personal experiences with opium and, in doing so, anticipated by more than sixty years scientific reports of certain psychological phenomena associated with drug taking. In one example, called drug dissociation or state-dependent learning, memories of events occurring under the effects of the drug cannot be retrieved when the drug has worn off but can be retrieved when the drug is reintroduced. In *The Moonstone,* the principal character, Franklin Blake, is advised by a friend to take laudanum as a way of discovering where Blake had unwittingly hidden the famous diamond. The rationale is explained to him in this way: "You may remember, under the influence of the second dose of opium, the place in which you hid the diamond under the influence of the first."[34] Judging from biographical accounts of his life, Collins was as addicted to laudanum as Coleridge, and enormous quantities of opium were being consumed by him during the writing of *The Moonstone.*[35]

Eventually, the literary romance with opium collapsed in its own reveries. In 1870 Dickens would write of the opium addiction of John Jasper, a character in *The Mystery of Edwin Drood,* the last and unfinished Dickens novel, without himself being an opium user. Reportedly, he accompanied policemen on their rounds in London to see for himself the opium-smoking dens that existed in that city, but he never considered it necessary to experience the drug himself in order to write about it.[36] In a similar way, Charlotte Brontë could write about a character addicted to opium in her novel *Villette* entirely out of her personal imagination. In general, literary critics have considered this latter approach to be much the superior one. As Hayter has put it:

> Writers can still write, and in fragments write well, when they have been addicted to opium for many years; and this is not necessarily only during withdrawal periods, though these do in some cases provide the energy to commit to paper the imaginative creation which may otherwise stay uselessly imprisoned in the mind. But the holding-together is gone, the great luminous images which shed light and pattern across all the wide tracts of a writer's imagination do not radiate any more. The images are still there, but some are darkened, some are luridly spot-lit, all are enclosed.[37]

OPIUM IN AMERICA

In many respects, the consumption of opium in America paralleled the practice in England. In one survey of thirty-five Boston drugstores in 1888, 78 percent of the prescriptions that had been refilled three or more times contained opium. Large quantities of opium poppies were cultivated in Vermont and New Hampshire, in Florida and Louisiana, and later in California and Arizona. It was not until 1942 that the growing of opium poppies was made illegal in the United States. Females outnumbered males in opium use by as much as three to one, since in America and elsewhere alcohol drinking among females was not considered respectable. As Edward Brecher has expressed it, the consequence was that "husbands drank alcohol in the saloon; wives took opium at home."[38] As late as 1897 the Sears, Roebuck catalogue was advertising laudanum for sale without prescription for about six cents an ounce. Some of the other patent medicines were addressed specifically to the alcoholic. For example, Sears' "White Star Secret Liquor Cure" was advertised as designed to be added to the gentleman's dinner coffee so that he would be less inclined to join his friends at the local saloon. In effect, he would fall asleep at the table almost before the end of dinner, since the "cure" was opium. If he became dependent upon opium as a result of the "liquor cure," he could fortunately order "A Cure for the Opium Habit" on another page of the same catalogue. Chances are that the ingredients in this one would include alcohol.[39]

Given the openness in which opium eating and opium drinking took place in nineteenth-century America, it seems reasonable to conclude that a large part of the fanatical reaction against opium smoking was racially motivated. It was clear that an intense hostility existed toward the thousands of Chinese men and boys brought into the American West in the 1850s and 1860s to build the railroads. Through a system of a credit ticket, these Chinese immigrants owed the cost of passage to their employer and the wages of labor could in theory repay the debt and even finance a passage back to their homeland. Few of them, however, ever managed to accumulate the means to return. Since most of the Chinese workers were recruited from the Canton area, where opium traffic was particularly intense, the practice of opium smoking was well known to them and it served as a safety valve for an obviously oppressed society of men. In 1875 San Francisco outlawed opium smoking for fear, to quote a contemporaneous publication, that "many women and young girls, as well as young men of respectable family, were being induced to visit the dens, where they were ruined morally and otherwise."[40] A number of national laws forbidding opium smoking followed, while regulation of opium use by other means failed to receive any legislative attention. By the beginning of the twentieth century, however, the social control of opium dens became overshadowed by the emergence of drugs that were seen as more threatening than smoked opium.

MORPHINE, THE SYRINGE, AND THE ADVENT OF HEROIN

In 1803 a drug clerk in Einbeck, Germany, named Friedrich Wilhelm Adam Sertürner first isolated a yellowish white alkaline base in raw opium that turned out to be its primary active ingredient. He called it morphine in honor of Morpheus, the Greek god of dreams. For the first time, 75 percent of the total weight of opium—inactive

4. *Late-nineteenth-century illustration of young working girls in a New York City opium den, part of a widespread media campaign at the time to outlaw the smoking of opium. (The Bettmann Archive)*

resins, oils, sugars, protein—could be separated out and discarded.[41] Of the active opiate products that remained, morphine was clearly the most potent. It represented roughly 10 percent of the total weight of raw opium but was about ten times stronger. All the opiate products that were eventually isolated (codeine, for example, in 1832) were weaker than morphine and represented a far smaller proportion of opium weight.

In the scientific community, Sertürner's discovery was recognized as a major achievement of its time. It was as if the way had suddenly been found to strengthen the potency of wine by turning it into brandy. The most striking advantage of morphine crystals over opium itself was in the purity and consistency of potency that could be produced. One of the problems in administration of opium had always been the variability in its effect from batch to batch. In 1831 the Institute of France awarded Sertürner a prize of 2,000 francs "for having opened the way to important medical discoveries."[42] Yet, within the medical profession, there was no great enthusiasm for switching from opium to morphine in the treatment of patients. Since a chemical process had to be performed, morphine ended up being more expensive than opium. Besides, doctors were reluctant to abandon a drug that had been in the arsenal of medical treatment for centuries, had been emphasized so strongly in their medical training, and had been received so readily by their patients, in favor of a drug that had just been introduced. The medical profession was only beginning to be in a position to react to the development of new drugs.

Slowly, morphine became incorporated in the great variety of patent medicines available to the public. However, it was not until 1856, when the hypodermic syringe was invented in England, that morphine became a dominant medical drug and therefore within the province of the medical profession.[43] In America, the new potential of a morphine injection coincided with the traumas of the Civil War. In his book *The Opium Habit,* written in 1868, Horace Day expressed vividly the horrors that the war had brought to the nation:

> Maimed and shattered survivors from a hundred battlefields, diseased and disabled soldiers released from hostile prisons, anguished and hopeless wives and mothers, made so by the slaughter of those who were dearest to them, found, many of them, temporary relief from their suffering in opium.[44]

It is estimated that 10 million opium pills and more than 2 million ounces of opiate products were distributed during the war to Union forces alone. Opiate addiction became known as the "soldier's disease."[45] Information about the syringe may have come too late for morphine injections to be widespread during the war itself, but it was readily available to those who during this period had become opium addicts.

By 1880 practically every American physician owned a syringe, and the new option of giving a morphine injection, with its powerful and rapid ability to relieve pain and produce euphoria, transformed medical practice. David Courtright has expressed the revolutionary change that occurred:

> The patient, instantly reinforced by the relief of pain and infused with a sense of well-being, would have remembered the wonderful effect of the drug administered in this way and would likely have requested the same treatment in the future, particularly if he suffered from a chronic disease and experienced recurring pain. The physician, for his part, was also reinforced by the injection. His patient responded quickly; pain disappeared and mood improved. Praise was effusive and patronage continued. More important still was the sense, which must have been precious for the nineteenth-century physician, that he could at last do something for the patient; for the first time in the entire history of medicine near-instantaneous, symptomatic relief for a wide range of diseases was possible. A syringe of morphine was, in a very real sense, a magic wand.[46]

A distinguished physician of his day, Sir William Osler, referred to these injections as "G.O.M."—"God's Own Medicine." A popular medical textbook in 1880 listed fifty-four diseases that could be treated with morphine injections, ranging from anemia and angina pectoris through diabetes, nymphomania, and ovarian neuralgia, to tetanus, vaginismus, and morning sickness.[47] David Macht, writing a historical review in a 1915 issue of the *Journal of the American Medical Association,* declared that "if the entire materia medica at our disposal were limited to the choice and use of only one drug, I am sure that a great many, if not the majority, of us would choose opium."[48] Yet there were also some prominent physicians who recognized the dangers of addiction from these drugs. In a speech delivered in 1860, Oliver Wendell Holmes, Sr., dean of the Harvard Medical School, had issued his own concerns:

The constant prescription of opiates by certain physicians . . . has rendered the habitual use of the drug in that region [the Western United States] very prevalent. . . . A frightful endemic demoralization betrays itself in the frequency with which the haggard features and drooping shoulders of the opium drunkards are met with in the street.[49]

The introduction of injectable morphine had made matters worse. By 1900 John Witherspoon, later to be president of the American Medical Association, was moved to warn his colleagues:

Ah, Brothers! we, the representatives of the grandest and noblest profession in the world . . . must . . . warn and save our people from the clutches of this hydra-headed monster. . . .

The morphine habit is growing at an alarming rate, and we can not shift the responsibility, but must acknowledge that we are culpable in too often giving this seductive siren until the will-power is gone.[50]

Against a background of increased worry about morphine addiction, a new pain-killing morphine derivative called heroin was introduced in 1898 by the Bayer company in Germany.[51] It was developed in the laboratory of chemist Heinrich Dreser, who earlier in the 1880s had been successful in developing aspirin (acetylsalicylic acid) as an analgesic. Twenty to twenty-five times stronger than morphine, and believed to be free of morphine's addictive properties, heroin (from the German *heroisch,* meaning "powerful") was hailed as an entirely safe preparation. It was even recommended as a treatment for morphine addiction. From 1898 to 1905 no fewer than forty medical studies concerning injections of heroin failed to report its potential addiction.[52] The powerful addictive properties of heroin, about twice those of morphine, were not fully recognized until as late as 1910.[53]

The end of the nineteenth century represented a turning point in the history of opium and its derivatives. Once viewed with concern but not alarm, opium and morphine addiction was never again to be treated casually. By 1900 there were an estimated 250,000 addicts in the United States.[54] The size of this population alone would probably have been sufficient grounds for reformers to seek some mechanism for drug control, but there was also a growing fear that, in spite of the popularity of opiates among all levels of society, the problem of opiate addiction was now closely associated with "the lower classes"

5. *A pharmaceutical advertisement by the Bayer Company, circa 1900,* listing heroin and aspirin as two of their products. The location on Stone Street is purely coincidental. (The Bettmann Archive)

or "the underworld." In addition, a reform movement was beginning against what was perceived as a corporate disregard for the public welfare. The dangers of wholesale, unregulated distribution of patent medicines, many of which contained opium, was the subject of a widely publicized series of articles by reformer Samuel Hopkins Adams in *Collier's* magazine from 1905 to 1907. Upton Sinclair's exposé of the meat-packing industry through his novel *The Jungle,* written in 1906, had led to the quick passage of the Meat Inspection Act. The Pure Food and Drug Act, passed in the same year, was part of this program of social reform. It was now required that labels specify how much alcohol or opium, as well as other substances, was contained in a particular medicine; opium could still be sold in these forms as long as the phrase "habit-forming" appeared on the label. As expected, sales of such patent medicines dropped in a few years by about a third.[55]

In addition to the domestic pressures, international developments at the time had a significant influence on what would eventually be legislative efforts to control opiate use. The twentieth century had ushered in a new American role as a world power. By taking control over the Philippines as part of the treaty ending the Spanish-American War in 1898, the United States gained an important foothold in potentially lucrative commercial markets in Asia. Financial interests within the United States, looking specifically toward China, sought diplomatic initiatives to pave the way.

The primary strategy was the announcement of American support for China's struggle to rid itself of opium addiction, and in order to show its sincerity the United States began to call for an international conference on the issue of opium traffic. It was a gesture, however, that proved a bit awkward. As historian David Musto has expressed it, "The United States, on the eve of entering an international conference it had called to help China with its opium problem, discovered it had no national opium restrictions. To save face, it quickly enacted one."[56]

The legislation that satisfied the needs of the moment was a prohibition of opium intended for smoking, passed in 1909. It would have little domestic effect, since few Americans used opium in this way. Nevertheless, the momentum was being gathered for the first important enforcement program aimed directly at opiate addiction. In 1914 the Harrison Narcotics Act was passed, prohibiting opium, heroin, and morphine (as well as cocaine, marijuana, and several other substances) from nonprescription preparations, and making the possession of opium or its derivatives without a prescription a criminal offense. Musto has described the public perception toward this new law:

> Passage of the Harrison Act came after consultation with the trade and professional interests concerned, from the obligation of America to other nations, and with the support of reform groups, but it was not a question of primary national interest. Although drugs later became a great popular issue, the passage of the Harrison Act in 1914 seemed a routine slap at a moral evil, something like the Mann Act or the Anti-Lottery Acts. It went largely unnoticed because the question of controlling narcotics had none of the controversy associated with the prohibition of liquor. . . . Almost no one ever used the term temperance in discussing the use of

opiates or cocaine after 1900; by the teens of this century both classes of drugs were deemed in public debate to have no value except as medicine.

. . . The only question publicly debated with reference to narcotics was *how* to control, not (as in the case of liquor) *whether* to control.[57]

It was at this time that treatment programs for the rehabilitation of opiate addicts were begun on an organized basis.[58]

PAIN-KILLING, ADDICTION, AND ENDORPHINS

After the disappointment with heroin as a potentially useful pain-killer, the search continued for alternatives that might not have addictive properties. When meperidine (brand name: Demerol) was discovered in 1939 (originally as an antispasmodic), hopes were high that its analgesic effects might also be nonaddicting. Not long after, however, it was recognized that Demerol addiction could occur. If anything, the new classes of synthesized pain-killers have been seen as more dangerous than any that have existed in nature because the effects can be felt in unbelievably minute quantities. A case in point is a synthetic drug called etorphine, which is five thousand to ten thousand times more potent than morphine and relieves pain with a dose of as low as one ten-thousandth of a gram.[59] There is no question that a substance of this type would be extremely addictive.

Why is there a seemingly inescapable link between the killing of pain and physical addiction? What is there about the brain that responds so willingly to these chemicals? In 1973 the scientific breakthrough on this question occurred. Three laboratories—in New York, Baltimore, and Uppsala, Sweden—simultaneously and independently of each other reported an astounding discovery.[60] While their approaches were somewhat different, they all found specific receptor sites in the brain and spinal cord that were sensitive to the opium derivative morphine.

It would seem highly unlikely that an opiate receptor system would have evolved simply to receive the juice of a poppy flower. The existence of a lock implied the existence of a key (or keys) within the nervous system itself. By 1975 the basic picture started to emerge. John Hughes and Hans Kosterlitz at Aberdeen, Scotland, announced their discovery of a substance in the brain with opiate-like properties: It mimicked the effects of morphine.[61] Within five years, several other opiate-like chemicals were identified with similar properties. Together, they became known as endorphins, from the contraction of "endogenous morphine."[62] The simplest model appeared to be that opiate receptors were really endorphin receptors, sculpted coincidentally so as to have an affinity for opiates derived from the opium poppy and opiates created in the laboratory.

With the development of insight into the functions of endorphins, the story of opium arrives full circle, back to those laborers working in the poppy fields around the world. Long ago, some unknown adventurer tasted the juice of the poppy and the brain recognized it as a creature of itself. By some quirk of nature, that plant yielded a substance that corresponded with something already in the brain. We now can start to understand why opium, morphine, and its related chemicals are addictive. According to a widely cited theory, the brain essentially gets fooled.[63] The chemicals are mistaken for what the brain has produced on its own. As a consequence, the brain stops its internal production and begins to rely upon the external source. As more from the outside is required, a vicious cycle is created. Since internal production has been curtailed, stopping becomes unacceptable to the brain. That is why presumably the abstinent addict goes through the throes of "withdrawal."

Why, then, do we not become addicted to ourselves? That is a nagging question that underlies this entire biochemical point of view. The easiest way of answering is to assume that the quantities in which these endorphins normally operate are worlds apart from the quantities of morphine or heroin that arrive in the brain from the outside. If this hypothesis proves to be true, the next task will be to develop a drug that operates at a more nearly identical level of functioning to the endorphins already in the brain. If this can be achieved, the dream of the nonaddicting pain-killer may be realized at last. We would then be able finally to surpass the standard set by the English physician Thomas Sydenham, who wrote in 1680, "Among the remedies which it has pleased Almighty God to give man to relieve his sufferings, none is so universal and so efficacious as opium."[64] We would finally have an indisputable milk of Paradise.

2

The Brain as an Evolutionary Journey

We might imagine that when the psychiatrist bids the patient to lie on the couch, he is asking him to stretch out alongside a horse and a crocodile. . . . Little wonder that the patient who has personal responsibility for these animals and who must serve as their mouthpiece is sometimes accused of being full of resistances and reluctant to talk; or that the psychiatrist's interpretations and diagnosis suggest a certain lack of training in veterinary neuropsychiatry!

PAUL MACLEAN, "New findings relevant to the evolution of psychosexual functions in the brain," 1962

The cursed crocodile became to me the object of more honor than all the rest. I was compelled to live with him; and (as was always the case in my dreams) for centuries.

THOMAS DE QUINCEY, *Confessions of an English Opium-Eater,* 1821

It is hard to imagine someone proposing that an organ of the body other than the brain might be responsible for the way we think and feel. If we were to speak today of the seat of the mind, few of us would look beyond the brain. Yet it is clear that many civilizations and cultures at one time or another have thought otherwise. The Melanesians considered memories to be stored in the stomach, probably on the assumption that a repository of food would hold ideas as well. Likewise, the larynx was thought to be the seat of the intellect, since it was associated so closely with the production of speech. The predominant view among the ancient Hebrews, Chinese, and Hindus was that the heart was the seat of the soul. The ancient Egyptians so venerated the heart and the aorta leading from it that special containers held them next to the bodies of their pharaohs so as to secure their souls everlasting. The brain was casually thrown away.*

We seem to hang on to a "cardiocentric" view of the mind when we choose the words to express our private notions of thoughts and feelings. We have "a change of heart," for example, when we change our minds. We give our "heartfelt thanks" when we wish to indicate our sincerity. We speak of an inherent characteristic in a person as being "in his blood." The brain does not figure conspicuously on St. Valentine's Day in the messages of affection we send, nor do we sing of leaving our brains in San Francisco. We do not belong to "lonely-brains clubs," coyly insist that "my brain belongs to Daddy," or harmonize to the tune of "brain of my brain." It is obvious that we carry the baggage of an earlier time.

We have Aristotle essentially to blame for all this. Aristotle believed in the heart over the head as the center of life, and his writings in the fourth century B.C. influenced practically the entire spectrum of intellectual thought for well over a thousand years. From his observations, the peculiar rhythmic contractions of the heart possessed the essence of life, while the brain could be touched and probed and

---

* Copies of the Egyptian Book of the Dead were placed in the sarcophagus as a handy reference source for incantations that would prevent demons from stealing away the heart. Later, during the act of Judgment, the heart of the deceased was weighed on Sacred Scales against the Feather of Truth. If the heart were so burdened with sin to outweigh the feather, the Eater of the Dead would devour the heart and the chance for life in the netherworld would be gone.[1]

show no response at all. Aristotle concluded that the brain served only to cool off the hot gases of the body, like some kind of radiator. As late as 1588 anatomy students at the University of Padua were being taught Aristotelian dogma that the heart was not only the origin of arteries and veins but of nerves as well.[2]

Not all the Greek philosophers shared Aristotle's point of view. Nearly a hundred years earlier, the writings of Hippocrates (460–377 B.C.) showed insights into issues ranging from medical ethics to a renunciation of a divine origin in diseases such as epilepsy and stroke. He had ideas that are, even by today's standards, startlingly modern. One of Hippocrates' teachings was that disorders of the mind were disorders of the brain. He wrote:

> Men ought to know that from the brain and from the brain only, arise our pleasures, joys, laughter and jests, as well as our sorrows, pains, griefs and tears. Through it, in particular, we think, see, hear, and distinguish the ugly from the beautiful, the bad from the good, the pleasant from the unpleasant. . . . In these ways I hold that the brain is the most powerful organ of the human body, for when it is healthy it is the interpreter to us of the phenomena caused by the air, as it is the air that gives it intelligence. Eyes, ears, tongue, hands and feet act in accordance with the discernment of the brain.[3]

Plato agreed with Hippocrates, though on nonempirical grounds. Plato believed that the brain's roughly spherical shape and relative proximity to the heavens made it the ideal candidate as the place for reason and insight. Neither encephalocentric (brain-centered) view of Plato or Hippocrates, however, could compete in authority with the cardiocentric view of Aristotle.

By the second century A.D., there were new stirrings of interest in the brain, and a new authority: a Greek physician and surgeon to gladiators named Claudius Galen. Nevertheless, the imagery of the heart still guided his theorizing. Galen saw the nerves as simply hollow tubes that delivered fluids and gaseous material to muscles so that the muscles could expand and contract like little balloons. If the heart gave life by the fluid of the blood, Galen reasoned, then the brain must contain fluids of its own. He found them in the cerebrospinal fluid circulating in chambers within the brain that we now call ventricles. Consequently, the focus of attention became directed toward the brain ventricles rather than brain tissue, an error in judgment that was to delay the understanding of brain function for about fifteen hundred years. Thomas Willis, an English anatomist, began to theorize in 1664 that mental acts might be the results of activity in brain matter itself. As physiological psychologist Elliot Valenstein has remarked, "Galen's 'hydraulic theory' of the nervous system was so generally accepted prior to the eighteenth century that, had it occurred to anyone to stimulate the brain, he might have attempted to use a pump."[4]

Even after the acknowledgment that brain matter was the appropriate area to study, there still seemed to be ample opportunity to go astray. A case in point is the strange history of Franz Joseph Gall and Johann Spurzheim, two German anatomists of the late eighteenth and early nineteenth centuries, who proposed a theory that took Europe and later America by storm: the idea that bumps and depressions on the skull surface indicated traits of personality and moral character. The pseudoscience associated with the study of the skull and personality became known as phrenology.

It is a good example of how a basically correct premise can sometimes lead to a wrong conclusion, and how persistent these conclusions can remain even if they are wrong, as long as they appear to be intuitively reasonable. Gall and Spurzheim made the assumption that certain functions were localized in certain areas of the brain, an idea that we accept today. Clearly not all functions are understood to be localized (as the phrenologists believed), but many are. It was then believed, erroneously, that a localized function would produce a larger region of the brain associated with that function and as a result the skull would bulge at that spot.

Concepts in phrenology were developed in a hopelessly unsystematic fashion. Reportedly, Gall had noticed some skull prominences in local pickpockets and labeled the spot for "personal acquisition." A prominence in the skull of a particularly lively hostess in the community where Gall lived became the location for "sociability." After the introduction of these ideas, it became great sport to probe the skulls of one's friends and relatives and speculate about their personalities, much as we might read astrology tables for guid-

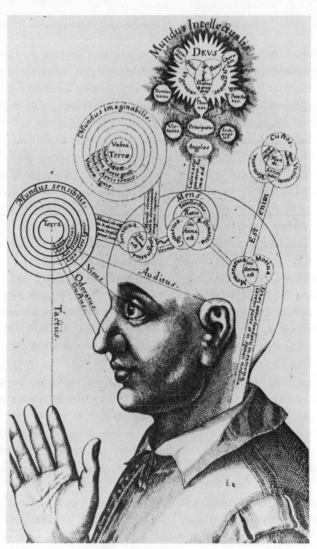

6. The "orbits of the mind" according to mystic Robert Fludd (1574–
1637), who related astronomical notions of his time with the idea that
the brain consisted of three psychic cells. (From C. Blakemore, Mechanics of the Mind. *New York: Cambridge University Press, 1977, p.
18)*

ance into the future.† As late as 1907 bumps on the head were still being measured with great seriousness (now with "advanced technology," as shown in the photograph), despite denunciations by the scientific establishment. The British Phrenological Society did not disband officially until 1967.[6]

7. An early-nineteenth-century parody on the popularization of phrenology. (Culver Pictures)

PAUL BROCA AND THE DAWN OF MODERN NEUROLOGY

Phrenology was an example of a theory, as psychologist E. G. Boring put it in 1929, that was "essentially wrong [but] . . . was just enough right to further scientific thought."[7] One of those who believed in a scientifically based concept of brain localization was a remarkable French physician and surgeon named Paul Broca.

Broca would have been classified by today's professional criteria as a neurologist, but in the mid-nineteenth century the field of neurol-

† The world couldn't quite decide what to do with Franz Joseph Gall. Physiologist and writer Gustav Eckstein summed it all up: "Gall was driven from Vienna as a quack, honored in Germany, died rich in Paris. Goethe was impressed by him but laughed at him. Flourens had no faith in phrenology but admitted he never truly looked at a brain till he saw Gall dissect one, and Flourens was a great neurologist."[5]

8. *Lavery Electric Phrenometer, a "high-tech" measuring device for phrenological examinations, circa 1907. (The Bettmann Archive)*

ogy had not been defined, and indeed the idea of medical specialties was yet to be accepted. His passion was anthropology, the "study of man." He was also what was called in those days a "freethinker." In 1859, despite resistance from the conservative French government, Broca had managed to organize a group of intellectuals to discuss and debate, on a regular basis, a wide range of scientific, social, and political issues. Broca's group, the Anthropological Society of Paris, soon became the champion of often unpopular points of view.

When Darwin's *Origin of Species* was published in 1859, the society offered its public support for the evolutionary theory. Broca himself said, "I would rather be a transformed ape than a degenerate son of Adam."[8] The most memorable event, however, occurred on April 18, 1861, when Broca made a startling report that would mark a turning point in the history of the brain sciences.

On the first day of 1861, Broca had assumed the post of surgeon at a hospital near Paris called Bicêtre. The place was more accurately a nursing home than a hospital, where patients with chronic ailments could be (and are today) cared for over an extended period of time. One of the patients at Bicêtre who had attracted Broca's attention was a man named Leborgne, who had been admitted more than twenty years earlier after having lost the capacity for speech.‡ Attendants nicknamed him "Tan Tan" because these words were the only ones he could utter, even though there was no paralysis of the articulatory tract and no loss of comprehension or intelligence. By April of 1861 Leborgne's condition had deteriorated. Death was imminent, and Broca ordered a confirmation of Leborgne's status for language expression. When Leborgne died on April 17, a postmortem examination of his brain was made immediately. On the very next day, Broca reported to the society that Leborgne had suffered primarily from a deterioration of a portion of the frontal lobe of the left hemisphere and that it was this area of the brain that was responsible for expressive language.[10] By 1865 several more case histories and brain examinations similar to that of Leborgne were consistent enough to narrow down the location to what has since been known as Broca's area and established the importance of this area for a type of language disorder called Broca's aphasia.[11] It was a breakthrough of enormous proportions that would usher in the modern era of our understanding of the physical basis for language. Fittingly, Broca's brain itself lies

‡ Broca had a particular interest in the relationship of brain to language. During his medical education, he had been associated with the few scholars of the time who believed that the basis for language could be found in the brain. It was quite controversial then whether there even existed regularities in brain structure from individual to individual.[9]

preserved to this day in the Laboratoire d'Anthropologie of the Musée de l'Homme (Museum of Man) in Paris.[12]

Today, the technology of imaging the brain is a far cry from the extreme of postmortem examination that was the only alternative of physician-scientists of Paul Broca's era. It has become commonplace (in a matter of five years or so) for neurologists to obtain CAT-scan pictures of the brain of living people that can show brain structures from any desired level in a matter of minutes. Hundreds of X-ray pictures, taken from different orientations around the head, are analyzed by computer, and an image of the brain results. The patient is given an intravenous injection of a contrast dye, but otherwise the CAT scan is accomplished without interfering with brain matter in any physical way. In a newer imaging technology called magnetic resonance imaging (MRI), the use of a combination of a magnetic field and radio-wave energy makes the injection of a dye unnecessary. The quality of the MRI images is astounding (figure 10). No longer do we have to undergo the risks of exploratory neurosurgery to localize brain tumors and other neurological problems.

Interestingly, it is the recent application of modern brain-scan technology that has served to confirm the specific anatomical conclusions that Broca could have made only by visual inspection. In 1984 Jean-Louis Signoret and his colleagues at the Salpêtrière Hospital in Paris conducted a CAT scan of the preserved Leborgne brain that Broca had studied in 1861.[13] The purpose of the study was to test a contention, made in 1908 by neurologist Pierre Marie, that Broca had erred in his judgment that Leborgne's brain was a result of a lesion in the left frontal cortex. The CAT-scan results showed clearly that the damage was exactly where Broca had said it was. Marie was wrong; Broca had been right.

THE EVOLVING ORGANIZATION
OF THE HUMAN BRAIN

If the science of brain function can be viewed as a historical journey of ideas stretching back to the earliest notions of what constituted the mind or soul, then the brain itself can be viewed as a result

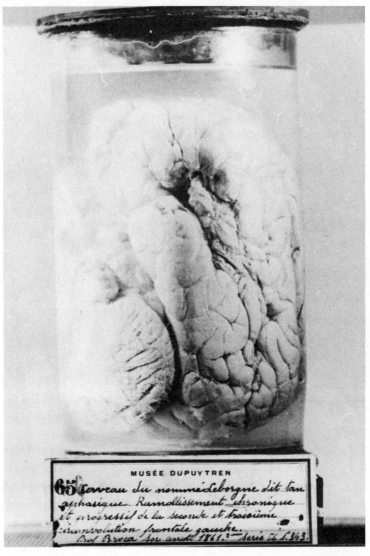

MUSÉE DUPUYTREN

65 Cerveau du nommé Leborgne dit tan
aphasique. Ramollissement chronique
et progressif de la seconde et troisième
circonvolution frontale gauche.
Prof Broca Soc anat 1861. — Serie 76 L 343.

9. The preserved brain of Leborgne, nicknamed Tan Tan, from the autopsy examination performed by Paul Broca in 1861. (Courtesy Francis Schiller, M.D., University of California, San Francisco)

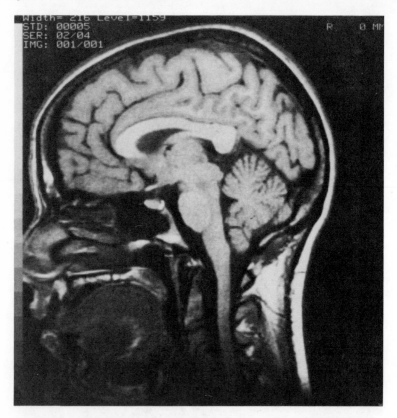

10. A side view, produced by magnetic resonance imaging (MRI), of a living, intact human brain. (General Electric Medical Systems)

of a kind of journey of its own. The human brain is indeed a product of an evolutionary journey stretching back to the earliest neural forms that began to contend with the demands of a changing and usually hostile environment. In order to confront our evolutionary heritage and try to understand how we have progressed to where we are today, we need not look any further than our own brains. The past is all there.

Over the course of evolution, the changes in the development of an organism's brain have not occurred merely as a matter of replacing the neural systems of earlier forms. Rather, the changes have been

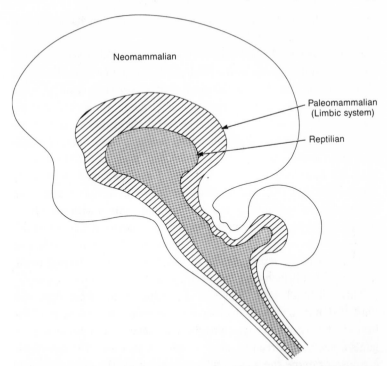

11. The "triune brain" model of brain evolution, as theorized by Paul MacLean, showing the three major thrusts of development over the course of vertebrate evolution. (From P. D. MacLean. "The Brain in Relation to Empathy and Medical Education," Journal of Nervous and Mental Disease, *1967, 44:377.)* © *by Williams and Wilkins.*

made through a series of enlargements and elaborations, *added on to the existing systems,* directed in a systematic way toward the head end of the organism. Brain anatomists call the directional development of new neural systems in the brain the principle of encephalization. As a consequence of encephalization, the present and most recent systems are in general nearest to the front and top, the ancient systems are nearest the back and bottom. It is as if the human brain can be viewed as an archeological dig, where the strata of past civilizations extend downward to greater and greater antiquity. The implication of all this, with regard to understanding our own brains, is that we still maintain and depend upon systems that have changed little in hundreds of millions of years.

Physiologist Paul MacLean—now head of the Laboratory of Brain Evolution and Behavior at the National Institute of Mental Health in Bethesda, Maryland—has theorized that this great march of brain evolution can be viewed essentially in terms of three fundamental stages.[14] The human brain can therefore be considered as a triune ("three-in-one") brain, a complex interaction of three neural systems that progressively hearken back to a distant past. In MacLean's system, the most primitive and oldest of these systems is a basically reptilian brain. The second most primitive is a paleomammalian ("old mammal") brain that is associated in evolution with the advent of primitive, largely nocturnal mammals. The third and most advanced is the neomammalian ("new mammal") brain, associated with the growing sophistication of advanced, largely diurnal mammals, up to and including the development of the human species.

Through MacLean's concept of the triune brain, we can develop a kind of dynamic view of neuroanatomy, seeing the structures of the brain in terms of the environmental challenges that a particular organism has been forced to meet in order to succeed as a species. We can also examine the way in which endorphins, the brain-produced opiate chemicals, have served in this great dynamic struggle of brain evolution. It will be argued in later chapters that endorphins have provided the foundation for the changes in brain structure that have occurred in the brain's long evolutionary journey and in the changes of behavior that have made possible our gradual mastery of the environment.

HINDBRAIN AND MIDBRAIN: STRUCTURES
OF THE REPTILIAN BRAIN

At the top of the spinal cord, neural tissue suddenly widens and enlarges into the first of three major divisions of the brain: the hindbrain. The medulla lies at the point of the hindbrain where this enlargement has just begun. It is in large part a continuation of the spinal cord, in that the major ascending and descending nerve pathways that connect the spinal cord with the brain course through the

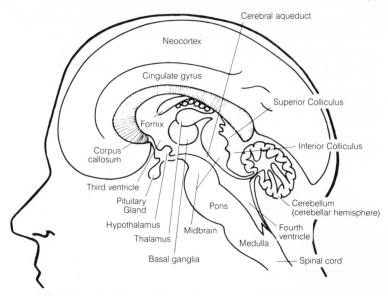

12. Principal structures in the human brain. (Modified from F. Leukel, Introduction to Physiological Psychology, 3d ed., St. Louis: Mosby, 1976, p. 94)

medulla. Cranial nerves that enable us to move our head and control our tongue and pharynx exit the brain at one end of the medulla, while the auditory nerve from the inner ear enters the brain at the other end. Aside from its importance in sensory and motor function, the medulla plays a crucial role in maintaining major biological systems of the body. It is literally the lifeline for any animal. Blood pressure is controlled here, as are the rhythms of breathing, heart rate, digestion, and the mechanism of vomiting. Thanks to all the cough syrup commercials television has exposed us to over the years, it probably comes as no surprise that the medulla also contains our "cough control center."

In general, we can view the medulla, this one-inch segment in the human brain, as the coordinator of the basic life-support systems in our body. Death would be seconds away were it not for the functioning of this basic structure of the brain. The action of alcohol illustrates this fact dramatically. Within a few seconds of alcohol ingestion, the activity of neurons begins to be depressed. The first area of the brain to be affected in this way, however, is not the medulla but rather the uppermost layer of the brain, the neocortex of MacLean's neomammalian brain. This is where the social inhibitions are gradually removed from our behavior. Progressively the depressant works downward toward the paleomammalian and reptilian structures, as if to allow a regression back to more primitive behaviors. When alcohol reaches sufficient levels to finally affect even the medulla, intoxication becomes lethal. The ultimate effect is asphyxiation as the respiratory system in the medulla ceases to function.

Above the medulla, the human brain widens further into another inch-long segment, the pons. An additional cranial nerve, one that controls our chewing movements, exists at this level; the number of pathways passing across the width of the pons gave the sixteenth-century anatomist Varolius the idea of calling it "the bridge" (formally, it is called the pons varolii, or bridge of Varolius). The nuclei within the pons control the cycle of wakefulness and sleep. Lesions in this area can produce extreme levels of insomnia. Since the neurons that communicate via the neurotransmitter serotonin (Chapter 3) arise from areas of the pons, serotonin has been implicated in the control of normal sleep patterns. Chemical inhibitors of serotonin act in the same way as lesions, in that sleep time is reduced significantly.

To one side of the medulla and pons is the cerebellum, a word in Latin meaning "little brain." It represents about one eighth of the weight of the entire brain and lies under the skull approximately at the nape of the neck. A primary function of the cerebellum is to help govern motor coordination, integrating sensory information from the gravitation-sensitive structures of the inner ear and from limb joints with the excitation of body musculature. Serious motor-control problems, ranging from equilibrium disturbances to flaccid muscles or tremor, result from lesions in the cerebellum. Recently, Richard F. Thompson and his associates at Stanford University have identified specific nuclei in the cerebellum that appear responsible for the learning of simple conditioned responses. In this light, the cerebellum can be considered not only as the brain's first attempt at connecting sensory information with appropriate motor responses but also as the brain's system for adapting certain reflexive reactions to new situations and circumstances. The kind of learning that Thompson has linked to the cerebellum is commonly called Pavlovian or classical conditioning. This kind of conditioning is often considered the most primitive kind of behavioral adjustment an animal can make.

Rising above the pons is the next principal division of the brain, the midbrain. As one follows the structures upward from the base of the brain, the midbrain is the last area that retains the tubular feature of the spinal cord. Lying on the front side of the midbrain, there are synapses for pathways that control body movement. One cluster of neurons in this region, the substantia nigra, is known to be necessary for motor control. We see the importance of the substantia nigra in those circumstances where the neurons mysteriously begin to degenerate and patients exhibit the tremor and rigidity of Parkinson's disease.

Two pairs of bump-like structures called colliculi (meaning "little hills") are situated on the backside of the midbrain, one pair above the other. The dominant theme here is not motor control, as is the case in other parts of the midbrain, but sensory function. The upper pair, or superior colliculi, comprise the processing system for vision in a large range of species of fish, birds, and reptiles—animals with little or no cortical development above the midbrain. In later evolutionary development, mammals would gradually develop another visual system, located in the neocortex, and just as gradually, the superior colliculi in the mammalian brain would become dominated by the new (and improved) system for visual processing. Nevertheless, the superior colliculi in the mammalian (and human) brain are still there. Their role in human vision centers on the control of eye movements; they allow us to fix upon an object we wish to see.

Twenty percent of optic nerve fibers from the human eye still go to the superior colliculi, with the rest routed to the new system in the neocortex, just a few dozen million years old. We have since transferred the responsibility of visual experience to the new system. We can observe the transition of power in the examination of patients with extensive damage in the cortical areas for vision. They are functionally blind, but if a light is moved in their field of view their eyes will follow it. The superior colliculi may no longer be able to bring the experience of vision, but they nevertheless are still intact and capable of performing basic reflexive tasks. The eyes move but they can no longer see.[15]

The lower pair of bumps on that side of the midbrain, the inferior colliculi, offer us a comparable story in the patterns of brain evolution. In those species with little or no brain development above the midbrain, the inferior colliculi serve as their system for hearing. (It is not surprising to find that the inferior colliculi in the bat's brain are unusually large.) For us, this area handles sound localization, the ability to identify the origin of sounds in the space around our heads. The responsibility for auditory experience, like that of visual experience, in the human brain has since been transferred to the neocortex.

One final region of the midbrain deserves particular attention. The periaqueductal gray, or PAG, takes its name from the fact that it surrounds the cerebral aqueduct, a tube of circulatory cerebrospinal fluid lying in the dead center of the midbrain. Since the late 1960s the PAG area has become an area of prime importance for those interested in the processing of pain. Electrical stimulation of the PAG appears to cause an animal to feel less pain than before. The analgesic effect of PAG stimulation has led to the idea that the PAG serves to inhibit the transmission of pain signals from the spinal cord. Just how this inhibition is accomplished will be described in Chapter 6.

Ahead of the midbrain area of the reptilian brain lies a rudimentary, yet-to-be-developed forebrain. It is a region dominated by a group of structures called the basal ganglia, whose function is to control movement. The substantia nigra, described earlier, projects to parts of the basal ganglia, and these two areas together make it possible to carry out complex, if somewhat stereotyped, motions necessary for defending a territory, fleeing an enemy, or feeding. It is clear that in later evolution a more sophisticated system for motor control will be necessary if behavior is to advance beyond simple stereotyped movement.

THE LEGACY OF THE REPTILIAN BRAIN

To say that mammals evolved from the reptilian species unfortunately leads to the common misconception that there is a direct line of evolutionary development from either forms of modern snakes or extinct dinosaurs. In reality we have to go back some 250 million years to see a point where a great many lines began branching from a common trunk. Mammals that would eventually include a human species are considered to have come out of a group of mammal-like reptiles called therapsids, who became extinct themselves by about 185 million years ago but nevertheless served as the ancestral relative of us all. One theory has it that the present-day mammals are isolated survivors of a group of mammal-like reptiles that lost out in an ecological competition with the ruling dinosaurs, gave up the diurnal niche, and retreated to a nocturnal existence. In their adaptation to a nocturnal life, they evolved into true mammals and developed the distance senses best suited for the nighttime: hearing and smell. About 65 million years ago, when the ruling reptiles that posed such a threat had become extinct, these nocturnal mammals could now reenter the diurnal environment.[16] No reptiles now exist that are identical to the therapsids, but, as MacLean has pointed out in his writings, the creature with the closest resemblance is the lizard.

We can imagine what the world would be like to a creature with a reptilian brain. It would be dominated by the sense of territoriality, an all-or-nothing distinction between a place of safety and survival and a place of danger and death. Behavior would be a matter of movements for approach or movements for withdrawal; life would be ritualized and routine. With the pain modulation in the midbrain PAG and other nuclei in the medulla, there would be a fundamental no-frills system for controlling pain. The creature could control some of the noxious signals arriving at the spinal cord and initiate simple stereotyped movements to escape back into its territory of safety. The beginning of Pavlovian conditioning, a capability made possible by the development of certain areas of the cerebellum, would provide the genesis of anticipatory learning.[17] Events would start to be predicted by precedent.

The legacy of these reptilian structures remains within components of the human brain. The parallels in human behavior cannot be easily dismissed. "No one would argue," MacLean has said, "that instincts, as generally understood, play a significant role in human behavior. But how should we characterize those proclivities that find expression in the struggle for position and domain: obsessive-compulsive behavior; slavish conformance to old ways of doing things; superstitious actions; obeisance to precedent, as in legal and other matters; devotion to ritual; commemorative, ceremonial reenactments; resort to treachery and deceit; and imitation?"[18] Chapter 6 will take up in detail the question of the role of the endorphins in the context of the reptilian brain.

THE LIMBIC STRUCTURES
OF THE PALEOMAMMALIAN BRAIN

Surrounding the structures just described as the reptilian brain lies a near-complete circle of brain tissue that Paul Broca in 1878 called the great limbic lobe, from the Latin for "forming a border around."* It has since become referred to as the limbic system to avoid confusion with the later development of lobes on the neocortex. Created in the early days of "old mammals," this region is remarkable because it is a kind of common denominator of all mammalian brains that have followed.

From a biological standpoint, the most important change in the paleomammalian brain is the elaboration of an area lying in front of the limbic system—the hypothalamus. Its functioning in guiding motivation and emotion far exceeds its size, barely 3 percent of the total brain. Feeding behavior, drinking behavior, temperature control, and sexual behavior are controlled by nuclei within the hypothalamus, and damage to these nuclei produces gross behavioral abnormalities. An animal (rats are studied most often) might suddenly eat enormous amounts of food and become obese, or eat nothing at all until it totally starves to death, increase its sexual activity to include inanimate objects, or suddenly refuse to copulate at all. The hypothalamus also controls the behaviors and acts we would call rage, as well as autonomic changes of increased heart rate and blood pressure that accompany emotional excitement.

* The word "limbo" derives from the same Latin root. In some Christian theologies, certain individuals would be forced to reside in a region called limbo, bordering the gates of hell. It has come to represent the epitome of being "neither here nor there."

Early ideas about the limbic system centered around the fact that output from the olfactory bulb (processing the information of smell) fed into the limbic system. At one point, the entire region was referred to as the rhinencephalon, or nosebrain. In 1937 neuroanatomist James W. Papez proposed that its functional role lay beyond the simple sensation of smell and instead was a system that formed the basis for emotionality. It has since been determined that three major areas of the limbic system feed into the hypothalamus and in effect provide the driving emotional input that is then coordinated and integrated within hypothalamic nuclei. One of these "drivers," originating in a structure called the amygdala, appears to be involved in oral (food-related) aspects of emotionality, a powerful factor in ensuring the preservation of the individual animal's life. Another "driver," originating in a structure called the septum pellucidum, appears to be related to the genital aspects of behavior, which ensure the preservation of the species. The close connection between the olfactory sense and orogenital emotionality is a reflection of the anatomical proximity of olfactory bulb and limbic areas.

Interestingly, there is a third "driver" into the hypothalamus that relates more to the visual pathway than to the circuits of smell. It is unique in that its anatomical prominence increases during the evolution of higher mammals (reaching its peak in the human brain); the other drivers appear to have remained stable.[19] Thus a part of the limbic system stands at a place of transition. Like the two-faced god Janus, the limbic system looks back to the olfactory dominance of the beginnings of animal evolution, and it looks ahead to increasing reliance upon the visual forms of information that are necessary for a creature to venture forth from its nocturnal environment into the light of day.

The limbic system is transitional in another sense. While the reptilian brain seems oriented to the negative pain-and-withdrawal consequences of its existence, there is a suggestion that the paleomammalian brain through its limbic structures accomplishes a turnaround to an orientation in which pleasure and euphoria can be experienced. Near the side of the hypothalamus runs a pathway, called the medial forebrain bundle, that has a very special property. If this pathway is electrically stimulated, the animal reacts in such a way that the stimulation can be viewed as a reward. As first observed by James Olds and Peter Milner in 1954, animals will learn to press a lever as frequently as seven hundred times per hour for such stimulation. It is clearly the system that underlies the process of positive reinforcement. It is possible that it underlies the phenomenon of pleasure as well, the euphoria of a positive experience in our lives, the achievement of a positive goal. The limbic system, in general, can be envisioned as part of a momentous evolutionary process that slowly repositioned the organism toward (as opposed to away from) its environment. From the joyless emotions associated with the stress of raw survival in the reptilian world emerged eventually the joyful emotions associated with the stress of accomplishment.† Chapter 7 will deal with the role of endorphins in a paleomammalian system that combines for the first time the emotionality of preservation and the emotionality of euphoria.

THE STRUCTURES OF THE NEOMAMMALIAN BRAIN

With the emergence and development of neomammalian structures, we are now literally at the roof of the brain. Stretched over the human brain is a wrinkled, convoluted surface of neural tissue, about as thick as the height of a capital letter on this page. It is called the neocortex, or new cortex, in order to distinguish it from an earlier cortex in the limbic system. Approximately three fourths of all the neurons in the human brain reside in the neocortex. Of these, about three fourths are tucked away in the recesses of cortical convolutions; a total surface of "unconvoluted" neocortex would hypothetically extend over an area of more than two square feet. Neurophysiologist Theodore Bullock has said, "We are entitled to awe at the contemplation of the dependence of our history and civilization upon a sheet of cortical tissue little more than 2 millimeters thick."[21] In the neocortex we indeed have reached the pinnacle, after a long evolutionary journey. If you gauge the length of time that this slow jour-

---

† One major theorist in the area of stress and behavioral health, Hans Selye, distinguished between distress (negative stress), on one hand, and eustress (positive stress).[20] In effect he was referring to the double-sided aspect of emotionality, created by the evolutionary transition of the reptilian and paleomammalian systems.

ney has taken, the development of the neocortex seems to be occurring virtually overnight. Anatomist C. Judson Herrick remarked in 1933 that its explosive growth "is one of the most dramatic cases of evolutionary transformation known to comparative anatomy."[22]

As you examine the neocortex across the higher mammalian species to the human, the convolutions deepen and grow in number. It is as if the drive for more cortical surface had to be satisfied without resorting to the enlargement of total brain and expansion of the skull. Any further enlargement of the skull would not be supportable by the neck, nor would the newborn be allowed down the birth canal of its mother. The gyri (convex loops) and sulci (concave loops) of the neocortex proved a perfect solution. With the new luxury of cortical space, cortical areas could now be established for a sophistication of sensory coding and motor control. In the back, in the occipital lobes, are the primary visual systems; to the sides, in the temporal lobes, are the primary auditory systems. In the human brain, each system has now gradually supplanted the older sensory areas of superior and inferior colliculi in the midbrain. For vision, the new pathway from retina to cortex (synapsing along the way in a specific area of forebrain thalamus) turns away from a functional priority of knowing *"where* a thing out there is" to knowing *"what* the thing out there is."* Localization has been replaced by object recognition. Visual detectability of object presence has been replaced by visual acuity of object detail. In a primarily diurnal environment, where objects must be discriminated on a basis beyond simple brightness, color has taken on great importance.

On the rear side of the fissure of Rolando, on the parietal lobes, lies the somatosensory system, with a newly acquired mapping of the body onto the cortical surface. We can imagine a grotesque-looking homunculus (literally "little man") projected upon this area of the human neocortex, with greater surface given to those parts of the body (face, tongue, and pharynx) whose disproportionate sensitivity appears critical to our adaptation to our environment. On the forward side of the fissure of Rolando, on the frontal lobes, lies the motor cortex, with a mapping of a homunculus of its own, only now it is the disproportionate space devoted to the lips and fingers of the hand that produces the grotesque image. It is clear that motor control for handling and speaking is being given the highest priority.

The human neocortex reveals the extent of another evolutionary adaptation: the creation of functional asymmetry in its cortical hemispheres. In effect, the development of different functional roles in the left and right hemispheres of the neocortex has accomplished more "cognitive space" without enlarging the surface area of the brain. In the growth of neocortex in the evolution of the later mammals it is apparent that two hemispheres comprise the cortical surface, separated by a long fissure running the length of the brain from front to back.‡ Yet until a middle stage in the evolution of primates, the two hemispheres appear to be functionally identical, with information essentially stored and processed "in duplicate" on each side. Communication between the two hemispheres is achieved via transverse pathways called commissures, the major one being the corpus callosum. With the advent of orangutans and gorillas, however, there begin the first signs of an asymmetry in both behavior and brain anatomy. Certain types of gorillas, for example, show skull asymmetries and an indication of a preference for using one hand over the other. It is the beginning of the human behavior commonly referred to as motor dominance.

With the human brain, the most recent step in the long evolutionary journey, we are witness to an explosion of cortical specialization. For most of us the left hemisphere is inclined toward the processing of verbal and symbolic information and behaviors that encourage analytical skills; the right hemisphere, toward the processing of nonverbal and concrete information and behaviors that encourage intuitive, synthetic skills. With these hemispheres functioning in concert with each other, the human being is now capable of expressing itself not only on a nonverbal, gestural level (with behaviors that link us with nonhuman primates) but on a verbal, symbolic level as well. Through the symbols of language, we have managed to compensate for serious deficits (relative to other animals) of strength, swiftness, and size. But the result is obviously more than that. With the capac-

‡ The double, wrinkled surface of the human neocortex looks like a giant walnut, a resemblance that prompted herbal physicians in the Middle Ages to prescribe walnuts as medicine for diseases of the brain.[23]

ity for symbolic thought, we can attain levels of behavior that liberate us from the constraints of biological evolution. We can create an environment of our own making, seeking solutions to problems that bother us or merely interest us. At the pinnacle of neomammalian development, the human neocortex can now consider questions about the mind and how it works, and can even come up with the curious thought, "What's so special about the brain?"[24]

As we will see in Chapters 8 and 9, even at this level of brain functioning, endorphins are now understood to have important roles to play.

3

The Chemistry of the Brain

There is no virgin forest, no clump of seaweed, no maze, no cellular labyrinth that is richer in connections than the domain of the mind.
PAUL VALÉRY, quoted in Jean-Pierre Changeux's
Neuronal Man, 1986

Ideas and images exist in the twilight realms of our consciousness, that shadowy half-being, that stage of nascent existence in the twilight of imagination and on the vestibule of consciousness.
SAMUEL TAYLOR COLERIDGE, quoted in Otto Loewi's
From the Workshop of Discoveries, 1953

At around three in the morning of March 27, 1921, a German physiologist named Otto Loewi was awakened by a strange dream. As it happens so often in the lives of scientists, after repeated attempts without success to solve a problem for a long time (in Loewi's case, over a span of seventeen years), a solution had come when he was totally off-guard. The unhurried images of a dream, that twilight realm of our consciousness, had suggested a simple but ingenious experiment. The events of the next few hours would clearly be a turning point in his life. The insights that followed would eventually lead to his receiving the 1936 Nobel Prize. It would also be the beginning of a modern era of research that has since 1921 given us the basic understanding of how chemicals work in the brain. For Loewi, it was a double dose of good fortune since he had had the same dream the night before, only then he had trusted his memory and a few words on a scrap of paper to recall the experiment. He had gone back to sleep and, to his dismay the next morning, he could make no sense of his notes and considered his opportunity lost. The second time, he left nothing to chance. He got up and performed the experiment then and there.[1]

The experiment in Loewi's dream was to arrange two dissected frog hearts in a trough of salt solution that could sustain their beating for several hours. It had been known since 1845 that if the vagus nerve, a branch of which leads to the heart from the brain, was stimulated electrically, the heart rate would slow down. Loewi left the vagus nerve intact for the first heart and removed it from the second. He then stimulated the first heart via the vagus nerve and discovered that a short time later the second heart was slowing down as well. The only contact the second heart had had with the first was the salt solution in the trough. The explanation was that when the nerve stimulated the first heart, it released some chemical substance that traveled via the solution to the second heart. In other words, the real effect of vagal stimulation was not an electrical phenomenon at all but rather a matter of releasing a chemical. Loewi cautiously dubbed the chemical "Vagusstoff," but later studies identified it as acetylcholine, a substance first synthesized in the laboratory by a German chemist, Adolf von Baeyer, in 1867. It had been known that acetylcholine existed in the body, but more than sixty years had been necessary to establish a connection between acetylcholine and biological functioning.

Loewi's studies demonstrated that chemical substances were the messengers, or neurotransmitters, by which the nervous system exerted control over the rest of the body. Acetylcholine, in particular, was identified as the neurotransmitter for the control of all skeletal muscle in the body (the diaphragm, for example, and all the muscles associated with movement), and shared with another chemical called norepinephrine the responsibilities for the control over smooth muscles (the walls of internal organs and blood vessels) and the cardiac muscle. The tantalizing question remained, however, as to the role of chemical neurotransmitters not merely at the muscular level but inside the brain itself.

A cardinal principle in the study of brain chemistry is that you have to settle first *where* a chemical exists in the brain (if it exists there at all) before you can try to understand *how* the chemical works there. Brain chemistry, it has been said, is a little like real estate, in that the three most important factors are "location, location, and location."[2] Ironically, acetylcholine, the earliest-known neuroactive chemical, has been one of the later ones to be localized in the brain. It turns out that in the case of other substances the task has been a good deal easier.

In the early 1960s two Swedish scientists, Bengt Falck and Nils-Åke Hillarp, developed a method called histofluorescence in which brain tissue treated with formaldehyde was made to fluoresce, or glow brightly, when examined under ultraviolet light. The bizarre combination of formaldehyde and ultraviolet light suggests that this method could not possibly have been deliberate. Like a good many valuable accomplishments in science, it was probably a lucky accident. Whatever the manner in which it was discovered, this method showed that the chemical serotonin glowed a bright yellow. The opportunity then arose to search for areas of the brain that displayed the characteristic serotonin "marker." Areas where serotonin was highly concentrated in the brain were readily apparent. Two other chemicals, dopamine and norepinephrine, glowed a characteristic green, and they too could be localized in the brain.[3] Through other techniques, the separate locations for dopamine and norepinephrine could be teased apart.

The current state of brain chemistry rests upon a wide assortment of localization methods besides histofluorescence, and with the proliferation of methods has come a multiplication in the number of known brain chemicals. Presently, thirty or so chemical substances seem to be functioning within the brain, some better understood than others but all apparently serving to control the way the brain works. Some neuroscientists predict the number to rise eventually above one hundred.

What do they all do, and why are they there? We know that the brain takes information in from the outside environment around us, processes it, integrates it, remembers some of it, and in turn controls a body that must respond to that environment, change its response if the circumstances warrant, and in short survive. The brain handles this formidable task through the operation of specialized cells called neurons, and these neurons are connected to each other in a complexity that is practically incalculable. If these neurons are the processors of information, then the brain chemicals are the languages through which information processing is carried out. As we will see, these chemicals enable one neuron to communicate with another, just as Loewi's "Vagusstoff" enables the vagus nerve to slow down the muscle of the heart.

THE NEURONS OF THE BRAIN

The sheer quantity of neurons in the brain (estimated range from 10 billion to 100 billion), added to the number of interconnections that exist among them all, makes the brain not only the most complex organ of the body but also the most complex known entity in the universe. Fortunately, the basic unit of the brain—the neuron itself—can be understood in relatively simple terms. For one thing, the neuron at any moment in time is either on or off, like a light switch. There is nothing in between. In this respect, the brain is similar to a computer, since a computer consists simply of electrical circuits that are permitted only two states, open or closed. From this simplicity of an electrical switch arises the complexity of information processing in the computer as a whole. From the simplicity of the neuron arises the far greater capability of the brain.

The structure of an individual neuron can be understood practically as easily as its function. The role of a neuron is to receive information *from* outside and to transmit information *to* the outside. The structure of a neuron is beautifully organized for this purpose, through its three fundamental parts: the cell body, the dendrites, and the axon. The cell body contains the elements (like a cell nucleus) that relate it to other types of cells (muscle cells, skin cells, blood cells, etc.) in the body. Extending from the cell body is a group of appendages, some rather short and one quite long. The short ones are called dendrites. Together with the cell body, the dendrites are the parts of the neuron receiving information from the outside.

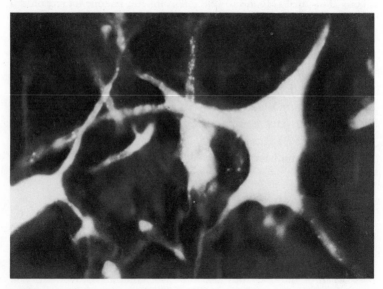

13. Single neurons in intercellular space, images that are products of new techniques in histofluorescence. (Courtesy L. Schmued and J. Fallon, University of California, Irvine)

The long extension, called the axon, is the part that transmits the information outward. It is eventually the carrier of the messages of the neuron. Sometimes a considerable distance needs to be covered before the message is delivered. In one extreme example, axons from motor neurons in the spinal cord pass down the leg to the toes of our feet, a distance of about three feet, making us able to wiggle our toes. A blue whale needs a comparable axon of thirty feet in order to wiggle its fin. The Stegosaurus dinosaur had a brain in its head the size of a walnut and another one twenty times larger near its hip. The latter controlled the animal's large spiked tail, a major defense against its enemies. Fortunately, the idea of multiple brains did not catch on.[4]

Neurons in the brain are special in a number of respects. First of all, their appetites for oxygen and glucose (simple sugar) are enormous. For example, the brain consumes 20 to 25 percent of the oxygen in the body and receives about 15 percent of the blood supply (the delivery route for glucose): this, even though the brain represents only a little over 2 percent of the body's weight.[5] During the first four years of life, the relative amount of oxygen consumed by the brain exceeds 50 percent. It has not been possible to measure relative metabolic rates prior to birth, but it must be quite impressive, considering that, over nine months of development, the embryonic brain gains neurons at the average rate of 250,000 per minute.[6] Second, unlike most other cells in the body, neurons in the brain and spinal cord cannot easily replace themselves. When a neuron in the brain dies (and about 10,000 of them apparently do each day), there may be some "sprouting" of axon terminals of adjacent neurons, but there is always a net loss.[7] If a motor nerve in the spinal cord is cut, there is no chance of recovery. The behavioral damage, usually in the form of paralysis, is permanent. If a nerve is cut more peripherally, however, as in the wrist, the nerve can regenerate and its function can return. We see this phenomenon in recent advances of microsurgery, where under the right circumstances amputated fingers and limbs can be reattached so that eventually there is sensation and movement.*

* An early experimental psychologist, E. G. Boring, in 1913 severed a nerve in his own forearm and observed the progression of sensations as the nerve recovered. It was his doctoral dissertation, from Cornell University.[8]

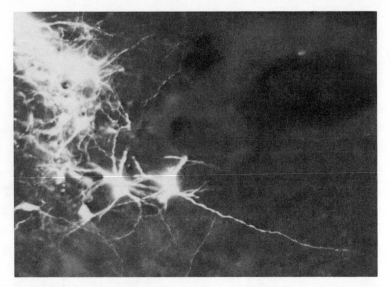

14. More neurons imaged by histofluorescence. Notice the long axon stretching out from the neuron in the center of the photograph. (Courtesy L. Schmued and J. Fallon, University of California, Irvine)

SYNAPSES AND THE LANGUAGES OF COMMUNICATION

Surrounding the cell body of a neuron, as well as all its extensions, is a thin net-like covering called the nerve membrane. This membrane defines not only the separation of "outside-the-neuron" from "inside-the-neuron" in a physical sense but the electrical quality of the neuron itself, a characteristic that is critical to the neuron's ability to function as a processor of information. For most of the time, the neuron is slightly more negative on the inside than the extracellular space is on the outside, the difference being about seventy thousandths of a volt (seventy millivolts). The slight negativity defines when the neuron is at rest (or, in the terminology of the electric switch, when it is off). When the neuron is not at rest (when "the switch" is on), the membrane has changed some of its properties so as to allow small amounts of sodium, a positively charged particle, to stream into the interior of the neuron. The result is that the neuron on the inside is now slightly more *positive* than the outside, a matter of forty millivolts. This active state, when the neuron is polarized to the positive, occurs at a small location in the surface of the membrane, and we call this event the action potential. Within a tenth of a second, the action potential has ended and that position of the neuron's membrane has returned to its rest state. The circuit is no longer closed; the switch is once again turned off.

In the meantime, the action potential has influenced surrounding areas of the membrane to allow sodium into the neuron, whereupon the polarity to a positive state occurs in those places as well. The action potential has spread, and we can imagine an action potential (also called the nerve impulse) eventually traveling down the length of an axon until it reaches the end point with no farther place to go. Animators have created images of crackling sparks moving like a lighted fuse toward some unseen bomb to give us the idea of an action potential coursing its way at speeds up to 120 meters per second (roughly 270 miles per hour).

Toward its end, the axon starts to diverge like the branches of a tree. The action potential moves along each branch as easily as the main trunk. At the terminal points of these branches are small button-like structures called synaptic knobs. It is here that the chemistry comes in, for inside each knob are miniature factories and warehouses (synaptic vesicles) for the chemicals we know as neurotransmitters. Without neurotransmitters, the action potential would sputter out like a wet fuse and the neuron would have no function at all. Across a tiny space of extracellular fluid, however, lies the membrane of another neuron, usually the dendrite or cell body. The overriding function of the neuron is to communicate information, and the neuron lying across that extracellular gulf (we call it the synaptic cleft) is the recipient of that information. When the action potential has reached the synaptic knob, the neurotransmitter spills out of the vesicles into the cleft, and special receptor sites on the other side are ready to receive it. The interiors of these receptor sites are designed to match the molecular structure of the neurotransmitter. When the neurotransmitter has successfully made it into the receptor site, a change occurs in the membrane of the receiving neuron.[9] Neuron A has now communicated with neuron B.

What exactly is the message? It takes basically one of two forms, either a message to *excite* or a message to *inhibit*. The receiving neuron (like all neurons in the nervous system) is continually creating action potentials. In other words, it is continually firing. (If it is not, the neuron is dead.) This leaves two alternatives for change: either an increase in the firing rate or a decrease. Excitation, therefore, is not creating an action potential out of silence but rather making the neuron emit a *greater number* of action potentials per second's time. Yet a message to excite does not guarantee an excitatory effect. The changes in the membrane of the receiving neuron are usually not enough to produce by themselves an action potential. The excitatory message merely increases the *probability* that an action potential may occur, just as the inhibitory message *decreases* the probability that an action potential may occur. The actual outcome in the receiving neuron is a sum total of both excitatory and inhibitory messages from neurons having synaptic communication with it. A typical neuron may have a thousand synaptic knobs near its membrane surface; some neurons have more. Add to this complexity the fact that the receiving neuron itself has thousands of synaptic knobs of its own that can communicate with other neurons and it is easy to see how the idea of many billions of neurons in the nervous system cannot begin to convey the *functional* complexity that is involved. In fact, according to one estimate, the number of possible different synaptic connections in a single human brain is greater than the total number of atomic particles in the known universe.[10]

If the principle of communication between neurons is to excite or inhibit, why are there dozens of neurotransmitters when it seems that any two would have been sufficient to do the job? In truth, we don't know. It may be that the subtleties of the brain are not yet fully appreciated or understood. One way of looking at it might be to assume that there exist two classes of neurotransmitters: "encouragers" (which are excitatory) and "discouragers" (which are inhibitory). In an analogy to human communication, different arguments could exist to provide encouragement (or discouragement), each effective in their own way in their particular circumstance. So it may be in the brain.

We have spoken of an image of the brain in terms of a computer, but somewhere along the line the metaphor breaks down. The superiority of the brain over the computer as a processor of information lies in a difference that is more than quantitative, for a computer with as many elements as a human brain has neurons would probably still not be able to think in the way we do. There is a *qualitative* difference in the way the brain and a computer operate. The computer is able to calculate an answer from known information and relationships already stored in its memory. Its usefulness arises from the almost inconceivable speed with which it can accomplish these calculations. The brain, on the other hand, is able to yield an answer from the use of relationships not originally tied to information already stored. The result is a synthesis, a creation. In short, the neurons of the brain make us able to imagine.

DRUGS AND BRAIN CHEMISTRY

One of the advantages in knowing the basic functions of the synapse is to help us to understand how certain poisons in the brain work. One of the better-known ones is an extract called curare, obtained from a poisonous South American plant. Indian tribes in that region discovered long ago that even a slight wound from a curare-treated arrow tip resulted in sudden paralysis and death. We know now that curare interferes with the action of acetylcholine on skeletal muscle. It works because curare greatly resembles acetylcholine on a structural basis but has none of its functional characteristics. As a consequence, curare binds itself to receptor sites and in effect bars the way for the real acetylcholine to do its work. It is as if a locked door cannot be opened with an available key, close enough in shape to fit into the keyhole but not close enough to move the lock mechanism. Curare poisoning, at sufficient dosages, results in death by suffocation, since the diaphragm muscles needed for breathing cannot function without acetylcholine. Botulinus toxin poisoning (botulism) has the same effects on its victims, the reason in this case being that acetylcholine cannot leave the synaptic vesicles when the action potential arrives at the synaptic knob. The electrical signal is intact, but the chemical messenger at the synapse cannot be released.

Quite aside from the story of poisoning that can result from changes in the synapses of neurons, the most gratifying application has been the understanding and development of drugs that help people with severe mental disturbance. The best example is the treatment of schizophrenia.

DRUGS TO CONTROL SCHIZOPHRENIA

Psychiatric institutions have never been wonderful places, but in the years between 1950 and 1955 there must have existed in them an air of pessimism and despair of crisis proportions. The dominant mental illness of patients then, as now, was schizophrenia, a mixture of agitation, disorientation, delusions, and, frequently, hallucinations. The principal methods to treat schizophrenia included heavy administration of barbiturates and a variety of surgical interventions that included prefrontal lobotomies. The effects of either of these treatments produced a patient abnormally apathetic and sedated. By 1952 it was clear from a widely respected study called the Columbia-Greystone Project (named for the university in New York and the state hospital in New Jersey that collaborated on the data) that a

REPRESENTATIVE ANTIPSYCHOTIC (ANTISCHIZOPHRENIC) DRUGS

GENERIC NAME	BRAND NAME*	MANUFACTURER	CLASSIFICATION
chlorpromazine	Thorazine	Smith Kline	phenothiazine
fluphenazine	Prolixin	Squibb	phenothiazine
	Permitil	Schering	
haloperidol	Haldol	McNeil	butyrophenone
prochlorperazine	Compazine	Smith Kline	phenothiazine
thioridazine	Mellaril	Sandoz	phenothiazine
trifluoperazine	Stelazine	Smith Kline	phenothiazine
triflupromazine	Vesprin	Squibb	phenothiazine

* Some of these drugs are available in generic form.

scientific argument for prefrontal lobotomies could not be maintained.[11] At the same time, the hospitalized psychiatric population by 1955 had risen to about 560,000 in the United States, roughly 50 percent of the entire population in hospitals for any reason. It seemed inevitable that the number of beds for psychiatric cases would soon outstrip the number for all other physical disorders.[12] Yet around 1956 the numbers turned dramatically, so that by 1971 the number had declined to 330,000, despite a doubling in the hospital admissions in general during this period. It can be reasonably argued that the primary reason for the turnaround was the introduction of psychiatric drugs for schizophrenia as well as for the psychiatric disorders of depression and mania. Pharmacologist Conan Kornetsky expressed in 1976 the impact of this revolution in mental health treatment:

> Today it is rare that one sees the type of florid psychotic behavior in mental hospitals that was so common only two decades ago. The Martha Washingtons and the Napoleons are not with us anymore. Also the straight jackets, hydrotherapy, and padded restraint rooms are all gone, and one seldom is overcome by the smell of human excrement when walking in the wards of a mental hospital today.[13]

One of the first drugs to treat schizophrenia, chlorpromazine (brand name: Thorazine), is still one of the leading drugs for this use today. Like most of the drugs developed in the 1950s that would later be used to treat psychiatric patients, chlorpromazine was first identified for use in an area unrelated to psychiatry: in this case, as a remedy for extreme vomiting. When it was administered to schizophrenics, the patients' improvement was dramatic. Moreover, it did more than merely mask symptoms; it seemed to alter the process of the disorder itself. How did chlorpromazine, and the other antipsychotic drugs like it, work so effectively in the brain? Until the 1960s the mechanism for their actions were not well understood. The answer came indirectly from discoveries in the field of neurology concerning a baffling motor disorder called Parkinson's disease.

Parkinson's disease is named for an English physician, James Parkinson, who wrote in 1817 *An Essay on the Shaking Palsy,* a monograph that described the major symptoms. Today, the diagnosis rests upon three major clinical symptoms: tremor, rigidity, and a slowness of bodily movement. The deficiency lies not in movement per se (it is not the same as a paralysis) but rather in the *control* of movement. Trembling is often observed in the hand or foot when it is at rest and disappears during movement. Limbs seem unable to relax. There is a lack of spontaneity and integration in ordinary movements, as in the swing of the arms during walking or in facial expressions.[14] In 1939 a German pathologist, R. Hassler, reasoning on the basis of autopsy examinations of the brains of Parkinson patients, connected the symptoms to a degeneration in a small area of the brain called the substantia nigra.[15] When this brain area was found to contain the neurotransmitter dopamine, it began to seem likely that Parkinson's disease could be attributed to a specific chemical deficit. In 1963 Oleh Hornykiewicz, at the University of Vienna, found that Parkinson patients had a striking deficiency in brain dopamine.[16] His later studies showed that this deficiency correlated with the degeneration in the substantia nigra.[17]

If this dopamine deficiency could be remedied, so reasoned the researchers, then symptoms of Parkinson's disease might be reduced. The most logical strategy, treatment with dopamine itself as a simple replacement therapy, could not work since dopamine in the bloodstream fails to cross into the brain. However, a precursor of dopamine (i.e., a related chemical that changes into dopamine) would have the ability to cross over into the brain and, once it was there, the necessary enzymes would be available for dopamine to be created. In 1967 the precursor in question, called levodopa or simply L-dopa, began to be used as an anti-Parkinson drug. Its success quickly revolutionized the ways in which Parkinson's was understood and treated. Earlier surgical approaches that had been popular in the late 1950s were seen to have been useful only for the relief of tremor and rigidity in general and not for the specific dysfunctions of the disease.† It was clear that the root of the disorder was a wayward

† Public awareness of Parkinson's disease can be credited to *Life* magazine staff photographer Margaret Bourke-White, who contracted the disorder in 1952. In 1959 she underwent a surgical operation in which an area of the thalamus in her brain was destroyed. Her experiences with Parkinson's disease and her subsequent improvement were documented in magazine articles, books, and a TV play.[18]

chemical process in the brain. Today, while Parkinson's disease has yet to be fully understood, the development of new anti-Parkinson drugs still rests upon the idea that a dopamine deficiency is a principal mechanism for this disease.[19]

REPRESENTATIVE ANTI-PARKINSON DRUGS

GENERIC NAME	BRAND NAME*	MANUFACTURER	CLASSIFICATION
benztropine	Cogentin	Merck	anticholinergic
bromocriptine	Parlodel	Sandoz	dopamine receptor agonist
carbidopa with levodopa	Sinemet	Merck	combination of L-dopa with an enzyme inhibitor
levodopa	Larodopa Dopar	Roche Norwich Eaton	L-dopa

* Some of these drugs are available in generic form.

The linkage between Parkinson's disease and schizophrenia had been a surprising one, from the earliest days of antipsychotic drug treatment. One of the side effects observed subsequent to chlorpromazine treatment was the appearance of problems with motor control that strongly resembled Parkinson's disease. In most cases these symptoms were mild and gradually went away, but the resemblance to a known disorder was enough to start a series of investigations into the possibility that schizophrenia was related to dopamine in the brain. The theory went that, if Parkinson-like symptoms were appearing when patients were being relieved of their schizophrenic behavior, and if Parkinson's disease was associated with a dopamine deficiency, then perhaps the antipsychotic drugs were actually reducing the effects of dopamine in the brain. The implication of all this was that schizophrenia could be due to an excessive level of dopamine, and the treatment for schizophrenia would hinge upon bringing the level of dopamine down.

The evidence in support of this rather simple model of schizophrenia in terms of brain chemistry has accumulated over the last twenty years to such a degree that, while there are researchers who argue that it may be only part of the story, no one any longer questions the basic premise that dopamine is a very important factor.[20] On a practical level, the dopamine theory has helped in the development of new generations of antischizophrenia drugs that maximize the benefits while minimizing the side effects. The problem remains, however, that while a drug may bring dopamine levels down, the risk increases that a dopamine deficiency (and Parkinson symptoms) will arise. Two principal neuronal pathways exist in the brain that use dopamine as their neurotransmitter, one associated with emotionality and the other with motor control.[21] If it were possible to "dissect them out" on a chemical basis, it would be desirable to reduce any excessive dopamine in the emotionality system in a schizophrenic patient while leaving the motor control system alone. Likewise, it would be desirable to raise the level of dopamine in the motor control system in a Parkinson patient while leaving the emotionality system alone. This scenario has yet to be realized, and, until then, the treatment of schizophrenia and the potential for a loss of motor control will be closely linked.

DRUGS TO CONTROL DEPRESSION AND MANIA

Any survey of history can show many examples of psychopathic personalities who have wrought havoc upon society and served as catalysts for some of the darker moments of civilization. It is less obvious that some of the heroes (or at least more benign figures) of history have suffered from another type of mental disorder: depression. Descriptions of depression date back to the fourth century B.C. in the writing of Hippocrates, making it probably the earliest account of any psychiatric condition. The Roman emperor Tiberius and Louis XI of France are among the famous depressives of history. More recently, Abraham Lincoln, who suffered periodic bouts of severe depression, would write, "If what I feel were equally distributed to the whole human family, there would not be one cheerful face on earth."[22] Winston Churchill would refer to his "mad dogs of depression."[23] The feelings of hopelessness and worthlessness, with the disturbances of sleep and appetite, that constitute the symptoms of depression make it a devastating phenomenon. As one pharmacologist has put it, "Feelings of sadness are a common human experience, but for some the extent of the sadness is a pit of deep depression that is beyond the range of normal experience."[24]

REPRESENTATIVE ANTIDEPRESSANT DRUGS

GENERIC NAME	BRAND NAME*	MANUFACTURER	CLASSIFICATION
amitriptyline	Elavil Endep	Merck Roche	tricyclic
desipramine	Norpramin Pertofrane	Merrell Dow USV	tricyclic
imipramine	Tofranil Janimine	Geigy Abbott	tricyclic
isocarboxazid	Marplan	Roche	MAO-inhibitor
tranylcypromine	Parnate	Smith Kline	MAO-inhibitor

* Some of the drugs are available in generic form.

REPRESENTATIVE ANTIMANIA OR ANTIMANIC-DEPRESSIVE DRUGS

GENERIC NAME	BRAND NAME*	MANUFACTURER
lithium carbonate	Eskalith Lithane	Smith Kline Miles

* Some of these drugs are available in generic form.

Historically, the pharmacological remedy for depression has been alcohol. It does, of course, produce a temporary feeling of euphoria and does appear to be a temporary stimulant, but in fact it is a brain depressant, and studies have shown that alcohol has no long-term effect on depression other than to provide another problem to worry about. Stimulants such as amphetamines have been available since before the 1950s, but they have addictive properties and undesirable physical side effects.

The first antidepressant drug was, like chlorpromazine first introduced for a nonpsychiatric purpose: in this case as a treatment for tuberculosis. Its name was iproniazid (brand name: Marsilid). The elevation of mood in patients treated with iproniazid at first was attributed to the improvement in the tuberculosis rather than anything associated with the brain.[25] We know now that iproniazid and similar antidepressants developed in this period were inhibitors of an enzyme called monoamine oxidase (MAO). Since MAO exists in the brain to break down the neurotransmitters norepinephrine and serotonin, it was soon conjectured that antidepressants like MAO-inhibitors worked because they allowed these neurotransmitters to rise. In other words, iproniazid was inhibiting an inhibitor, with the effect of this "double negative" being equivalent to a positive. Depression itself was then considered to be some combination of a low level of norepinephrine and a low level of serotonin in the brain.

On a practical level, however, MAO-inhibitors have had to be used with great caution, because MAO acts as an enzyme in other places in the body besides the brain. In the liver, MAO serves the useful function of breaking down a dietary amino acid called tyramine; an elevation in tyramine can produce highly toxic effects. When taking the MAO-inhibitor medication, the patient has to be very careful to avoid foods that contain large amounts of tyramine: certain fermented cheeses, chicken livers, certain wines, and pickled herring, to name a few of the foods on the "caution" list. The potential side effect is a severe rise in blood pressure and the risk of a stroke. As a consequence, there has been only limited use of MAO-inhibitors for controlling depression. Iproniazid itself has been withdrawn from the market, due to its side-effect problems. Other MAO-inhibitors, like tranylcypromine (brand name: Parnate), have been restricted to use only with closely watched depressed patients. Eventually a new class of antidepressants was developed that served to raise the levels of norepinephrine and serotonin in the brain without interfering with the functions of MAO. These drugs, called the tricyclic antidepressants, include imipramine (brand name: Tofranil) and amitriptyline (brand name: Elavil), to name just the most prominent examples.

Imipramine appears to act predominantly on serotonin, and amitriptyline on norepinephrine, though both neurotransmitters rise with use of both drugs.[26] The distinction is important because depressives often respond better to one tricyclic drug than another. It may be, as some have argued, that there are two subtypes of depression, similar enough in behavioral terms to be indistinguishable by even the best clinician but separable in terms of brain chemistry. One subtype might be the result of a serotonin deficiency; the other, of a norepinephrine deficiency.[27]

The urgency in understanding the possible subtypes of depression is easily seen in the current work on a serotonin linkage to suicide. It has been recently found that a lower level of serotonin activity is found in the brains of suicides than in individuals who have died by other means.[28] However, lower serotonin levels have also been observed in the brains of highly aggressive and impulsive personalities, a parallel that has led National Institute of Mental Health (NIMH) psychiatrist Frederick K. Goodwin to speculate that "suicide is a reflection of not just depression, but of some kind of interaction of depression with aggression and impulsivity."[29] The task ahead would be to develop specific antidepressant medication for a high-suicide-risk population that focused upon a serotonin deficiency.

DRUGS TO CONTROL ANXIETY

If the 1950s became known as "the age of anxiety," it is then appropriate that this period also was marked by the development of tranquilizers (or as they are more precisely called today, antianxiety drugs). The first drug, meprobamate (brand name: Miltown), was synthesized in 1951 as a muscle relaxant, and its effect on anxiety was realized a few years later. It was an important breakthrough, since anxiety had been treated previously only through barbiturate sedation. Meprobamate is still prescribed today, often for insomnia, but it has since been overshadowed by a newer class of drugs called the benzodiazepines. The best-known examples are chlordiazepoxide (brand name: Librium) and diazepam (brand name: Valium). Since their introduction in the early 1960s, the sales of both of these drugs have grown to enormous proportions, current prescriptions totaling more than 100 million per year worldwide. It has been estimated that between 10 and 20 percent of all adults in the Western world consume antianxiety drugs on a fairly regular basis.[30] Until 1981, Valium alone was the best-selling prescription drug of any kind (including

REPRESENTATIVE ANTIANXIETY DRUGS

GENERIC NAME	BRAND NAME*	MANUFACTURER	CLASSIFICATION
alprazolam	Xanax	Upjohn	benzodiazepine
chlordiazepoxide	Librium	Roche	benzodiazepine
clorazepate	Tranxene	Abbott	benzodiazepine
diazepam	Valium	Roche	benzodiazepine
meprobamate	Miltown	Wallace	propanediol
	Equanil	Wyeth	

* Some of the drugs are available in generic form.

antibiotics) in modern history.‡ In that year, the intestinal-ulcer drug called Tagamet replaced Valium as number one. It is interesting and important to note that Valium's successor is also related to the burden of stress in a modern society.

The chemical basis for antianxiety drugs has been focused on a neurotransmitter called gamma aminobutyric acid (GABA), one of the inhibitory neurotransmitters in the brain. It appears that these drugs enhance the activity of GABA and produce an increase in some kind of inhibitory control. We have recently learned that there are receptors in the brain that are specific to diazepam, dubbed "Valium receptors" by the popular press. Evidently, the potency of a wide range of antianxiety drugs in relieving anxiety closely parallels the drugs' ability to fit into these particular receptor sites in the brain.[31] It appears then that the brain has special receptors for drugs that reduce anxiety. If the receptors exist, could there be a chemical in our brains that serves as a natural tranquilizer? It turns out that there has been isolation of a natural substance that is associated with these receptors but its effect induces rather than relieves anxiety. Researchers at the NIMH laboratories recently identified a "diazepam-binding inhibitor," produced in the brain, whose function may be to counteract GABA's inhibitory effects.[32] While it may be disappointing that we do not have (or at least it has not yet been found that we have) a natural tranquilizer in the brain, it makes sense in the context of evolution that a brain chemical may be specifi-

‡ Valium was approved in 1985 for marketing in its generic form of diazepam, thus ending Roche's exclusive rights to its distribution and sales.

cally anxiogenic (anxiety producing). As researcher Phil Skolnick has expressed it, "We probably wouldn't be here if our ancestors hadn't had a little bit of anxiety."[33]

BRAIN CHEMISTRY AND THE FUTURE

It is obvious that while the strides that have been taken in the last thirty years have been enormous, we are still far from a complete understanding of mental disorders in terms of brain chemistry. It seems quite unlikely that one or even two neurotransmitters in the brain will be found to be responsible for a particular array of behaviors as complex as a mental illness. As one researcher has put it, "A few years ago everybody was running around battling for his sacred neurotransmitter. There was the cholinergic theory, the dopamine theory, the serotonin theory—but life is just not that simple. No neurotransmitter ever acts in isolation."[34] Already, it is clear that neurotransmitters interact with each other and it is their combinational effects that serve best to explain the effectiveness of a particular therapeutic drug or the variability in a patient's symptoms. "Schizophrenia may be like mental retardation," psychiatrist Richard Haier has said, "with many identifiable causes. It may be 30 percent of schizophrenics have a dopamine disease, and that 30 percent have something else wrong—perhaps a nutritional disorder. Maybe 10 percent have brain damage."[35] So much remains to be known.

Undoubtedly, a major advance in the field of brain chemistry has been the discovery of substances called brain peptides. So revolutionary has been the impact of this newly opened territory on neuroscience research that one pharmacologist has likened it to the discovery of America.[36] Unlike acetylcholine, dopamine, and the other "classic" chemicals that have a complex molecular structure, peptides are simply chains of amino acids strung together in a linear arrangement. There are a few dozen brain peptides presently isolated that serve as messengers of information; one prediction is that there may be more than one hundred. It is an embarrassment of riches, and a tremendous challenge. Some of these peptides, as we will see, have turned out to be our own internal opiates.

4

Days of Discovery: 1971–1973

. . . *it's smarter to be lucky than it's lucky to be smart.*

STEPHEN SCHWARTZ, *Pippin,* 1972

In the fields of observation, chance favors only the mind that is prepared.

RENÉ VALLERY-RADOT, *The Life of Pasteur,* 1900

Popular ideas about how modern science works are often built more upon myth than reality. There is the well-ingrained image, to quote one writer, "of the scientist in the aseptic white coat, the emotionless automaton who sits in his laboratory and with equal detachment watches rats drown or run mazes."[1] Here, scientific discovery is conceived as a linear process, exceedingly boring, where fact A leads to fact B then finally to discovery C. At the opposite extreme, we imagine an episode of high drama in which a discovery comes into being out of a seeming vacuum, the ideas guided as if by divine intervention. The reality of science is that scientists are neither coldly objective about their work nor unmoved by the excitement of doing something really important. They are also not unmindful of the possibility that someday they could be, in their own community of scholars or for that matter the world at large, household names. The prize of recognition, the dream of someday being "the one who . . . ," is the food that feeds the emptiness of frustration and disappointment along the way. They are as ambitious and competitive in their own careers as young executives eyeing the rungs of the corporate ladder. Science itself is a product of a cast of many thousands, with a million interconnections, and the origins of a scientific discovery are most often complex and controversial.

Occasionally books come along that provide a window into the reality of science and scientists themselves. Probably the most famous one is *The Double Helix,* published in 1968, by James Watson, Nobel laureate for his co-discovery (along with Francis Crick and Maurice Wilkins) of the structure of the DNA molecule. It was the first time that someone so prominent in the scientific community wrote about his colleagues not only as scientists but also as *personalities.* The book was clearly a sensation as well as a popular success. A number of those described in the book were fiercely annoyed. When shown a draft of the manuscript in 1967, Crick wrote angrily:

> Should you persist in regarding your book as history I should add that it shows such a naive and egotistical view of the subject as to be scarcely credible. Anything with any intellectual content, including matters which were of central importance to us at the time, is skipped over or omitted.[2]

Watson's opening *The Double Helix* with the line "I have never seen Francis Crick in a modest mood"[3] hardly helped. Watson's intention, however, was to convey the sense of excitement and competition of the time. A new field of research, molecular biology, was being born. The structure of the DNA molecule was a formidable problem that was on the verge of being solved, and, since DNA in many ways seemed to represent life itself, it was widely felt that the solution would be considered worthy of a Nobel Prize.

The struggle for discovery even took on a kind of David-and-Goliath feeling. Here were Watson, an American biologist on a post-doctoral fellowship, arriving in Cambridge, England, in the fall of 1951 at the age of twenty-three, and Crick, eleven years Watson's senior but yet to earn a Ph.D. Up against them was Linus Pauling, a giant in the field of physical chemistry and a world-renowned figure of science, whose achievements in almost thirty years at the California Institute of Technology (he had joined the faculty at the tender age of twenty-one) would earn him a Nobel Prize for chemistry in 1954.[4] Competition was indeed the key factor in those events of 1951 to 1953. In an interview with Watson in 1971 for the book *The Eighth Day of Creation,* Horace Freeland Judson relates Watson's personal view of the role that competition played in the race for DNA:

> I [Judson] remarked that some former colleagues say *The Double Helix* exaggerated the competitiveness of science. Watson's manner changed. He bit the words out sharply. "I probably understated it. It is *the dominant motive* in science. It starts at the beginning: if you publish first, you become a professor first; your future depends on some indication that you can do something by yourself. It's that simple. Competitiveness is very, very dominant. The chief emotion in the field. The second is you have to prove to yourself that you can do it—and that's the same thing. You've got to keep doing it; you can't just—once."[5]

In a recent book, *The Nobel Duel,* Nicholas Wade relates a famous case in which the competition in science turned bitter and hostile: the rivalry between biochemists Roger Guillemin and Andrew Schally and their race to discover the identity of the hypothalamic hormones that control the pituitary gland. It was a struggle that spanned more than twenty years and was marked by angry accusations and mutual dislike. Often information from each of the laboratories would be withheld from scientific meetings—a practice more characteristic of industrial laboratories than of basic research centers—for fear of alerting "the opposition" to a fruitful advance.[6] In the end, both Guillemin and Schally achieved their goal, one winning the race over the other by a matter of days. In 1977 they shared the Nobel Prize that they had coveted for so long, but as Wade reflects, even that international achievement was not enough. "Fierce ambitions are seldom fully sated. In attaining even that award, they were denied the victory that each also craved, the final triumph over the other."[7]

In a number of significant ways, the atmosphere in 1970 was identical to that of molecular biology in 1950. The competitiveness and ambitions were all there; the excitement was no less intense. And just as the new field of molecular biology had brought together physicists, chemists, geneticists, and biologists for the first time, a new hybrid of research had been formed as the neurosciences—an amalgam of pharmacologists, psychiatrists, psychologists, endocrinologists, biochemists, and others—joined in a collaborative effort to study the functioning of the human brain. We will see that as late as the early months of 1973, major laboratories were working on essentially the same problem—the possible existence of an opiate receptor —with a total lack of awareness of the work going on in other laboratories. It was as if a broad river were about to be created seemingly overnight from a number of isolated streams that were now flowing along as completely independent entities.*

This chapter is the story of the major discoveries in opiate research in terms of those streams that eventually combined to create neuroscience. A good beginning is the set of events that led to the announcements in 1973 from researchers at three major laboratories: Candace Pert and her mentor Solomon Snyder at the Johns Hopkins University; Eric Simon at the New York University Medical Center; and Lars Terenius at Uppsala University in Sweden. All can claim to be discoverers of the opiate receptor.

* A good illustration of how quickly the concept of the neurosciences took hold can be seen in terms of the professional organization that sprang up as its representative. In 1970 the Society for Neuroscience was formed with an initial membership of just over 200. By 1986 its membership had grown to more than 10,000. Its annual meeting in Washington, D.C., was attended by nearly 12,000 people. Approximately 13,000 papers and 4,900 poster presentations were listed in the program.

A FOUNDATION FOR DISCOVERY: THE IDEAS
OF AVRAM GOLDSTEIN

Well before 1973 it was assumed that an opiate receptor *should* exist. There was no question about the idea that opiates ought to work in the nervous system by virtue of attaching themselves as molecules to a receptor that, for some reason or another, was constructed so that an opiate could "fit in." The metaphor of a key and lock (or hand and glove) was commonly used to illustrate the basic principle.

One line of evidence arose from the crop of synthetic opiates being created in the laboratories of pharmaceutical companies during the 1960s. Probably the most dramatic example to this day is called etorphine, first synthesized by American Cyanamide. While it has a molecular structure similar to morphine's, etorphine has a tremendously greater potency, from 5,000 to 10,000 times as great. A dose of etorphine can be effective in an amount of less than one ten-thousandths of a gram. Even LSD-25, often considered among the most powerful psychoactive drugs, requires a higher dose to be effective. With such small doses involved in the case of etorphine and other related drugs, it was reasonable to think that highly specific receptors in the brain must be involved.

And yet, as late as 1968, there were those who thought that the discovery of receptors in the brain could never be actually accomplished. In a highly influential textbook on the study of drugs, Stanford University pharmacologist Avram Goldstein (along with Lewis Aronow and Sumner Kalman) reflected upon the prevailing view among scientists in the field: "Some think that receptors of this type may be impossible, in principle, to be isolated. If separated from the integrated system of which they are a part, they would lose all function, it is argued, and could not even be identified as receptors any longer. Only future research will tell if such pessimism is warranted."[8] In about three years, however, the picture suddenly looked much brighter. Ironically, the turnaround was due to the efforts of the person who had voiced such pessimism in the first place. In August of 1971 Goldstein and two of his colleagues published an article in the *Proceedings of the National Academy of Sciences* that contained a remarkable solution to the problem.[9] Goldstein proposed an ingeniously simple experiment. His proposal was based upon a characteristic feature of opiates that had been known since 1954, when the structure of the morphine molecule was beginning to be understood.[10] This feature is called stereospecificity.

Stereospecificity, as a concept, originates from the observation that some opiate drugs have powerful behavioral effects (reducing pain, producing euphoria), while others are either very weak or have no effect at all. The difference seems to depend not only upon the type of atoms in the opiate molecule but, more important, upon the spatial arrangements of atoms in relation to each other within the molecule. Figure 15 shows two forms, or isomers, of morphine: the one on the left being the active form (having all the functional properties of morphine); the one on the right being totally inactive (having none of the functional properties). It is possible to distinguish the two isomers, without seeing the atoms directly, by projecting a beam of polarized light on the substance; each isomer will cause the light to rotate from its polarized plane toward one direction or the other. If the light rotates to the left, the molecule is called the levorotational isomer (levo meaning "to the left"); if the light rotates to the right, it is called the dextrorotational isomer (dextro meaning "to the right"). In the case of morphine, the levo or L-form is the functional one, while the dextro or R-form is not.† The fact that the isomeric form can be so crucial is usually referred to as stereospecificity. It is as if a receptor existed that, like a left-handed glove, could tell the difference between a left hand that fit and a right hand that did not.

The design of Goldstein's experiment followed directly upon the stereospecificity idea. First, you would homogenize whatever you thought might contain opiate receptors (a section of animal brain, for example). Then you would take two isomeric forms of an opiate, one being an active analgesic and the other being inactive and a mirror image of the first. Goldstein used levorphanol (a powerful, synthetic analgesic drug) and its mirror image, dextrorphan (a decent cough

---

† Amphetamines yield another example of stereospecificity. D-amphetamine (the dextro isomer of it) is the form of amphetamine that is powerful. L-amphetamine is considerably less so.

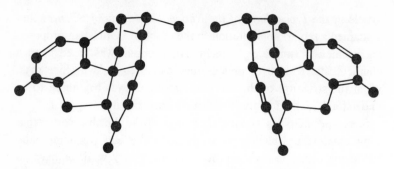

LEVO ISOMER (ACTIVE)   DEXTRO ISOMER (INACTIVE)

15. The two isomorphic mirror images of morphine. The levorotational form, at left, is the only form that produces the pharmacological and behavioral effects of morphine; the dextrorotational form, at right, is largely inactive.

medicine but not an analgesic). The levorphanol was made radioactive (or hot, as scientists like to call it) so that the substance could be traced by special geiger-counter-like devices called scintillation counters. The hot levorphanol was then combined with the homogenate and divided into two samples. To one sample, you would add nonradioactive (cold) dextrorphan and to the other sample nonradioactive (cold) levorphanol. If there existed an opiate receptor, then the cold levorphanol would displace some of the hot levorphanol in the receptor site; cold dextrorphan would be unable to do this since the shape of the dextrorphan molecule would not fit that of the receptor. Comparing the amount of displaced levorphanol in the two samples would indicate what is generally referred to as stereospecific binding.

Goldstein's experiment showed only a 2 percent difference, hardly enough to prove anything. The first attempt to observe stereospecific binding was essentially a failure. But it did establish the basic procedure that others would later modify. The historical importance of the attempt lay in its substantial influence on the opiate receptor research that was immediately to follow. Goldstein had obviously missed a wonderful opportunity, the discovery of the opiate receptor. His methodology, however, was so elegant that it was clear to others that the receptor could eventually be found, if just the right kind of modifications were made. Goldstein had come so close.

CANDACE PERT AND SOLOMON SNYDER AT JOHNS HOPKINS

Candace Pert is a feature writer's dream. She combines the scientific credentials of having been at the center of opiate research and the distinction of being the youngest of those credited with a milestone discovery in the field. There is an earthy humor and enthusiasm about her that lets one know she thoroughly enjoys what she is doing. At the same time, she knows how to communicate an idealism about her chosen area, an area that promises to shed light on so many aspects of human suffering and misery. ("I have a mystical streak," she is quoted as saying, "about what I'm here to do.")[11] Pert's career has had, in the eyes of many of her colleagues, a kind of symbolic importance. When the discovery of the opiate receptor was made, Pert was a graduate student (indeed, the discovery represented her doctoral dissertation) in a discipline where graduate students are usually overshadowed by the senior researcher in whose laboratory the work is done. Pert has had to protect the record of her involvement in the discovery. Moreover, she has struggled in a professional environment where sex discrimination might make itself felt in any number of ways. "If I had known just one woman scientist with a husband and children, but in those days you weren't supposed to be both," Pert has remarked when telling of the early days of her scientific career.[12]

Candace Beebe had planned to major in English at Hofstra University in Long Island, New York. "My goal in life was to be an editor of *Mademoiselle* magazine,"[13] she has said. Her future husband, Agu Pert, now a prominent neuroscientist in his own right, was a psychology major. When Agu went on to Bryn Mawr for graduate work in psychology, Candace transferred to Bryn Mawr and switched to biology. In 1970 she began the graduate program in pharmacology at Johns Hopkins University, where the main attraction for her was the work of Solomon Snyder. "I came because I had heard about this psychiatrist who was interested in doing biochemistry of the brain. I was just there to work with Sol."[14]

Solomon Snyder had come to the Johns Hopkins Medical School faculty in 1965 as an assistant professor of pharmacology, having completed medical training and two years of research at the National Institute of Mental Health in Bethesda, Maryland. By 1970 his prominence in the field of pharmacology had been well established, but he had done no work specifically on opiates.‡ In large part, it was the social and political climate at the time that influenced the turn of events that directed Snyder's attention toward opiate research. He recalls:

> There was a lot of interest in the drug abuse of soldiers in Vietnam. Richard Nixon had declared war against heroin and appointed a czar of drug abuse, Jerry Jaffe, who was a good friend of mine. He had a special action office in the White House which he headed, with the authority to coordinate literally in a czar-like fashion all drug-abuse research efforts. A Manhattan project sort of thing, a lot of funding. One of the things that they did was to allocate to the NIMH, to the part that became the National Institute on Drug Abuse, to actually create drug abuse research centers. Hopkins was one of them. At that time, the only research I had done related to drug abuse was on catecholamines and amphetamines. So in actually writing the application, I was trying to think of some new areas that might be interesting to try out and the notion of looking for opiate receptors seemed interesting.[15]

He had also read the Avram Goldstein paper in 1971. The impact of the Goldstein paper for Snyder, despite its report of failure, was to suggest that the opiate receptor was really there but that the failure to detect it was due to some technical reason, some procedural quirk that remained at the time a mystery.

Fortuitously, the laboratory next door to Snyder's was headed by a renowned pharmacologist, Pedro Cuatrecasas, a naturalized American, born in Spain, who had come to the Hopkins faculty in 1970 to fill the chair of professor of clinical pharmacology, a position endowed by the Burroughs Wellcome pharmaceutical company.[16] Cua-

‡ In 1977 Snyder would assume the post of distinguished service professor of psychiatry and pharmacology and in 1980 direct the newly formed Department of Neuroscience at Johns Hopkins.

trecasas had discovered the insulin receptor in the pancreas, and Snyder was anxious to adapt some of Cuatrecasas's techniques to the problem of the opiate receptor in the brain. As Snyder has said, "We would collaborate with Pedro, that is get Pedro's advice on how to do the experiments and master the technique."[17] From Snyder's point of view, after the techniques were learned from the Cuatrecasas laboratory in 1971 and 1972, it was clear why someone would look for the opiate receptor and not find it.

For Candace Pert, as a graduate student in pharmacology, the Cuatrecasas connection was crucial:

> We had a one-year rotation, where you had to work in three labs before you did your dissertation. . . . Five months into my rotation, I worked for Pedro Cuatrecasas. Now, Pedro had developed the methods for finding the insulin receptor, the first peptide hormone receptor. Not only the methods but the whole conceptualization. I took every seminar that the guy offered. I sat there constantly listening. Then in the doctoral dissertation I adapted that methodology and that strategy and that thinking to the opiate receptor."[18]

At first, Pert and Snyder used radioactive dihydromorphine as the opiate to bind to the receptor site, but it failed to show the stereo-specificity they were looking for. As they were to realize later, dihydromorphine was a perfectly good opiate for the purpose but it was light-sensitive, so that all the fluorescent lights in the laboratory interfered with the experiment.[19] At that point, they decided to try a different approach. They knew that a drug called naloxone was a pure antagonist to morphine; that is, whatever morphine the agonist could do, naloxone the antagonist could undo. With a composition very much like that of the morphine molecule, naloxone was thought to be able to fit into the receptor and cause the receptor to react in a way diametrically opposite to the way it reacted to morphine. By filling up the spaces in the receptor sites, so the theory went, morphine would be prevented from getting in.* Hoping that naloxone would show a strong affinity for the opiate receptor, Pert and Snyder

---

* From a practical standpoint, naloxone (brand name: Narcan) could act as an emergency antidote to a morphine overdose. Indeed, Endo Laboratories (now part of Du Pont) had been marketing naloxone for this purpose since the later 1960s.

started to try it instead of dihydromorphine. Another factor worked in their favor. The radioactivity level was raised to such a magnitude that very low levels of naloxone needed to be used for the experiment. At these low levels, the hot naloxone found its way to receptors specific to morphine with a minimum of nonspecific binding along the way. When the crucial study was performed, as much as 70 percent of the hot naloxone (actually, very hot naloxone) was knocked out by the cold levorphanol and not by the cold dextrorphan. Goldstein's 1971 blueprint for stereospecific binding made the Pert and Snyder findings clear beyond any doubt.

That experiment began on Friday, September 22, 1972,[20] but it was not known until the following Monday that it had come out so well. Pert recalls her feelings at that time:

> Monday morning I came in and got the counts, began to look them over. As I was copying the numbers down I couldn't believe that it was working out so beautifully and my friend Ann Young, now Dr. Ann Young, sitting at the next desk said, "What's the matter?" And I said, "Do you know where the nearest bar is," and she said, "Is it that bad, is it that awful, do you need to get drunk?" I said, "No, I want to buy a bottle of champagne, I can't believe that it worked."[21]

The follow-up experiments confirmed that the newly discovered receptors were not sensitive to any nonopiate molecule: serotonin, norepinephrine, or a number of other substances then known to exist in the brain. The report of their data was submitted to the journal *Science* on December 1, revised on January 15 of 1973, then published on March 9. Johns Hopkins arranged a press conference for Pert and Snyder when the news of an opiate receptor in the brain finally was made public. Astonishingly, two other laboratories had meanwhile discovered the same thing: one in Uppsala, Sweden, under the direction of Lars Terenius; the other in New York under the direction of Eric Simon.

ERIC SIMON AT NEW YORK UNIVERSITY

If Solomon Snyder had arrived at the opiate receptor from the avenue of pharmacology, Eric Simon approached it from the orientation of biochemistry. Of all the opiate receptor discoverers, Simon was the only one who had done any work on opiates prior to 1970. Trained with a Ph.D. in organic chemistry, he had switched to biochemistry by 1958 and accepted a research post at the New York University Medical Center. He was hired by Lewis Thomas, then chairman of the Department of Medicine, a physician who was later to direct the Memorial Sloan-Kettering Cancer Center and become a distinguished essayist on science and medicine. Thomas was particularly interested in research on narcotic addiction, and at that time New York City had just created a Public Health Research Institute that would fund the salaries of researchers on selected topics relevant to social issues. Thomas has recalled this period as chairman of the drug addiction committee for the institute:

> The committee met several times, during the summer [of 1962], finding the heroin problem more complicated at each meeting and finding, as well, very few openings for real research work. We were not even sure it was a medical problem as much as a social dilemma. I persuaded Eric Simon, a young Ph.D. biochemist . . . to take an interest in opiate addiction as a biochemical problem, and placed a laboratory and fellowship at his disposal. It was a considerable gamble for him; to leave his present line of work and take on a brand-new, obviously intractable problem was a high risk. He took it on with some zest, however, and kept at it for the next twenty years.[22]

By 1966 Simon reported some evidence that an opiate (he used dihydromorphine) could bind itself to some kind of receptor in the brain, but it was never clear whether the binding was stereospecific.[23] As was the case with Pert and Snyder in Baltimore, the 1971 Goldstein paper galvanized him to return to the receptor question, pushing it back to the forefront. "We were stimulated to try harder," Simon has said. "We had been doing the next to the nearest thing to it all along."[24]

From Simon's standpoint, the most important step was a change in how people had conceptualized the nature of the opiate receptor up to that time. Goldstein had predicted the receptor to be "loose"; that is, it was thought that opiates fit into a receptor but could be easily dislodged by even a relatively minor disturbance in the solution. It turned out that just the opposite is the case: The opiate receptor is very tight and molecules that fit into the receptor can resist quite a bit of disturbance. The distinction is crucial because Goldstein, in an effort to prevent the receptors from losing the opiate, was careful not to wash the homogenate before doing the dextrorphan-levorphanol test. One consequence of this decision was to keep the "noise" level, the amount of extraneous data, so high that the tests to determine stereospecificity could never work; indeed they were doomed to failure. If the receptor was tight, repeated washings could be performed, the opiate molecules would still be inside the receptors, and the noise level could be brought down. With a low noise level in the homogenate, the scintillation counts after mixing cold levorphanol in one sample and cold dextrorphan in another could be distinguishable, just as in a good-quality radio the distinction of two radio stations close to each other in frequency can be made. The idea of "looseness" also influenced another modification. The opiate Simon decided to make radioactive and to use in the receptor binding was the most potent opiate then known, etorphine. It was reasoned that if the receptor was loose at all, and washings had to be done, at least the use of an extremely powerful molecule like etorphine would be able to "hang on" inside the receptor. When Simon and his postdoctoral student Jack Hiller did the experiment in 1972, it worked perfectly. As in the findings of Pert and Snyder, the stereospecificity was clearly demonstrated. Simon used the opiate agonist etorphine to bind in the receptor, while Pert and Snyder used the opiate antagonist naloxone, but the methods were remarkably similar. Simon and Hiller were influenced by the issue of receptor "tightness," while Pert and Snyder were influenced by Cuatrecasas and his experiments with receptors in the pancreas. Nevertheless, both laboratories reached the same point at practically the same time. When the results were made public, the two laboratories were joined by a third, the laboratory in Uppsala, Sweden, directed by a man neither Simon nor Snyder had known personally and whose reputation up to 1972 and 1973 had been in an entirely different area of research.[25]

LARS TERENIUS AT UPPSALA, SWEDEN

The primary influence behind Lars Terenius's approach to the problem of the opiate receptor was his prior work with hormones. He had been one of the pioneers in the development of biochemical techniques to study the receptors for steroid hormones and the effects of these hormones on tumor growth and fertility. Despite his prominence in his own field, however, Terenius was geographically and academically distant from the other researchers working at the time in the opiate field. He recalls:

> I started around 1970, to begin with, as a side project. . . . The estrogenic steroids and congeners form a very heterogenous bunch of compounds sharing one (or apparently one) receptor. It occurred to me that the opiate group might be similar. This gives certain advantages in defining receptors by chemical means. . . . Also, when I researched the literature, opiate pharmacology had not really advanced for the past twenty years, and biochemical (mechanistic) explanations were very vague.[26]

His success in identifying the opiate receptor came about without his ever knowing the American research efforts then under way.

> I did not know Snyder personally, although I had met him, and I did not know that he (or rather Pert) or Simon worked on the problem. Being in Sweden, I could work in isolation, [unaware] of a race. I knew of the Pert and Snyder paper after mine had been published. I had no reason for disappointment.[27]

REALITY AND PERCEPTION—THE QUESTION OF PRIORITY

If the events leading up to the spring of 1973 could be considered a race, it was a race against the clock and oneself rather than a race against an opponent. The Goldstein paper was the opening gun, the call to succeed where he had failed, but one took up the challenge without knowing who else might also be involved. The lines of communication were not yet established. Within a year, the cast of characters in the opiate research story would be fully apprised of who the competition was, but in the summer and fall of 1972 one seemed pretty much alone. It is quite likely that Snyder knew that Simon was working on the opiate receptor problem. Simon had visited Snyder's laboratory in Baltimore and Simon himself had previously published work on receptor binding. But there was no reason to think Snyder was involved, for his reputation had been built on amphetamine research. And no one recalls having heard of Terenius at all.

A strange historic three-way tie—crucial experiments carried out in three laboratories completely independently of each other. That is the reality. It is sometimes easy, however, to view Snyder as being the first, and ahead of the others. If you read the review article "Opiate Receptors and Internal Opiates" that Snyder wrote for *Scientific American* in March of 1977, where the experiments of Pert and Snyder are discussed along with the events that would eventually follow, neither the name of Eric Simon nor that of Lars Terenius is even mentioned.[28] It is a glaring omission that has rankled many people in the field, since the example is not a trivial one. *Scientific American* is often cited as a definitive source by the scientific community outside particular specialized fields of research and is often reprinted for use in university courses. Therefore, the article seemed to establish a priority (indeed an exclusivity) in the discovery that had no basis in fact.

It is clear that by September of 1972 stereospecific binding had been confirmed at both Simon's laboratory in New York and Snyder's in Baltimore. Simon was invited to give a major address on opiate receptor research at a special symposium at the annual meeting of the American Society for Pharmacology and Experimental Therapeutics the following April. It was seen as a good opportunity to present his findings, and, since the symposia of this type were typically published at a later date, the presentation was anticipated to be the appropriate time for the initial statement that the receptor had been finally found. In December, Simon reportedly was called by the organizer of the symposium, who told him that a call had come in from the chairman of the Pharmacology Department at Johns Hopkins to the effect that Solomon Snyder had just made some new findings. Could he, Simon was asked, relinquish part of his allotted time so Snyder could speak as well? Simon consented, unaware of the fact that the Pert and Snyder paper that would come out in *Science* in March had already been submitted to the journal on December 1. When Simon finally presented his findings on April 18, 1973, the Pert and Snyder paper had been out for about five weeks. Simon lost no time in establishing a published record of his contribution. On April 19, one day following the symposium, immunochemist Michael Heidelberger communicated the Simon data to the National Academy of Sciences, and the written version (coauthored with Jack Hiller and Irit Edelman) came out in the *Proceedings of the National Academy of Sciences* in July. From the standpoint of publication dates, the image could have been construed as Simon merely confirming in a different way what Pert and Snyder had discovered earlier in 1973. But a problem really would not have existed if Snyder reportedly had not persisted for a time in crediting his laboratory with the primary discovery and referring to the New York (and Uppsala) laboratory as having a more subsequent than simultaneous contribution. The *Scientific American* version of opiate research history that Snyder wrote in 1977 made matters worse.

Ironically, in light of the question of priority on the American side, it is worth noting that the Terenius paper on the opiate receptor was submitted on November 6, 1972, and accepted for publication on November 8. Therefore, it is Terenius who technically came in first. His "mistake," however, lay in the fact that he submitted the paper to the relatively obscure journal *Acta Pharmacologica et Toxicologica,* published in Denmark. If it had been published in a widely read source such as *Science* or *Nature,* it is certain that the impact would have been felt instantly.

While the months of 1972 and 1973 were heady times for the main protagonists in opiate research, the intensity was typical of how science works when a field suddenly breaks open. Those were days of real discovery. They were also days that showed the human side of modern science. Scientists, it has been said, "have the same faults as anyone else, sometimes magnified by the hothouse atmosphere of scientific competition. . . . But they also have a kind of quiet mirth, a subtle joy in existence."[29] And the discovery of the opiate receptor, however important, was only the first step. The obvious inference was that something in the brain existed to fit into those receptors. Now, if only that something could be found.

Another race was on.

5

Days of Discovery: 1973–1979

Is it significant that the discovery of the enkephalins was made by a team of young and mature scientists? The combination of enthusiasm and experience has been of great importance.

HANS KOSTERLITZ, A thought for present and future investigators upon a ceremonial planting of a camellia in the gardens of Chikusuikai Hospital near Kurume, Japan, 1981

I think it's very rare that a scientist is privileged to watch the birth of a new era . . . in his or her field, that was something like waiting for the sun to come out and all of a sudden it does. It had that feeling about it. We knew it was there. We knew it was important but nobody could quite get a hold on it, and then all of a sudden there it was in your lap and I remember thinking I'm never going to forget these days because I may never live through anything like that ever again.

HUDA AKIL, *The Keys of Paradise* from the television series "Nova," 1979

By the summer of 1973 the idea of opiate receptors in the brain had moved from hypothesis to reality. This was a milestone, but a much greater one lay ahead. The next obvious step was to identify the chemical substance that fit into these receptors. No one could now doubt for a moment that an opiate-like substance was being produced by the brain. Why else would there be receptors? It was absurd to think that there would be any evolutionary advantage in having receptors that waited patiently for the juice of the opium poppy plant to come around to fill them up.

On the other hand, there were those in neuroscience research who were not in the least surprised in 1973 by the discovery of opiate receptors.[1] For them, a biochemical system inside the brain that mimicked the action of morphine *had* to exist. From the experiments they were doing and from other evidence gathered quite independent of receptor research, there simply was no logical alternative. In these laboratories, the seeds for this viewpoint had been planted well before attempts to find an opiate receptor had even begun. One such laboratory was headed by physiological psychologist John C. Liebeskind at UCLA.

THE LIEBESKIND GROUP AT UCLA

In 1969 David Reynolds at the NASA Ames Research Center in Mountain View, California, published a striking and puzzling experimental effect.[2] By electrically stimulating the periaqueductal gray (PAG) region (an area surrounding the cerebral aqueduct) in the midbrain of rats, Reynolds was able to produce a significant elimination of responses to pain. So great was the analgesia that Reynolds successfully performed abdominal surgery on these rats during the brain stimulation without the need for any chemical anesthesia. When brain stimulation stopped, normal reactions to painful stimuli returned.

Stimulation of no other region of the brain had ever produced analgesia in this way. Yet for about a decade and a half it had been known that motivated behavior could be guided by electrical stimulation of the brain. In 1954 James Olds and Peter Milner, then working at McGill University in Montreal, had discovered certain areas in the rat brain that, when electrically stimulated, appeared to be providing genuine reinforcement.[3] In a later study, Olds reported that rats pressed levers, sometimes at rates of five thousand times per hour, in order to receive this stimulation.[4] We will never know what the rats were experiencing during the stimulation, but there was an unmistakable feeling among the researchers that when rats were self-stimulating these areas of their brain they were "enjoying" it. With or without the approval of the author, the *Scientific American* article written by Olds in 1956 was entitled "Pleasure Centers in the Brain."[5] Through the 1950s and 1960s, the "Olds Effect" was replicated and extended to a wide range of species (including the human); extensive mapping of the positive (rewarding) and negative (punishment) areas in the brain was carried out.[6] Could the self-stimulation phenomenon be related to the effect that Reynolds had discovered?

When the Reynolds finding became public, David Mayer was a graduate student in John Liebeskind's lab at UCLA, having arrived there in 1966. Mayer set out to replicate the Reynolds effect and determine how it fit into the self-stimulation literature, which by 1969 was quite advanced. At first his attempts were unsuccessful, and it looked as if the analgesia phenomenon might not be genuine. "We had gotten to the point," Mayer would later relate, "where we couldn't believe that he [Reynolds] got that. It took us a while before we came to agree with him."[7]

Eventually, the right procedure and electrode placements were found, and a consistent analgesia was finally achieved. When the stimulation was present, tail shocks produced no signs of pain on the part of the animal. When rats were placed in ice water, a normally painful state for any animal, no signs of discomfort appeared. "One animal," the published report in *Science* later described, ". . . ate a food pellet for over 5 minutes while standing on its hind legs in a shallow trough of ice water. Approximately 30 seconds after brain stimulation was turned off, the animal suddenly dropped the pellet and jumped out of the trough."[8]

Clearly, the possibility that pain relief could be accomplished by electrical stimulation of points in the brain rather than by administering addictive drugs like morphine was of great importance for people suffering from chronic pain. In the meantime, however, the big theoretical question was why the effect was working in the first place. How could electrical stimulation stop pain?

The consensus among important physiologists in pain research at the end of the 1960s was that morphine acted in the brain much in the same way as a local anesthetic like novocaine acted on a peripheral nerve—by stopping the transmission of nerve impulses.[9] From this point of view, electrical stimulation could be seen as simply a kind of nonspecific "static" introduced into the system, jamming up the transmission of pain signals. Mayer thought otherwise. From his point of view, the electrical stimulation was not stopping the action of a neurotransmitter; it was allowing another to act. The stimulation was activating a neural system that functioned normally in the blockage of pain. *A natural analgesia system was being created.*

The idea was pretty radical. Liebeskind recalls his initial reaction: "I kept looking to see [if there was] some hole in this argument. I couldn't necessarily believe it. I saw that it was important, but I couldn't accept it because I thought this was too big a statement. Someone was going to get burned."[10] Mayer's hypothesis, however, soon became the official explanatory concept of Liebeskind's research group. After destroying the PAG area in the rat brains and finding no analgesic effect at all, they were persuaded the jamming idea could no longer be defended.[11] A careful parallel could now be drawn between the properties of what became known as stimulation-produced analgesia (SPA) and the properties of morphine-induced analgesia. Perhaps the electrical stimulation, they argued, was activating a morphine-like factor (substance?) in the brain. There seemed to be no turning back from the idea that analgesia, the blockage of pain, was an active, not a passive, process in the brain.

Another of Liebeskind's students, Huda Akil, sought to explore the pharmacological aspects of stimulation-produced analgesia for her dissertation, just as Mayer had established the basic phenomenon for his. If SPA was acting like morphine (if a morphine factor was involved), would there be a tolerance to SPA over repetitions just as there is a tolerance to repeated doses of morphine? If the effects of morphine could be reversed by opiate antagonist drugs, naloxone, for example, could these same drugs reverse the effects of SPA?

Akil's decision to use naloxone in an attempt to reverse the effects of SPA is an interesting example of how a decision could be completely logical from one point of view and completely illogical from another. If morphine and SPA were actively setting off a common system of analgesia, naloxone should indeed reverse the processes of both. Yet it was known among most pharmacologists at the time that naloxone produced no significant behavioral effects in normal animals. It simply reversed the effects of morphine. Therefore, it seemed to them quite irrelevant, from a strictly behavioral point of view, to choose to test naloxone's effect on the SPA phenomenon. Nevertheless, it did indeed work; there was, if not complete, at least partial reversal of SPA by naloxone.[12] Even though the possibility of naloxone reversal had been hypothesized, the success of the experiment took Akil by surprise. "I thought, 'Oh, I don't believe it, it's not true,' " she later would say, "so I did another animal, then another animal, then another animal and I ended up doing the whole study that evening, just testing one more animal. I was very thrilled, and at the same time I kept thinking, 'Well, maybe there is another explanation.' So, it was a mixture of feelings, but I was very happy."[13]

Early in 1972, while on academic leave in Paris, Liebeskind first published (along with Akil and Mayer) the finding that naloxone partially reversed the effects of SPA.[14] It was a crucial step in the whole sequence of events that would lead up to the discovery of endorphins. To the extent that naloxone could reverse this process, a morphine-like factor had to be involved. When Akil presented her data at a meeting in San Francisco later in the spring of 1972, there was one particular individual in the audience who immediately saw the implications. Hans Kosterlitz, who was later to be one of the discoverers of the substance Akil was reversing with naloxone, rose to ask the fundamental question, "Are you looking for that factor?"[15] Reportedly at that point he was convinced that a morphine-like factor or substance existed and that Liebeskind's group at UCLA had been the ones who had identified it. It soon became evident, however, that an identification by the Liebeskind group or by anyone else had *not* been made. Even so, it was obvious to these people that the events of neuroscience research were quickly converging on the critical discovery. Less than a year would pass before the opiate receptor would be identified. The Goldstein paper on the strategy of stereospecific binding for finding the opiate receptor had already been out, and interested parties in at least three laboratories around the world were hot on the trail. It seemed to Kosterlitz that, if a morphine-like factor in the brain was to be discovered, he had better move fast.

THE MEN AT ABERDEEN

Hans Kosterlitz, at the time of the San Francisco meeting where Akil had presented her data, was almost sixty-nine and approaching the age of retirement as chairman of the Pharmacology Department at the University of Aberdeen, an institution in Scotland he had been associated with for almost forty years.[16] His interest in morphine had its roots in experiments on the responses of isolated sections of ileum tissue (the lowest part of the small intestine) in the guinea pig. He had found that the reflex contractions of ileum to electrical stimulation could be closely calibrated and that morphine (as well as other opiates) selectively inhibited these contractions. It was essentially an effect that was first observed by a physiologist named Trendelburg in 1917.[17] In Kosterlitz's hands, however, the inhibition of the guinea pig ileum contraction became a powerful way of measuring the potency of a wide range of opiate substances. (The greater the potency of a particular opiate, the greater would be the inhibition of the ileum contractions.) In 1962, responding to a challenge from an American pharmacologist who had been skeptical of the usefulness of the ileum preparation in opiate research, Kosterlitz had succeeded in identifying a set of unmarked chemical substances entirely on the basis of their observed effects on ileum tissue. The successful test was a triumph for Kosterlitz and his ileum preparation.[18] Here was a key anatomical entity to test out any new opiate-like substance that might eventually come along. The two criteria would be to inhibit the contractions and then to see the inhibition reversed by naloxone, the pure antagonist to morphine. As a result of his extensive experience with the properties of this ileum preparation, Kosterlitz was in an ideal position to screen out the countless candidates for a morphine-like factor in the brain. The possibility had been discussed, according to his colleagues, as early as 1966.[19]

With "retirement" looming one year away, Kosterlitz was determined to continue his morphine work into a future that could see the fruition of his speculations over the years. Obtaining funding from the University of Aberdeen and the U.S. National Institute on Drug Abuse, Kosterlitz set out to establish a new research organization that focused upon the search for this chemical substance that acted like morphine. For the final assault on the problem, as Kosterlitz saw it in 1972, he would choose the best collaborator and together they would find the opiate in the brain that was gradually becoming less and less hypothetical with each passing day. The collaborator he chose was John Hughes, a thirty-year-old lecturer in pharmacology at Aberdeen. From Hughes's recollections, the plans for the joint venture began aboard a British Airways flight from London to Bucharest, Romania, where both were going to deliver lectures at an international conference on brain research.[20] Earlier in 1972, Hughes and Kosterlitz had collaborated on a paper showing that the mouse vas deferens, a tiny tube-like bit of muscle that delivers sperm from the testes to urethra, was also highly reactive to morphine. Like the ileum contractions, the contractions of the vas deferens could be inhibited by morphine and other opiates.[21] Now there would be two preparations that could be used to test a potential morphine factor. It would be a perfect match: Kosterlitz with his ileum and vas deferens preparations as tests for opiate substances and Hughes with his biochemical expertise in extracting chemical substances from animal brains. In October of 1973, at the age of seventy, Kosterlitz opened the Unit for Research on Addictive Drugs at Marischal College, University of Aberdeen, with Hughes as his deputy.

From the outset, the accommodations for the unit were picturesque but considerably less than ideal. The laboratory was housed in an old neo-Gothic, gray-granite castle of a building in the center of Aberdeen. With twenty-foot-high ceilings and a dilapidated electrical system circa 1900, Hughes would later recall that the setting was worthy of a scene from *Frankenstein*. Adding to the setting was the macabre task of obtaining the necessary brain material for purification. Hughes needed about thirty pig brains every day, obtained from the local slaughterhouse.* At first he had to hacksaw the brain out of

---

* An enormous quantity of raw materials is often needed in bioassay work. Biochemist Roger Guillemin reportedly needed a quarter of a million sheep brains, fresh

the skull himself. "After only a few days I learnt that a bottle of whiskey a week would buy me the right to get heads neatly severed in half by the chainsaw as the pigs came through the production line, so I was spared the more gruesome aspects of the dissection," he later said. Apparently, few citizens of Aberdeen during those early morning hours seemed to be bothered by the sight of a man with thirty frozen pig brains on the back of his bicycle.[23]

Despite the accommodations, by November of 1973 Hughes had managed to achieve a partial purification of a brain material that, when applied to vas deferens tissue, inhibited the contractions like morphine.[24] The fact that he had succeeded when others (including Avram Goldstein) had failed did not seem to surprise people who knew the complexities of finding a morphine factor. While Goldstein had by then formulated a hypothetical model of a chemical that would have the necessary properties to fit into the newly discovered opiate receptor, Hughes had gone on with the search without a model as a guide. "The thing that was unique about Hughes and Kosterlitz," Huda Akil would later say, "is that they had no preconceived notion about what the factor was. . . . They searched for it whatever its size or its nature, unlike Avram [Goldstein], who was almost too logical about it—so logical that he wasn't biological."[25]

By March of 1974, at an international conference on pharmacological research in Cocoyoc, Mexico, Hughes and Kosterlitz were excitedly telling their colleagues about their progress.[26] The formal presentation was made in May at a neuroscience research meeting in Boston.[27] At the same conference, Terenius from Sweden reported that together with Agneta Wahlström, he had found a "morphine-like factor" that seemed similar to the extract found in Aberdeen.[28] It was starting to look as if the substance was a peptide (a simple string of amino acids) rather than a molecule with a more complicated structure.

The first glimmer of the discovery was beginning to be seen, but since the stakes were so high for all concerned, the atmosphere in that meeting in Boston was reportedly more tense than jubilant.[29]

from the slaughterhouse, to isolate about one ten-thousandths of an ounce of a hypothalamic hormone, so that an identification could be made. Over the course of three years, an estimated two to five million hypothalami were needed for this research.[22]

And, as in a high-stakes game, the players wanted to get more information without divulging their own positions. The goal of final discovery was so close that victory could easily tilt toward a number of the participants.

Avram Goldstein recalls the feelings during the meeting: "It meant they were ahead of us in the race, and science is just like that —a race. It's cooperative, but it's competitive too, and probably more of the latter because scientists are by nature competitive people. Since there isn't much in the way of monetary rewards for what they do, they go for the ego rewards."[30]

About a year later, at a meeting held in Airlie, Virginia, in June of 1975, Hughes and Kosterlitz announced that they had succeeded in identifying the amino acids in the morphine-like peptide that they had been studying since the previous year, but the actual amino acid *sequence* still remained to be worked out.[31] A month earlier, on May 2, Hughes had published the essentials of the Aberdeen discovery in the journal *Brain Research,* in an article originally submitted the previous December.[32] By June, Terenius and Wahlström had published another article on their "morphine-like factor" in samples from human cerebrospinal fluid, and the Snyder group had published its discovery of a similar substance from extracts of calf, rabbit, and rat brains.[33]

On December 18, 1975, the final step was made public in the journal *Nature.* The peptide that acted like morphine was actually five amino acids long and consisted of two forms. Hughes and Kosterlitz had the privilege of naming their creation and chose the term "enkephalin" (from the Greek *en kephale,* meaning "in the head").[34] To the end, consistent with their whole approach, they wanted to imply no preconceived function in the name itself. Yet enkephalin was indeed an endogenous opiate, an opiate created by the brain itself. It inhibited the ileum and vas deferens contractions like morphine, and like morphine it was completely reversed by the action of naloxone.

If there were to be undisputed winners in the endorphin story, it would be Hughes and Kosterlitz for the definitive identification of enkephalin. Lars Terenius had in late 1974 found a morphine-like factor, as had Solomon Snyder in 1975, but they had not made the identification of its exact composition. The race this time was won in Aberdeen.

What were the two enkephalins that Hughes and Kosterlitz had found? One of them was a pentapeptide with the following five amino acids in sequence: tyrosine - glycine - glycine - phenylalamine - methionine (Tyr-Gly-Gly-Phe-Met, for short). This was to be called methionine-enkephalin or simply met-enkephalin. The other form had a different fifth amino acid, leucine instead of methionine, making the sequence Tyr-Gly-Gly-Phe-Leu. The second type was thus called leucine-enkephalin or simply leu-enkephalin. Each form was a very small molecule, ideally formed to have functional significance as a neurotransmitter. After Aberdeen, the next burst of discovery would come virtually simultaneously from San Francisco and London. Enkephalin would soon prove to be one of several chemicals that worked like morphine in the brain.

THE LABORATORIES OF C. H. LI AND DEREK SMYTH

When Choh Hao ("C.H.") Li, director of the Hormone Research Laboratory of the University of California at San Francisco, discovered in 1964 a new ninety-one-amino-acid-long peptide hormone from experiments on sheep pituitary glands, he was following a strategy that was more chemical than biological.[35] In other words, rather than starting from an idea that a chemical substance must be present in the body because there already existed a known biological function, Li would extract and purify a substance from body tissue and then try to determine what its biological function was.†

Like a mountain climber, Li would undertake to isolate a compound or molecule simply because "it was there."[37] With this kind of approach, however, there would be inevitably a number of risks. A period of time might pass in which you would have essentially "a hormone without a function" as you waited for the biologists to take notice of your discovery and fit it into the context of life outside the

† Earlier successes had included the identification of the structure of the pituitary hormones ACTH and human growth hormone.[36] Ironically, it was later to be the function of ACTH in stress and the association of ACTH with beta-endorphin that would start the theorizing on how stress and endorphin functioning were intertwined.

test tube. Because the new peptide hormone Li discovered in 1964 appeared to increase the movement of fat (lipids) away from fat tissue to the liver where it was metabolized, it was called beta-lipotropin.[38] But beyond a vague association with fat metabolism, beta-lipotropin could not be tied in to classic pituitary activities. For the ten years that it passed in relative obscurity, beta-lipotropin lay like an uncut diamond in Li's laboratory, ninety-one amino acids long but with a function that was only a matter of vague conjecture. "You must have faith in science. You know what faith is? You have to be optimistic," Li would later emphasize. "I *believe* in this molecule. In 1967 I wrote an article saying that someday this molecule will be very important."[39]

In 1972 Li's optimism about beta-lipotropin began to pay off. On a hunch, Li asked an Iraqi student who had worked in his laboratory to send some camel pituitary glands for analysis. He reasoned that since camels were tough, fat-conserving, lean animals, strongly adapted to live in one of the world's harshest environments, then it was possible that levels of beta-lipotropin would be particularly high. Eventually a package of two hundred or so camel pituitaries did indeed arrive, probably one of the more interesting parcels cleared by U.S. Customs.[40] When the material was purified, however, only the last thirty-one amino acids (amino acid sixty-one through ninety-one) of beta-lipotropin were found. The function of this fragment remained obscure until December 1975 when the five-amino-acid sequence of enkephalin that had been finally determined in Aberdeen was published.

Page proofs of the *Nature* article were sent by Hughes and Kosterlitz to Goldstein at Stanford, and events at Li's laboratory moved like lightning.[41] "I remember that Avram Goldstein called me about the enkephalins," Li has said. "He read me their amino-acid sequences over the telephone and I thought, 'Yes, I already have that on my shelf.' . . . When Goldstein called and told me beta-lipotropin contained the enkephalins, I knew my camel material must be very active. I let him test it and it was."[42] Indeed, the astounding finding was that met-enkephalin consisted of the first five amino acids (numbers sixty-one through sixty-five) in the camel peptide from Iraq.[43] Upon the suggestion of Eric Simon at New York University Medical Center,[44] Li drew upon the generic name that Simon had created for the growing number of morphine-like factors. The new name was endorphin, from the contraction of "endogenous morphine."‡

When Goldstein tested the thirty-one-amino-acid fragment—which C. H. Li would eventually call beta-endorphin—as an analgesic, it proved up to one hundred times more effective than morphine. It was clearly secreted by the anterior pituitary and could be measured in the bloodstream and cerebrospinal fluid. It would eventually be identified in brain tissue as well.

Virtually at the same time, in England, beta-endorphin was being discovered by an equally strange series of coincidental events. Derek Smyth and his colleagues at the National Institute for Medical Research in London had been working on pituitary hormones for some time. In 1974 they had separated out several portions of the beta-lipotropin, one of which was comprised of amino acids sixty-one through ninety-one. They called it the C-fragment, and it was identical to beta-endorphin. Yet, as was the case with Li, it was not until late 1975 that Smyth knew the significance of this particular fragment.[46] One of the central figures in the Hughes and Kosterlitz identification of enkephalin, Howard Morris of Imperial College, University of London, was attending a lecture given by Smyth where several of the peptide fragments were being studied.* When the sequence of Smyth's C-fragment was shown to Morris, it was obvious (but no less surprising) that the first five amino acids matched those of met-enkephalin. It was as if Morris were watching a long thirty-one-car train go past at a railroad crossing and noticed that a short portion of it, with cars marked Tyr-Gly-Gly-Phe (with a Met-marked caboose), was leading the others. Smyth's reaction was immediate. "Naturally

‡ In the last few years, researchers in this field have tended to prefer the term "endogenous opioid peptides" for the overall category of substances produced in the body that have opiate-like properties. Nevertheless, the simpler term "endorphins" will be used here.[45]

* In retrospect, the reason the identification of the two enkephalins had taken as long as it did was it had originally been thought that the two peptides with five amino acids each were really one peptide with ten amino acids. It was the application of a newly developed technique called mass spectrometry by Howard Morris in late 1975 that made possible the identification of the two sequences.

at once I went back home," he recalls, "and we at once tested our peptides for binding . . . and of course for the whole range of properties that morphine has, such as analgesia, and effects on the blood pressure, and so on, and as you may already know, . . . our peptide proves to be the most powerful analgesic agent, naturally occurring analgesic agent, that's been known [as of 1979]. It proved to be a hundred times more potent than morphine."[47]

The results of Smyth and his colleagues A. F. Bradbury and C. R. Snell were ready to be submitted to the British journal *Nature* in February 1976 and appeared in the issue of April 29.[48] By that time, however, Li and his colleague David Chung had already published their beta-endorphin work in the American journal *Proceedings of the National Academy of Sciences* earlier in April, having submitted their results in January.[49] As a consequence of the slim lead in publication dates, Li's laboratory had effectively won over Smyth's laboratory in the race for rights of priority over this new brain opiate. Like the events of 1973, however, when the opiate receptor was unveiled, the research activity in the two laboratories had been virtually simultaneous.

Later, in June 1976, it became clear that Li's beta-endorphin was also identical to one of two morphine-like substances Avram Goldstein at Stanford had been studying (without knowing its exact structure) since the summer of 1975.[50] Thus, in a final sweep together, three major laboratories converged in the summer of 1976 to establish a new, very potent endorphin substance called beta-endorphin, a peptide that contained one of the two enkephalins discovered in Aberdeen. While the concentration of beta-endorphin in the brain was to be only one tenth that of the enkephalins, it was several times more potent—obviously a new peptide to be reckoned with and a critical factor in the endorphin story.

THE GOLDSTEIN LABORATORY AND DYNORPHIN

Ironically, one of the last major endorphins to be identified was one of the first opiate-like substances to be discovered. At the Airlie meetings in 1975 Avram Goldstein reported on his work on two substances he had extracted from pituitary tissues—POP-One and

POP-Two he had called them, from the words "pituitary opioid peptide." POP-One had turned out to be beta-endorphin, but POP-Two
had resisted identification for four years.[51] In 1979 Goldstein and his
associates had succeeded in identifying the first thirteen amino acids
of what appeared to be a seventeen-amino-acid-long peptide. It was
named dynorphin (from the Greek, *dynamis,* meaning "power") on
the basis of its extraordinary potency in inhibiting the stimulated
twitch of the ileum preparation, by then the standard determination
of the opiate-like properties of any new substance. Dynorphin's potency was demonstrated to be 730 times that of leu-enkephalin, 190
times that of morphine, and 54 times that of beta-endorphin.[52] Only
certain synthetic opiates like etorphine (the substance Eric Simon
had used so successfully in his opiate receptor work in 1972–73) were
more powerful. While it is now known that this incredible effectiveness was largely due to the interaction of dynorphin with smooth
muscle tissue (such as the ileum) and that the binding of dynorphin
to opiate receptors is roughly comparable to that of the other endorphin peptides, the discovery of dynorphin nevertheless established a third substance in the growing endorphin family. Interestingly, the first five amino acids of dynorphin were none other than
leu-enkephalin; just as the first five amino acids of beta-endorphin
had been shown to be met-enkephalin. The endorphins were suddenly multiplying on the scene in a seemingly bewildering fashion.
How were they all related to each other?

A GROWING SENSE OF ORDER—1980 AND BEYOND

By the end of the 1970s the field of the neurosciences was about a
decade old and with it there was a slightly younger entity under the
umbrella of the neurosciences—endorphin research. The expansion
of interest had been so explosive that, by the beginning of the 1980s,
there were more than a thousand published articles that in one way
or another involved the investigations of these morphine-like chemicals in the brain. There was also a certain degree of biochemical
chaos. The two enkephalins identified by Hughes and Kosterlitz had
quickly been joined by a variety of longer peptides. For example, at
about the time beta-endorphin was discovered, Roger Guillemin at

the Salk Institute in California had identified a peptide with sixteen amino acids he called alpha-endorphin and another one with seventeen amino acids called gamma-endorphin, both with opiate-like properties. The two Guillemin peptides could be seen as the initial sixteen or seventeen amino acids in the thirty-one-amino-acid sequence of beta-endorphin.[53] The full seventeen-amino-acid sequence of Goldstein's dynorphin had to be called dynorphin A, in order to distinguish it from a thirteen-amino-acid version (called dynorphin B).[54] There was also a shorter eight-amino-acid form of dynorphin called dynorphin (1-8), which was identical to the initial segment of dynorphin A.[55]

By 1982, however, a certain amount of order emerged. The enkephalins, beta-endorphin, and the dynorphins were shown to be originating from three large precursor molecules (see table), and the three opioid (short for opiate-like) families were found to be distributed in three separate anatomical pathways in the brain. In short, there were three interacting but distinguishable endorphin systems.[56]

Another complication arose in 1976 on the issue of the nature of the opiate receptor itself. William Martin and co-workers at the National Institute on Drug Abuse Addiction Research Center in Lexington, Kentucky, had proposed that different natural and synthetic opiates worked in such different ways that there must be not just one, but two different types of opiate receptors in the nervous system.[57] One of these proposed receptor types was called the mu-receptor since it was theorized that it would be sensitive primarily to morphine and similar drugs. A separate type, called the kappa-receptor (after the synthetic opiate ketocyclazocine) was proposed because ketocyclazocine and morphine acted in different ways on respiration, heart rate, and mood. If the two opiates worked on the same receptor, Martin reasoned, the physiological effects of the two drugs would have been more similar.†

Martin's idea of multiple opiate receptors was given considerable support in 1977 by the Kosterlitz group in Aberdeen, who showed that different receptor types could be anatomically as well as biochemically separated.[58] They found one receptor type in the guinea

---

† A third receptor type, the sigma-receptor, was proposed by Martin at the time, but it has since been shown not to be tied exclusively to opiate chemicals.

THE THREE FAMILIES OF ENDORPHINS

PRECURSOR	ENDORPHIN PEPTIDE	SEQUENCE OF AMINO ACIDS IN STRUCTURE*
Proenkephalin	Met-enkephalin	Tyr-Gly-Gly-Phe-Met
	Leu-enkephalin	Tyr-Gly-Gly-Phe-Leu
	Heptapeptide	Tyr-Gly-Gly-Phe-Met-Arg-Phe
	Octapeptide	Tyr-Gly-Gly-Phe-Met-Arg-Gly-Leu
Pro-opiomelanocortin	Alpha-endorphin	Tyr-Gly-Gly-Phe-Met-Thr-Ser-Glu-Lys-Ser-Gln-Thr-Pro-Leu-Val-Thr
	Gamma-endorphin	Tyr-Gly-Gly-Phe-Met-Thr-Ser-Glu-Lys-Ser-Gln-Thr-Pro-Leu-Val-Thr-Leu
	Beta-endorphin	Tyr-Gly-Gly-Phe-Met-Thr-Ser-Glu-Lys-Ser-Gln-Thr-Pro-Leu-Val-Thr-Leu-Phe-Lys-Asn-Ala-Ile-Val-Lys-Asn-Ala-His-Lys-Lys-Gly-Gln
Prodynorphin	Alpha-neo-endorphin	Tyr-Gly-Gly-Phe-Leu-Arg-Lys-Tyr-Pro-Lys
	Dynorphin A (1-17)	Tyr-Gly-Gly-Phe-Leu-Arg-Arg-Ile-Arg-Pro-Lys-Leu-Lys-Trp-Asp-Asn-Gln
	Dynorphin (1-8)	Tyr-Gly-Gly-Phe-Leu-Arg-Arg-Ile
	Dynorphin B (Rimorphin)	Tyr-Gly-Gly-Phe-Leu-Arg-Arg-Gln-Phe-Lys-Val-Val-Thr

* *Abbreviations:* Ala: alanine, Arg: arginine, Asn: asparagine, Asp: aspartic acid, Gln: glutamine, Glu: glutamic acid, Gly: glycine, His: histidine, Ile: isoleucine, Leu: leucine, Lys: lysine, Met: methionine, Phe: phenylalanine, Pro: proline, Ser: serine, Thr: threonine, Trp: tryptophan, Tyr: tyrosine, Val: valine.

pig ileum that was sensitive to morphine and easily antagonized by naloxone. In accordance with Martin's terminology, this type was called the mu-receptor. Another type, however, was found in the mouse vas deferens, more sensitive to enkephalin than to morphine, and not as easily antagonized by naloxone. The second type was called the delta-receptor, after the deferens tissue where it was originally discovered.

The combined effects of this research was the recognition of three receptor types (mu, delta, and kappa) coexisting with their own anatomical distribution in the brain as well as three separate families of endorphins. It would have been convenient (and tidy) if it were the case that a single receptor type were linked up with only one family of endorphins, but it seems that there is considerable overlap. The met-enkephalin and leu-enkephalin peptides are primarily attracted to the delta-receptors, while one of the variations of the enkephalin peptide seems equally attracted to the mu-receptors as well. Beta-endorphin is strongly attracted to both mu-receptors and delta-receptors, with a slight bias toward the delta type. All dynorphin peptides show a preference for kappa-receptors, but even here there are tendencies toward the other two receptors. Why there should be this range of receptor sensitivities for each endorphin group remains a mystery. It is possible that there is some gain in information conveyed by neurons in the brain by involving different types of receptors.‡ Multiple forms of endorphins are evidently released simultaneously in the brain, and perhaps slight differences in the proportional representation among the three families could have some physiological significance.[59]

Beyond their major biochemical properties, however, there has also been interest in the functional significance of opioid peptides in the physiological and behavioral life of the organism. The mu-receptor seems to be the classic morphine receptor, and the function of

‡ The situation of multiple receptors and peptides is a bit like trying to describe the linguistic characteristics of three neighborhoods in a multiethnic city. Residents of one neighborhood (receptor type) may speak a dominant language (opioid type) but have the capability to speak others under certain circumstances. Likewise, a given language (opioid type) may be spoken in two different neighborhoods (receptor type) but in different proportions according to the ethnic makeup within each neighborhood.

mu-receptors in general appears to be in the area of analgesia. Solomon Snyder and his associates have even shown evidence for two subtypes of the mu-receptor, one responsible purely for analgesia and the other for the inhibition of breathing (the principal cause of death from overdoses of morphine and heroin).[60] If a drug had a sensitivity for the first receptor subtype and not the second, obviously it would be an important clinical advance; but unfortunately no such drug has yet been developed. The function of the delta-receptor, it has been theorized, may be less involved with analgesia than with mood. It is possible that the euphoric feelings after taking morphine would be due primarily to binding at the delta-receptor, because at sufficient dosages both mu and delta types would be affected.

If there is a central thread running through the fabric of the endorphin story since these days of discovery, it is the connection between the function of endorphins and the concept of stress. It made intuitive sense, for example, to link up the reduction of pain and the feelings of euphoria with the stress of fighting for one's survival. When it was found in 1977 that beta-endorphin shares a place with ACTH (adrenocorticotropin, the hormone released by the anterior pituitary and delivered to the adrenal gland during times of stress) on the same precursor molecule, it became a real possibility that endorphin peptides (at least beta-endorphin) played a direct role in the stress response.[61] The reality of this possibility soon became established by the laboratories of Roger Guillemin and Floyd Bloom at the Salk Institute later in 1977, when they demonstrated that beta-endorphin and ACTH were secreted into the bloodstream from the pituitary gland *simultaneously,* and moreover shared the identical regulatory responses.[62] No more dramatic evidence could be presented that the endocrine (glandular) and nervous systems worked in a holistic way. As we will see, stress seems to be an important key in understanding what the endorphins do for us as humans, as well as for the range of vertebrate species that share these wondrous and mysterious substances.*

* Rabi Simantov and Solomon Snyder measured the relative concentrations of opiate receptors in a range of animal species, finding an equivalent level for all vertebrates from humans down to species as primitive as the hagfish (one of the oldest living

POSTSCRIPT TO THE DAYS OF DISCOVERY—THE 1978
LASKER AWARDS

For the neuroscience community and for the scientific world at large, the announcement by the Albert and Mary Lasker Foundation in November 1978 of the annual Basic Medical Research Award to Solomon Snyder, Hans Kosterlitz, and John Hughes was exciting news. It was, for one thing, a validation of the contribution that endorphin research had made to the neurosciences (and medical science in general) in the scarcely five years since the field had begun. But more than that was the meaning behind winning the Lasker. The prestige for this award is enormous. As of that year, fully twenty-eight of the former Lasker awardees had gone on to win the ultimate award, the Nobel Prize. (As of 1986, the number had grown to forty-four.) In other words, winning a Lasker seemed often to be a predictor for a future Nobel.

It was precisely the implications that could be read *into* the announcement of the 1978 winners that sparked the immediate controversy. No one doubted that Snyder should have been included, but what about Eric Simon and Lars Terenius, in whose laboratories the opiate receptor was also discovered? In fact, a slight edge in priority could have been given to Terenius, ahead of the other two. What about the contributions of Avram Goldstein, whose basic methodology made the receptor discoveries possible in the first place?

Beyond these obvious omissions, however, was the matter of acknowledgment *within* a particular laboratory group, and here was an issue that quickly became a cause célèbre: the lack of recognition accorded to Candace Pert. In an unusual step, Pert wrote to Mary Lasker after the announcement, expressing her disappointment over the foundation's decision. "I was angry and upset to be excluded from this year's Awards . . . as Dr. Snyder's graduate student, I played a key role in initiating this research and following it up."[65] She refused the invitation to attend the Lasker Foundation luncheon

---

vertebrates).[63] Since then, moreover, a few invertebrates with opiate receptors have been found.[64]

honoring the award-winners and a series of articles and letters to the editors protesting her omission soon appeared in the journals.† Some reporters saw Pert as a victim of sexist attitudes held by a male-dominated scientific establishment.[67] Others, however, saw the situation as another example of a scientific tradition where the graduate student in the laboratory does much of the actual experimental work and the senior investigator who oversees the work gets the credit.[68] Reportedly, Snyder at the time called the members of the Lasker Committee to reconsider including Pert, but the foundation stood by its decision. "It's kind of a philosophical issue," Snyder later explained when asked to comment, "usually it isn't discussed in the news media. It's like fraternities—that's the way the game is played. They [graduate students] figure that later, when they have students, it will be the same."[69] The chairman of the Pharmacology Department at Johns Hopkins, has recalled that when he put Snyder's name into nomination for the Lasker Award, "it never entered my perception of the staff in this department to include Dr. Pert in that nomination. There was just no reason I knew of to do that."[70] Hughes, it was said, was a collaborator with Kosterlitz, not his graduate student. Hughes had been the *sole* author of the pivotal May 1975 article in *Brain Research,* while Pert had been *senior* author of articles cowritten with Snyder.

It was a situation with many accusations and few easy answers. The Lasker Committee had no rules that limited the number of individuals that could have been honored (unlike the Nobel Committee, which must limit the number to three in any particular category), and it seemed clearly a mistake not to have included Goldstein, Simon, and Terenius. A major prize given the previous year, the National Institute on Drug Abuse (NIDA) Pacesetter Research Award, had included them, as well as Snyder, Hughes, and Kosterlitz. William Pollin, Director of Research at NIDA, writing to the *Science News* in 1978, had admitted regretfully that it was in retrospect a

† Pert reportedly kept for a time on a wall of her lab the postcard reading, "PLEASE —we have not as yet received your reply card for the Lasker Award Luncheon, Tuesday, November 21, 1978." The card was next to a poster with the slogan "If you are getting run out of town, get in front of the crowd and make it look like a parade."[66]

major omission that the Pacesetter Award had not included Pert as well.[71]

At the very least, the furor over the 1978 Lasker Awards demonstrated the contrast between the reality of modern scientific research and the fantasy of the ivory tower existence so many people envision. It also showed the difficulty faced by an organization that assumes the responsibility of bestowing awards for scientific accomplishment. If award committees cannot determine which laboratories are responsible for important discoveries, it has been asked, how can they sort out the individuals *within* the laboratories who are worthy of recognition? Science has changed since the day when one would never have questioned Einstein's solitary accomplishment on the theory of relativity. Modern-day science is now an international community and a team effort. No one works alone anymore.

There may have been winners and losers in the Lasker affair but fortunately no victims. All of those who were thought to have deserved the award but were left out have continued their distinguished careers. They continue in their work on the frontiers of brain chemistry. The Lasker affair is behind them. So far, the Nobel Committee in Stockholm has looked elsewhere.

In March of 1979 pharmacologist Thomas Maren would reflect on what could have been. "I do not quite know," he wrote, "what the Lasker Foundation should have done—taking all of [them] in means a pretty big gang—at least seven. But life is perhaps not so much unfair as it is unruly; science as well as art mirrors life, and the prize-giving foundations may have to join in."[72] It seems fitting that the Lasker Awards of 1978 would draw a curtain down on an era marked by intense personal competition along with scientific discoveries of truly historic proportions.[73] Neuroscientists who were at the center of the endorphin story—veterans of races won or lost—would, in looking back, call that period "the vintage years."[74]

PART TWO

Endorphins and Evolution

6

First Step Toward Paradise

THE STRUGGLE OVER PAIN

When I think of pain—of anxiety that gnaws like fire and loneliness that spreads out like a desert, and the heartbreaking routine of monotonous misery, or again of dull aches that blacken our whole landscape or sudden nauseating pains that knock a man's heart out at one blow . . . it "quite o'ercrows my spirit." If I knew any way of escape I would crawl through sewers to find it. But what is the good of telling you about my feelings? You know them already, they are the same as yours. . . . Pain hurts. That is what the word means.

C. S. LEWIS, *The Problem of Pain,* 1962

Your pain is the breaking of the shell that encloses your understanding.

Even as the stone of the fruit must break that its heart may stand in the sun, so must you know pain. . . .

It is the bitter potion by which the physician within you heals your sick self.

KAHLIL GIBRAN, *The Prophet,* 1923

Short-term pain may be a vital signal, built into our evolution, warning us that we are in some kind of biological danger, but long-term, inescapable pain is a curse, the worst curse we can ever conceive. Its torment is synonymous with the imagery of Hell itself. As physiologist Ronald Melzack once wrote, "Anyone who has suffered prolonged, severe pain comes to regard it as an evil, punishing affliction."[1] It is not surprising, therefore, that throughout history those who have had even the slightest degree of effectiveness in reducing the pain of others have gained enormous stature. They have been the shamans, faith healers, mesmerists, medicine men, and high priests. When morphine became available to the medical profession in the mid-nineteenth century, physicians could finally be true healers.[2] They could now at last do something magical for their patients by offering nearly instantaneous relief from chronic pain.

Until very recently, the natural environment has been the only source for drugs that reduce pain. When American pioneers traveled westward, they encountered Indian tribes who treated pain and fever by chewing willow bark, reminiscent of a remedy that had been popular in Europe from as early as 400 B.C. It turns out that willow bark yields an analgesic substance called salicylic acid, named from *Salix,* the botanical name for willow. The beneficial effect of pure salicylic acid on pain, however, was for a long time limited by the fact that most digestive systems could not handle it easily. In 1898 Felix Hoffman of the Bayer Company in Germany discovered that when an acetyl group was added (making the chemical product acetylsalicylic acid), the side effect was reduced without any decrease in its therapeutic power. When Heinrich Dreser, research director of the company, wanted a name that was easier to say, it was recalled that salicylic acid also came from spirea plants, and the name aspirin was invented, from the German *Acetylirte Spirsäure.*[3]

Drugs like aspirin, however useful they may be, have nowhere near the analgesic power of opium or morphine. The reason behind the effectiveness of these opiates was largely a mystery until the 1970s, when it was discovered that the central nervous system had the ability to produce its own natural substances called endorphins with analgesic properties virtually identical to those of the opiates originating either naturally from the poppy or synthetically from chemical laboratories. Here finally was the reason behind the power of opiate drugs. They would simply substitute for chemicals already within us. Armed now with an understanding of endorphins, we have advanced in our long quest for an effective treatment for chronic pain.

But why should such an internal "opioid" system of endorphins have ever developed? It seems to be a continual feature of the nervous systems of every vertebrate species one can find. Why has the opioid system been around for so long? The activation of this system seems to be inextricably linked to the circumstances of stress. Why is stress such an important factor? Behind all the speculation is the recognition that, in the spectrum of human experience, no feelings are as primitive and none can be felt so deeply as those of pain. In the entire range of animal behaviors, none is more basic to survival than the avoidance of pain. It is clear that endorphins can serve as a window into our evolutionary past.

In that past there is a world most of us are lucky enough never to have encountered, an environment in which we must fear a host of natural predators that could kill us at any moment. Imagine yourself as a small animal, a rodent or rabbit, for example, in that dangerous world. What would you do to protect yourself and survive? One possible defense would be to escape visual detection in the first place, to freeze. While you were immobile, the protective coloring of your fur would blend into its surroundings. Your breathing would be rapid and shallow. Beyond this defensive posture, however, something else would be happening that would prove extremely advantageous toward your survival—you would be temporarily analgesic. The reason is that pain would ordinarily produce behaviors that would hurt your chances for survival, not help them. If you licked your paw, the predator would notice the movement. If visual sighting by the predator did occur, your next strategy would be to flee as quickly as possible. If you limped away on an injured leg, your escape would obviously be slowed. If you were to have any chance of winning an actual fight, an injury would be best ignored. There would be a powerful evolutionary advantage for a species, any species, to have developed a degree of analgesia in times of stress.[4]

In an important sense, we as humans continue to function with a similar kind of analgesia during stressful periods of our lives. There are countless stories, most of them well documented, of soldiers who become oblivious to the pain of their injuries during the heat of battle. Athletes are sometimes aware of an injury only after the stress of the game is over. There are also cases of painlessness accomplished through the stress of religious ritual or primitive initiation rites. All of these examples link us to a fundamental biological relationship between stress and analgesia.

STRESS, PAIN, AND ENDORPHINS

In animal research, one of the ways stress can be simulated under laboratory conditions is to present animals with the possibility of receiving electric shock. No animals are injured by the shock, but it is obvious by their behavior that they don't like it, any more than we would. If you gave a laboratory rat, for instance, a choice between receiving a shock either *with* or *without* a warning signal, you would find (not surprisingly) that signaled shock would be preferred. If a shock had to be received, it seems to be only common sense that at least it would be better to have a warning just prior to its delivery. It is not so easy, however, to come up with the exact reason a preference for signaled shock should exist. It simply seems reasonable that it would be helpful to prepare oneself in some way for the shock and, in doing so, make it less aversive.

In 1977 physiological psychologist Michael Fanselow, then a graduate student at the University of Washington in Seattle, considered the possibility that a signal just prior to a shock might be giving an animal the opportunity to release endorphins. Perhaps a form of Pavlovian conditioning was taking place. Just as Pavlov's dogs had learned to salivate at the sound of the bell that signaled the delivery of food, animals receiving signaled shock could be associating the stress of shock to the signal; a resultant increase in the level of endorphins could be making the shock feel less painful. Using the by then standard procedure for testing the involvement of endorphins, Fanselow gave naloxone to his rats and discovered that the preference for signaled shock was abolished. After naloxone, rats did not seem to care whether shock was or was not preceded by a signal. If

the warning had triggered an endorphin-type analgesia and if naloxone had canceled this effect, then it was reasonable to assume that
the pain the rats felt in the two circumstances was now identical.[5]

The process of Pavlovian conditioning, probably the most primitive of all forms of association, seemed to hold an important key to
understanding the ways in which endorphins were related to stress-
induced analgesia. Subsequent studies showed that being in the same
place where shock had been previously experienced was enough to
produce an analgesia that was reversible by naloxone.[6] Moreover, the
scent of another rat that had experienced shock was enough to produce the effect in an unstressed rat (probably the closest you would
come to social empathy in a rat).[7] And rats tested in the presence of,
but protected from, a cat became analgesic, an effect that could be
blocked by naloxone.[8] It was clear that an emotion like fear could,
under the right circumstances, trigger the activation of an endorphin
system that would inhibit the processing of pain and any of the
behaviors associated with that pain. In other words, endorphins
would ensure that survival came first, and recuperation later.[9]

Fanselow's experiments had succeeded in establishing a *behavioral*
linkage between stress and endorphin release. In the meantime, stress
and endorphins were found also to share a close biochemical kinship,
at the level of the pituitary gland. In 1977 beta-endorphin and
ACTH, the classic stress hormone, were found to originate from the
same precursor molecule, a long peptide, with approximately 260
amino acids and the unwieldy name of pro-opiomelanocortin or simply POMC. This precursor molecule had been located in a range of
places in the body—the hypothalamus and other areas of the brain,
as well as several peripheral tissues including the placenta and gastrointestinal tract.[10] It was in the anterior portion of the pituitary
gland, however, that the last 134 amino acids of this giant peptide
would be found to break off from the rest in a characteristic way.
The split-off portion would consist of ACTH and beta-lipotropin,
two peptides joined end to end.[11] In 1976 C. H. Li's laboratory had
found that beta-lipotropin contained beta-endorphin, so it seemed
likely now that a further split-off would release beta-endorphin itself.
In the following year, studies by Salk Institute researchers had
shown that beta-endorphin and ACTH were secreted *together* from

the anterior pituitary as joint hormones of stress.[12] In effect, beta-endorphin and ACTH were "sibling peptides," coexisting on the same precursor molecule, ready to be released together as the need arose. Peptides inside other peptides; strings of amino acids broken off and routed to destinations of need: it was like boxcars splitting off from a long freight train. Or better, like some kind of biochemical dance designed to prepare an organism to deal with threats to its survival.

The areas of the brain that are involved in the release of endorphins for analgesia during stress—structures in the midbrain and hindbrain—are among the most primitive regions of our brains. These are parts of the brain whose development stretches back to very early days in vertebrate evolution, more than 200 million years ago. In the context of Paul MacLean's triune concept of brain evolution (see Chapter 2), these brain structures constituted the first of three major thrusts in the evolutionary development of the brain and were associated with the emergence of a range of reptilian species.[13] Our own brains still depend upon these neural systems, little changed in hundreds of millions of years. Thus, we can view ourselves as a part of that biological heritage that produced an endorphin system for analgesia.

It can be argued that endorphin systems formed the basis for a new element of control over an animal's environment, a crucial advance in the power that could be exerted over that which was potentially lethal in the world. In order to appreciate the impact of endorphins in this new kind of control, it is important first to examine what we think the world was like in that distant time.

ENDORPHINS AND THE PROTOREPTILIAN BRAIN

According to present-day evolutionary theory, the Age of Mammals began around 65 million years ago, when the dominance of the giant dinosaur reptiles over the natural world abruptly ended. Mammals may have begun their ascendancy at this time, but their evolutionary development could be traced back to a much earlier period. Approximately 250 million years ago a great many lines of evolutionary development began to branch away from a common ancestral trunk. Starting from a primal group of "stem reptiles" called cotylosaurs, some of these branches continued to evolve into the various forms of dinosaurs. Out of branches from this common stem also arose the evolution of crocodiles and birds around 190 and 150 million years ago respectively; snakes have a relatively recent history, beginning around 120 million years ago. With respect to mammalian evolution, the critical break-off happened around 250 million years ago, when a group of mammal-like reptiles called the therapsids appeared on the scene. They would become extinct themselves after 65 million years of existence on earth, but not after sowing the seeds for the Age of Mammals and our own evolution.

The era of the therapsids coincided with a geological period that preceded even the presence of separate continents; most of the land-mass on the earth's surface at that time was connected together in the giant supercontinent called Pangaea, and when the continents started to drift apart the therapsids followed. As a result, therapsid fossils are found in all parts of the world, in astonishingly large numbers. It is in the Karroo fossil beds of southern Africa—a massive area that comprises more than 200,000 square miles (covering about half the area of the present-day Republic of South Africa)—that we see the richest deposit of animal remains from this period. With deposits in layers to depths between two thousand and five thousand feet, the Karroo contains an estimated 800 billion fossils, a significant portion being therapsids. The first mammal-like reptile fossil was discovered there in 1838 by English paleontologist Andrew Geddes Bain.[14]

From a behavioral standpoint, we are not in a position to know directly much about the therapsids, not even whether or not they actually laid eggs. Nevertheless, the therapsids were so similar in structure to some types of present-day lizards that a fruitful avenue of behavioral research (to get some idea of this long-ago time) has been the study of lizard behavior, particularly one specific type called the Komodo dragon from Indonesia.[15]

It can be disconcerting to recognize that the closest linkage between ancient therapsids and an existing species should be a three-hundred-pound, ten-foot-long nightmare of an animal like the Komodo dragon (figure 16). It seems the epitome of a dark past that we would gladly deny or at least ignore. Nevertheless, the study of its behavior and the behavior of other lizard species has been extremely useful in understanding the behavorial capabilities and limitations of a protoreptilian brain, and in turn how the protoreptilian aspects of our own present brains have influenced our present behavior.

What were the behaviors of these extinct creatures? It is probable that, like the lizards studied by MacLean and others, the protoreptilians also lived a life of ritual and routine, an existence characterized by stereotyped movements rigidly governed by precedent. The most prominent behaviors would be oriented to the establishment of a defensible territory, an environmental space for the securing of food and for mating and breeding.[16] It is possible to speculate that this instinctive drive for territoriality might have been supported by an endorphin system oriented toward pain control. The mechanism of Pavlovian conditioning would enable an animal to associate a painful stimulus with the environment in which that stimulus occurred. Out of this simple form of learning, a dichotomous representation of the world could be generated. The world would be viewed as two basic territories: either a place of safety and security or a place of danger and potential death.

As MacLean has written, the struggle for territoriality may have served as the foundation for a general struggle for dominance, a natural will-to-power:

> In the world of animals, one can hardly find the will-to-power more dramatically expressed than in the behavior of some lizards. To see two rainbow lizards in their resplendent colors striving for dominance is like returning to the days of King Arthur. In a contest, once the gauntlet is thrown down, the challenge display gives way to violent combat and the struggle is unrelenting. Twice we have seen rainbow lizards humiliated in defeat. They lost their majestic colors, lapsed into a depression, and died two weeks later.[17]

We see the same struggle in our own behavior. We continue to maintain an intense identification with our geographical roots and a clear discrimination between "home" and "non-home." In sports events, we speak of advantages of playing on our "home field." The sense of

16. The Komodo dragon, Varanus komodoensis, *from Indonesia. (Courtesy Department Library Services, the American Museum of Natural History, New York)*

territoriality᠆has also become, as MacLean has pointed out, in-grained in our sense of legality.

> If human beings are not born with some degree of territorial itch, it is remarkable that there is so much preoccupation with trespass and non-trespass and that in every advanced culture complex legal systems and a whole body of law have evolved for settling disputes regarding ownership of lands and possessions. If all human behavior is learned, then human beings seem naturally to have learned very well to be territorial![18]

The behaviors connected to the workings of a protoreptilian brain may appear extremely primitive to us, but the truth is that a limited repertoire of responses enabled a group of species to survive for an astoundingly long portion of evolutionary history. Control over pain, as achieved by the functioning of endorphins, may have been only a small step in an accumulating history of control over environmental forces, but for a protoreptilian animal trying to survive it was enough.

The idea that this protoreptilian brain has since then intermeshed, as MacLean has put it, with the more recently evolved and "more enlightened" components of our brain forces us to confront the leg-acy of territoriality that our reptilian ancestors have left us. No one claims that it is easy to do, as MacLean has recognized:

> Man puts so much emphasis on himself as a unique creature possessing a spoken and written language that, like the rich man denying his poor relatives, he is loath to acknowledge his animal ancestry. In the last century, it almost killed him to admit his resemblance to apes, but the time is approaching when he must say "uncle" and admit to having far poorer relatives! Intellectually he has been aware of this for a long time, but emotionally he cannot bring himself to recognize it. It is a little bit like the "denial of illness."[19]

If the crux of brain evolution, as MacLean's triune brain concept has implied, is a three-step process of gaining control over one's environ-ment, then, according to the speculation here, endorphins helped to achieve that first step by providing the biochemical means for con-trolling pain.

WHAT IS STRESS?

It can be argued that part of the heritage of that protoreptilian brain is the inseparable linkage between stress and endorphins. Nevertheless, the question of what kind of stressor manages to activate the endorphin system is quite complex. Neuroscientists in endorphin research have had to grapple with the same long-standing problem that has concerned psychologists and physiologists over the course of stress research in general: How do you define a stressor?

It turns out that the concept of stress itself is very young. When Hippocrates wrote that disease was both a matter of suffering *(pathos)* and a matter of toil *(pónos)* as the body fought to restore itself toward a normal state, he was referring to a central idea about stress; but it was not until 1936 that the modern era of stress research began.[20] In that year, Canadian scientist Hans Selye began to demonstrate in his research and argue almost single-handedly that specific changes in bodily function, literally a "stress syndrome," would result as challenges arose to the well-being of the organism. "Stress," he wrote, "is the common denominator of all adaptive reactions in the body."[21] In the case of humans, stress is the reaction to the wear and tear of living; in the case of animals who live in the wild, it is the reaction to the demands of survival.

Yet the definition of a stressor inevitably rests upon the criterion of its ability to initiate the stress reaction. In the human experience of stress, it is the neocortex that accomplishes the interpretive judgment that a particular environmental event qualifies as a "stressor." The neocortex communicates neurally with the hypothalamus to stimulate the secretion of hormones by the anterior pituitary gland and later the adrenal glands.[22] Our bodies are reacting to the circulating levels of these hormones in the bloodstream, but the beginning lies in the interpretation of information in the neocortex of our brains.

"It is not what happens to a man that is important, it is what he thinks happened to him." This observation by the great nineteenth-century philosopher Arthur Schopenhauer arrives at the very heart of the problem of defining a stressor.[23] In one extreme instance, the intensity of a perceived stressor can lead to a disastrous fall in blood pressure or ventricular fibrillation of the heart that could be fatal. There are well-documented cases of "sudden death" (or in certain cultures, "voodoo death") in apparently healthy individuals who have died during times of extreme stress.[24]

Stressors can be so pervasive that whole communities of individuals are affected. During World War II, for example, epidemic-like outbreaks of "air-raid ulcers" in the blitzed areas of England involved thousands of civilians emotionally overwhelmed by the continual series of bombings, even though they escaped direct physical injury.[25] It was the atmosphere of uncontrollability that made these wartime circumstances so horrendous. People felt helpless in the face of unpredictable bombings.

When a similar degree of uncontrollability is created in animal studies of stress, an equivalent degree of physiological and psychological damage can be observed. Jay Weiss, at Rockefeller University, showed in 1971 that inescapable (and hence uncontrollable) shocks produced a greater degree of stomach ulcers in rats than escapable ones.[26] Martin Seligman, at the University of Pennsylvania, showed in 1967, with experiments on shock avoidance in dogs, that, when the animals experienced a series of inescapable shocks, they became simply helpless. Twenty-four hours later, they would be totally unable to learn to respond to a clear signal that reliably preceded shock in order to avoid it. This phenomenon—Seligman called it "learned helplessness"—would not be observed in animals that had been given either escapable shock or no shock at all in the earlier phase. These latter animals evidently learned to respond in an entirely appropriate and adaptive way, and as a result they avoided the shock.[27] Subsequent studies in several laboratories showed that learned helplessness could be created in a range of species: cats, rats, fish, and even humans (where an unpleasant noise was used instead of shock).[28]

When Steven F. Maier and colleagues at the University of Colorado demonstrated in 1979 that animals who had developed learned helplessness were also analgesic, a crucial linkage between stress and analgesia was finally complete. Most important, the analgesia was mediated by an endorphin system, by virtue of two important criteria. First, the effect could be blocked by either of the opiate antagonists, naloxone or naltrexone. Second, there was a "cross-tolerance" between the analgesia caused by the learned helplessness and the analgesia caused by morphine. That is, animals that had previously been addicted to morphine (they had developed a tolerance for morphine so that larger than usual amounts were needed for a given level of analgesia) were now *less* analgesic after inescapable shocks than animals having no previous experience with morphine.[29] It was clear that uncontrollability was the key. Something in the animal's evolutionary past had produced a protection against pain in circumstances when the noxious event could not be controlled by the animal's behavior.

It is not difficult to see the parallels in the animal studies of stress and situations in human society. Like the results of the Weiss studies on animals, surveys concerning the incidence of psychosomatic ulcers among corporate executives show a close association with the notion of uncontrollability. Contrary to what may be expected, it is not the top executive who shows the greatest frequency of stress-related disorders.[30] The level of a corporate hierarchy that produces the worst effects is middle management, since it is here that an individual must shoulder a great deal of responsibility and suffer substantial pressures without the benefit of having a sense of control over the policy-making process, which is reserved for top management. For a middle manager, uncontrollability would be a major component of the work environment. It would be interesting to see if middle managers have on the average a higher threshold for pain while at work!*

THE POSSIBILITY OF ANALGESIA WITHOUT ENDORPHINS

Until 1980 it was generally thought that stress-induced analgesia in laboratory studies necessarily involved an endorphin system. In that

---

* There is a cyclical pattern during an average twenty-four-hour day of both endorphins and the stress hormone ACTH. They rise and fall together in a diurnal rhythm, with their highest levels in the morning and the lowest in the afternoon and evening—probably the reason why pain sensitivity is lowest in the morning and highest later in the day.[31] The information may be helpful when scheduling a future visit to the dentist.

year it was discovered that, under certain circumstances, analgesia could also be produced independently of endorphins. One critical factor seemed to be the *temporal* pattern in the shocks. John W. Lewis in Liebeskind's laboratory at UCLA showed that *intermittent* foot shock to rats caused an analgesia within thirty minutes, reversible by naloxone and cross-tolerant with morphine. A comparable amount of *continuous* shock, however, produced an equivalent degree of analgesia, but the analgesia could not be reversed by naloxone and displayed no cross-tolerance.[32] In the first condition, endorphins had been triggered; in the second condition, they had not.

Perhaps, as has been speculated, those in the intermittent-shock group were in a better position to recognize the uncontrollability of their situation; or perhaps the presentation of intermittent shock was spread over a longer period of time so as to make the circumstances more aversive in general.[33] Whatever the reason for the difference, the important implication was that a stress-induced analgesia could be created without the participation of endorphins. At about the same time, David Mayer and Linda Watkins, at the Medical College of Virginia, Virginia Commonwealth University, found that brief mild shocks to either the front paws or hind paws produced analgesia equivalently, but only the analgesia from front-paw shock could be blocked by naloxone or could show cross-tolerance to morphine.[34] Again, a potent analgesia could occur without the involvement of endorphins.

Why would two physiological systems for stress-induced analgesia have evolved in the handling of pain? Was there a sequence of development with one system existing prior to the other? Unfortunately, it is impossible to find physical evidence, from either fossil records or comparative anatomy, that would indicate whether the two systems evolved in a serial or parallel fashion. Nevertheless, from the behavioral evidence, a case can be made that the endorphin system for analgesia evolved as a relatively more sophisticated process for controlling pain, with some unusual advantages. First and foremost, the fact that the Pavlovian conditioning of fear depends upon an endorphin system supports the speculation being developed here that endorphins may have provided a critical mechanism for avoiding potentially harmful elements in an animal's environment. In the long run, an animal would be in no position to avoid something that was painful unless there was a means for making the association between that pain and events that immediately preceded or accompanied it. Whatever the effectiveness of a non-endorphin analgesia system for short-term pain relief, there was clearly no capability for making associative links between events.

Mayer and Watkins have theorized that an endorphin analgesia system is activated when there is a substantial distance between the portion of the body being stressed (in their case, the front paws being shocked) and the portion of the body being tested for analgesia (usually the analgesia test used is the reactivity of the tail to either heat or a pinch). They have reasoned that hind-paw shock produced a non-endorphin analgesia because the two portions of the animal's body were close to each other.[35] Their theory may be correct, but in the context of an evolutionary account of endorphins and analgesia, another interpretation of their data can be considered. It may be that the key factor lies in the importance of front-paw sensations for general exploratory behavior. The association of something experienced during exploratory behavior with unpleasantness or pain would be an important element in the gradual gaining of control over that environment. It would no longer be a matter of escaping from a stressor but rather a matter of learning to avoid it in the future. The systematic exploration by front paws would expand an animal's sense of territoriality, its sense of what is safe and what is not. The endorphins would in that sense provide the means for proceeding from *pain experience* and *pain reaction* to *pain avoidance*. It is not inconceivable that this relatively small step would lead eventually to greater and greater use of front paws (and hands) to achieve increasingly powerful means of environmental control.

It is significant, with regard to these speculations, that hind-paw shock may also produce endorphin-mediated analgesia, provided that some conditioning process is involved. Exposure to a non-electrified grid floor produces an analgesia that is reversed by naloxone, after being paired with either front-paw or hind-paw shock.[36] Apparently, the feature of Pavlovian conditioning is an overriding criterion for triggering endorphins to reduce pain, regardless of what portion of the animal's body was experiencing the stressor. It is also significant that the analgesia produced in situations of Pavlovian conditioning, unlike some other forms of analgesia, is independent of hormones in the body.[37] It is a purely neural phenomenon. On the basis of these findings, therefore, it is reasonable to see an endorphin-mediated analgesia process as an evolutionary advance over the analgesia that functions independently of endorphins.

Beyond the theoretical significance of multiple systems for analgesia, however, is the fact that there is potential clinical importance in being able to produce analgesia outside the domain of endorphins. It may be possible someday to tap into this non-endorphin system in the treatment of pain and, let us hope, avoid the addictive side effects of present analgesic drugs. The magnitude and duration of non-endorphin analgesia in animal studies appear to be comparable to those of the analgesia produced with endorphins. But the neurochemistry of non-endorphin analgesia is virtually unknown. If we were to make progress in this area, we could begin to develop nonopioid analgesic drugs.[38] Consequently, the reality of non-endorphin analgesia provides an opportunity in our long battle against chronic pain. It is at least theoretically possible that pain inhibition need not be associated with tolerance and dependency.

ENDORPHINS AND THE ANATOMY OF PAIN CONTROL

The understanding we now have of effects of endorphins in the nervous system upon the processing of pain has revolutionized the conception of how pain is perceived from a neurological point of view and, more important, how chronic pain may be effectively treated. We no longer interpret the effectiveness of morphine and other opiates as a matter of stopping the transmission of nerve impulses in the central nervous system, as novocaine might act on a peripheral nerve. The discovery of endorphins made it clear that there were active processes whose purpose it was to inhibit the signals of pain. In this regard, the neural pathways underlying pain had to be considered quite differently from the pathways underlying the other major senses. Sensory systems like vision and hearing, for example, have well-defined pathways in the nervous system, leading from a well-defined sense organ (eye or ear) to receptive and integrating centers in the brain. Some degree of physical interruption in these pathways leads predictably to some degree of blindness or deafness. The processing of pain, on the other hand, makes use of pathways that also participate in the registration of touch, pressure, warmth, and cold—not surprising when you consider that it is the extreme degree of any of these tactile sensations that becomes uncomfortable or painful. The source of pain signals, called nociceptors (literally, "hurtful receptors"), are widely distributed as networks of free nerve endings embedded in the skin as well as in the walls of internal organs, on the surface of the cornea, and in the pulp sections of teeth. Yet the interruption of these sources of pain sometimes fails to dispel its effect.

The special nature of the pain pathway gives rise to some medical problems that have no precedent in clinical practice. One example is the phenomenon of the phantom limb. About one third of all patients having undergone an amputation of a limb report at least temporarily some degree of pain that feels as if it were originating from a part of the body that is no longer there. Arm amputees might say that a phantom hand is clenched and that phantom fingers are digging into the palm. Surgical procedures, such as the sectioning of sensory nerve fibers from the limb or even the sectioning of portions of the spinal cord itself, are often only partially successful in relieving phantom limb pain. In the disease trigeminal neuralgia, often seen in older individuals, severe pain is felt in the head or face, made worse by movements associated with eating or talking. Surgical separation of the sensory nerves from this area is frequently ineffective in relieving this pain.[39]

One way of making sense of pain perception and its disorders is to imagine the neurology of pain as a two-way street. When pain signals originate on the body, they are carried in the spinal cord upward to the brain along the spinothalamic pathway, so named because the destination is the thalamus.† This is the same pathway that carries ordinary sensations of deep pressure, and of warmth and cold. Another spinal pathway, called the dorsolateral columns, carries signals

† When pain signals originate at any location from the neck up, the input comes into the brain via the trigeminal (or fifth cranial) nerve. Pain inhibition, however, is accomplished in a similar way as in the spinal cord.

downward and acts to inhibit these pain signals. Therefore, in these circumstances, pain is processed as an interaction between ascending signals transmitting the raw information and descending signals serving as a means for modulation or control.

It is the descending information to control pain that lies at the heart of endorphin-mediated analgesia. We now understand three principal locations in this pain-control system. The first lies at the entry point of neural information in the spinothalamic pathway. At this level, an area called the substantia gelatinosa can act upon incoming pain signals virtually at the gates to the central nervous system. Not surprisingly, the substantia gelatinosa is heavily endowed with opiate receptors, and it is generally believed that endorphin substances, possibly enkephalin, inhibit neurons in the spinothalamic pathway at this site. The other two locations, also with high concentrations of opiate receptors, are deep in the lower portion of the brain. Neural centers in midbrain and hindbrain, they are essentially the top of the dorsolateral columns in that they provide the major inputs that can be carried down and serve to modulate pain. One of these brain areas is the periaqueductal gray (PAG) area in the midbrain and the other is a portion of the medulla called the nucleus raphe magnus (NRM).[40]

Studies of the midbrain PAG have figured prominently in the theoretical development of ideas about pain control. Even prior to the discovery of opiate receptors, studies had shown that electrical stimulation of this region led to a naloxone-reversible analgesia in rats. These findings gave initial support to the idea that an active system for the reduction of pain was operating.[41] When it was further established that an addiction to morphine greatly reduced the analgesia produced by PAG stimulation (in other words, that there existed cross-tolerance), it was logical to assume that a natural morphine-like chemical was responsible for the phenomenon.[42] After enkephalin and beta-endorphin were identified in 1975 and 1976, it was finally possible to confirm in a direct fashion that PAG stimulation had the capability of triggering endorphins in the brain.

Given the success of PAG stimulation in producing analgesia in animal studies, a crucial question was whether a similar procedure might have therapeutic value for patients suffering from intractable pain. Conceivably, it was now possible to offer significant relief to patients for whom morphine or other opiates at acceptable dosages had been unable to suppress their constant pain. One first report of success came in 1977 from a medical team headed by Yoshio Hosobuchi at the University of California, San Francisco.[43] Six patients suffering either from pain from cancer or from some peripheral nerve damage agreed to undergo a surgical implantation of stimulation electrodes in the PAG region. These electrodes were secured to the skull and connected by wires to a small radio-frequency receiver that was implanted in the patient's chest. A battery-operated, hand-held transmitter could activate the receiver and in turn trigger PAG stimulation. Five of the six patients reported total relief from the pain, while one reported only partial relief and had to supplement the stimulation with a nonopiate analgesic. It was no longer necessary for them to take opiate drugs. Their appetites, ability to sleep without medication, and general well-being all improved dramatically. It was necessary, however, to use the transmitter sparingly, with short durations and rest periods in between. Otherwise, they found that after four to five weeks a tolerance effect would set in; the stimulation would start to be ineffective and the quantity of morphine needed to control the pain would actually rise to levels higher than that needed prior to the surgery. When the patients were given a brief administration of naloxone, the PAG stimulation effects were blocked, so it was clear that an endorphin system was mediating their pain relief.

About a year later, neurosurgeon Donald E. Richardson at Louisiana State University Medical Center at New Orleans, along with Huda Akil, John Hughes, and Jack Barchas, found similar success with PAG stimulation in another group of patients. In their study, they found that the stimulation produced an increase in what was referred to as "enkephalin-like material" in the cerebrospinal fluid.[44] Hosobuchi and his research associates at the Salk Institute also reported a biochemical change in their patient's cerebrospinal fluid, only in their case it was an increase in beta-endorphin rather than enkephalin. Beta-endorphin in the Hosobuchi studies rose from two to seven times the level prior to the stimulation.[45] While disagreeing as to exactly which endorphin substance was being affected, the two studies demonstrated that the clinical treatment for pain could be linked to the body's endorphin resources. The brain stimulation had actually increased the level of endorphin functioning, in parallel to its ability to relieve the pain.

Richardson's data revealed that the baseline levels of his patients were abnormally low and that PAG stimulation could be interpreted as raising the levels back to a normal point.[46] The implication was that patients suffering from the kinds of chronic pain that were treatable by opiate drugs or PAG stimulation had a basic insufficiency in their endorphin systems for pain control. In effect, these patients could be viewed as having lost the normal ability to produce acceptable amounts of endorphins.

Support for an idea of endorphin insufficiency in chronic pain comes from several areas of research. Swedish researchers, for example, have reported a negative correlation, in general, between endorphin levels in the cerebrospinal fluid and the degree of pain an individual reported. That is, the pain reported tended to be less intense when endorphin levels were high, and vice versa.[47] In a study by medical researcher Charles W. Denko of Case Western Reserve University in Cleveland, serum endorphin levels, as measured in blood samples from patients suffering from arthritis or from gout, were on the average between 30 and 86 percent lower than levels from normal controls.[48] Denko noted that some gout patients had almost no detectable serum endorphin at all. The knowledge that certain forms of chronic pain can be identified with endorphin insufficiency has led to future clinical possibilities for remedying the biochemical problem. The question of whether the best treatment lies in the neurosurgical approach of PAG stimulation, or in direct injection of endorphins themselves, remains unanswered.

There is little doubt that we share with other animal species the capacity to become analgesic in situations where the body's resources are being called upon to deal with some kind of stressor. In that sense, many of those who suffer from chronic pain, for one reason or another, are victims of a failure of an endorphin system that was originally designed to protect the body in circumstances of short-term, temporary stress. The constancy of a pain stimulus seems to have been simply not a feature of the environment that an endorphin system was meant to handle. In some individuals, as mentioned before, the operating system of endorphins has literally collapsed. Only through extraordinary medical interventions, it seems, can the effectiveness of a biochemical process that developed over hundreds of millions of years be recaptured.

ENDORPHINS IN ACUPUNCTURE

More than two thousand years ago, the Chinese developed a method for analgesia called acupuncture (figure 17). This technique involves the insertion of needles into the skin at precisely defined points in the body. Sometimes the needle is rotated, other times heated or electrically stimulated, so that nerve endings in the vicinity of the placement are affected. While the effectiveness of acupuncture in producing analgesia (often in areas of the body far removed from the location of the needle) has been demonstrated for a long time in the Orient, only recently has the practice become accepted by Western medicine.‡ It was simply unfathomable for non-Oriental scientists that the insertion of long needles at specific sites in the skin and the stimulation of nerve fibers could stop the perception of pain. If nothing else, the new understanding of pain processing in the last decade or so has helped bring the practice of acupuncture closer into the mainstream of Western medical practice.

The first demonstration of an endorphin connection in acupuncture analgesia was reported by David Mayer in 1974. He found that when an acupuncture site called the ho-ku point, between the thumb and index finger, was stimulated with needles, a significant (28 percent) analgesia in the teeth could be achieved, an effect that was completely reversible by naloxone.[49] The ho-ku point was also found to be effective for acupuncture analgesia in mice (in the analogous location, between the first and second digit of the front paw). In a series of studies by Bruce Pomeranz at the University of Toronto with acupuncture in these animals, specific cells in the brain that responded to normal pain stimuli were identified and observed. The

‡ Perhaps the most revealing tribute to acupuncture's newly won status is that in California patients of acupuncture treatment are presently eligible for reimbursement through the major insurance carriers.

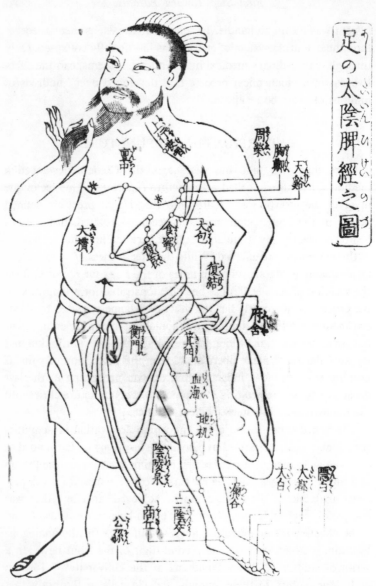

足の太陰脾經之圖

17. *A typical acupuncture chart, from* Kana yomi jushikei *by Kawatsu, published in Osaka in 1805. (National Library of Medicine, Bethesda, Maryland)*

firing of nerve impulses from those neurons slowed down during acupuncture.[50] Interestingly, however, when electrical current was used to stimulate the acupuncture needles, the mechanism behind the analgesia was a function of the electrical frequency of the current. At the lowest frequencies there was some degree of analgesia, which was reversible by naloxone. At higher frequencies the analgesia was greater and not reversible by naloxone. Instead, the latter analgesia was reversible only by an antagonist of the neurotransmitter serotonin.[51] Thus, acupuncture appeared to provide pain relief by two separable mechanisms, a moderate level mediated by endorphins and a more dramatic level mediated by serotonin. The fact that serotonin would be involved in acupuncture analgesia is consistent with other studies of pain control. Hosobuchi, in his treatment of pain through PAG stimulation, found that his patients developed fewer signs of tolerance if they had previously taken a precursor form of serotonin, the amino acid L-tryptophan. In studies of morphine-induced analgesia in animals, the effectiveness of this opiate was increased after injections of serotonin. From these observations, it is reasonable to conclude that serotonin shares with endorphins some of the same basic neural circuitry involved in pain control.[52]

ENDORPHINS AND LIVE BIRTH

In the evolutionary scheme of things, there is only one key word—reproduction. Even the slightest slackening of reproductive capabilities can have devastating effects; the potential for extinction can never be taken lightly. In the case of nearly all mammals, it is a live birth that satisfies that evolutionary requirement. But in order for this event to be accomplished, a relatively long period of gestation (as short as 12.5 days in Virginian opossums to as long as 645 days in elephants) must be completed within the female body, and during the birth itself the offspring must be pushed from the uterus to a birth canal that widens manyfold for the entrance of that offspring into the world. All of these processes put a biological stress on the mother, and it is not surprising that endorphins would be involved.

During the period of gestation for most mammals, it is the placenta that provides the necessary nourishment for the development of the fetus. The placenta contains the crucial precursor molecule POMC, from which beta-endorphin, met-enkephalin, and ACTH are all derived. It is reasonable to infer that these peptides function as agents of basic analgesia. Alan Gintzler at Columbia University found that pregnant rats become analgesic as early as the sixth day of a twenty-two-day gestational period (with a dramatic analgesia within forty-eight hours of giving birth), an effect reversible by naltrexone, a long-lasting version of naloxone.[53] A similar pattern shows up in the human placenta as well. Beta-endorphin and met-enkephalin are present in the placental tissue and placental blood at higher levels than usual during pregnancy and labor.[54] Huda Akil discovered that, when pregnant, her own endorphin levels were elevated:

> I carried out a study when I took some of my own blood and some blood from various people, females around me who were pregnant, and I started studying them from about six months of pregnancy on to the day of labor. Stan Watson [her husband and research colleague] collected . . . my blood at several stages during labor and after labor, and what we found was that throughout pregnancy as early as six months, possible even earlier but I don't know that, beta-endorphin is indeed quite high— higher than I've ever seen it in normal human blood.[55]

In a more systematic study in 1982, Cheryl Cahill and Akil reported an elevation in plasma beta-endorphin during pregnancy, a greater elevation during labor, plus a significant decrease twenty-four hours after the birth, though no systematic correlation with levels of pain perception was found.[56]

Beyond the significance of surging endorphins countering the stresses of live birth with their analgesic powers, there is something else happening—something else to consider. When the pain is gone, there is now new life to be cared for. For the offspring, there will be a period of helplessness, and in order for the survival of that next generation to be secured, there must be a guarantee of parental care and protection. This fact is a crucial difference between reptilian and mammalian species. As MacLean has pointed out, the "transition from reptiles to mammals, [the latter of which] developed a close

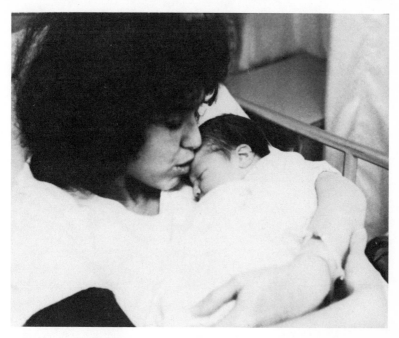

18. Mother and newborn, aged thirty minutes. (Courtesy Dr. & Mrs. Charles F. Levinthal)

parent-offspring relationship, represents a great evolutionary leap, a real quantum jump! Unlike the situation in birds, the continued evolution of mammals is distinctive because of the progressive increase in the time and care given to the young."[57]

In terms of MacLean's triune theory, that quantum leap in behavior has been tied to the second major thrust in the evolutionary development of the brain: the emergence of the limbic system. It is possible to consider something else that is equally dramatic: the emergence of a new role for endorphins in the brain. This role would no longer be linked only to the hostile aspects of one's environment but would now be focused upon the social behaviors and relationships that form the essense of mammalian life. A momentous evolutionary process would slowly reposition the organism toward, as opposed to away from, its environment. From the joyless emotions associated with the stress of raw survival in the protoreptilian world would emerge the joyful emotions associated with social bonding. Out of a biochemistry of analgesia would emerge a biochemistry of social reinforcement. Endorphins would be at the center of that next step toward Paradise.

7

Second Step Toward Paradise

SOCIAL COMFORT, ALIENATION, AND ADDICTION

There is something in staying close to men and women and looking on them, and in the contact and odor of them, that pleases the soul well,

All things please the soul, but these please the soul well.
WALT WHITMAN, "I Sing the Body Electric," 1855

The pain was so great that I screamed aloud; but at the same time I felt such infinite sweetness that I wished the pain to last forever. It was not physical but psychic pain, although it affected the body as well to some degree.

It was the sweetest caressing of the soul by God.
ST. TERESA of Ávila, *Autobiography*, 1587

"It's wild speculation," Candace Pert once said in an interview, "but it's very interesting to think about a fetus floating around with its opiate receptors loaded with endogenous endorphins. A fetus in that position would be sleepy, would be relaxed. Its gastrointestinal motility would be suppressed, would be calm. It wouldn't breathe; we don't want it to breathe when it's in the uterus surrounded by liquid; we want it to breathe when it comes out. It's fascinating . . . to think about the fetus in this blissful prenatal state medicated by beta-endorphin."[1]

Not a bad place to be, it seems. It is enough to encourage support for those psychologists who talk about unconscious yearnings to return to the womb. Here, at least, is a neurochemical reason for doing so. Yet the time arrives when we have to create our own safe haven outside the mother's body. As mammals, we are by definition nursed by the milk of our mothers (or, in some human cases, a modern equivalent). If there are multiple births (as is the typical case for most small mammals) there is a social unit in which to grow and develop, protected by the mother. Quite a contrast to a newborn reptile's introduction to the world. As Paul MacLean has pointed out, "The young of the Komodo dragon must take to the trees for the first year of life to avoid being cannibalized, while immature rainbow lizards must hide in the underbrush in order to prevent a similar fate."[2]

If nothing else, the development of the mammalian line brought a close to the pattern of potential cannibalism of the young. Only under the extraordinary circumstances of population overcrowding or other gross disturbances in the territorial needs of the new mother do we have occasion to observe instances of a female mammal killing or ignoring her young. In these instances, this aberrant behavior can be viewed as part of a general stress response, reflecting perhaps a retreat back to an earlier time of evolution.

Most paleontologists agree that early mammals were nocturnal creatures, hiding from the predatory dinosaurs under the protective cover of darkness. Unlike the case with reptiles, where separation from the parent was vital to the offspring and a vocalization or cry of the young would have had calamitous consequences, MacLean has theorized that, for the mammalian offspring, *separation itself* would

have been calamitous and that the production of some auditory signal would have been a significant behavior in order to keep in close
contact with the mother. It would be the cry of separation (particularly in the dark) that would get mother and newborn back together
again, and, if this was done, the safety and nurturance of the young
would be ensured (figure 19). The separation cry would represent,
therefore, the most primitive and fundamental form of mammalian
vocalization, eclipsing even the cry of hunger.[3]

Another feature emerging at this point in evolution seems to have
been the behavior of social play. You simply do not find playfulness
in any reptilian species existing today, and it is likely that none
existed at any stage of reptilian evolution. Mammals, on the other
hand, display this behavior almost universally, as a component of a
general sociability within the family unit. It appears to be a part of a
young mammal's emotional development to engage in play with its
siblings.

Maternal care, vocalization, and social play: a behavioral triad
never before seen in the natural world even in singular terms, much
less in combination. They represent a pervasive element of mammalian life, and a profound departure from the behavior of evolutionary
predecessors. Given these vast behavioral changes, it is not surprising that, at this point in evolutionary history, there was also an
astounding shift in brain anatomy. There began a development of
new neural structures, collectively known as the limbic system, that
literally surrounded the old protoreptilian brainstem. We will never
be able to resolve the question of whether the new behavioral demands of these mammals produced the evolutionary development in
the brain, or the opposite: that the new brain structures produced the
evolution of behavior. Nevertheless, it is clear that a significant
thrust of brain evolution—the second phase of the eventual triune
brain, according to MacLean—occurred more than 100 million years
ago.[4]

Paul Broca, the great French physician and scholar whose insights
illuminated so many areas of psychology and neurology, examined in
a paper written in 1878 the implications of what he called "the great
limbic lobe" of the brain. He chose the description from the Latin
word *limbus,* meaning "border or edge," because the brain tissue

19. The close bodily contact of monkey mother and infant, a critical ingredient in normal emotional development. (Harlow Primate Laboratory, University of Wisconsin)

appeared to encircle a central core. Characteristically, he was far ahead of his time in noting that this limbic lobe was a common denominator in the brains of all mammals (figure 20).[5] Today, neuroanatomists speak of a limbic *system,* in that there is a functionally interconnected grouping of brain structures that includes the "great limbic lobe" of Broca. The most prominent structures include the amygdala, septum pellucidum, hippocampus, and cingulate cortex—all interacting with the hypothalamus as the integrator of emotional responses. When experimental lesions are made in the cingulate cortex in particular, a number of the mammalian behaviors specific to maternal care, vocalization, and social play are lost.[6] The cingulate portion of the limbic system seems to be vital to the great behavioral transition that mammals were able to accomplish.

With the development of the limbic system, it might also be said that there began a new trend in an animal's emotional positioning toward the environment. Without abandoning the reptilian instinct for territoriality and a generally defensive posture toward the environment, mammals could now develop a posture of socialization and nurturance.* It appears no coincidence, as we will see, that the limbic system should hold the key to understanding the neural basis for *reward*-directed (as opposed to *punishment*-directed) behavior, nor that the limbic system should contain some of the highest concentrations of opiate receptors and endorphins in the brain.

ENDORPHINS AND SOCIAL COMFORT

"When mammals opted for a family way of life," MacLean has recently written, "they set the stage for one of the most distressful forms of suffering. A condition that, for us, makes being a mammal so painful is having to endure separation or isolation from loved ones and, in the end, the utter isolation of death. . . . It drives home what basically lonely creatures we are. As members of the class of mammals, we find our greatest warmth of companionship within the body of the human family."[8]

There is probably no more heart-rending scene in human experience than the persistent crying and panic when an infant or child is separated from its mother. Many animals show the same behavior

* Physiological psychologist Robert Isaacson has called the limbic system Lethe, after the Greek mythological river flowing through Hades, the waters of which produced a loss of memory in those who drank from it. Isaacson sees these structures as providing a way to inhibit the ancestral memories of the protoreptilian brain.[7]

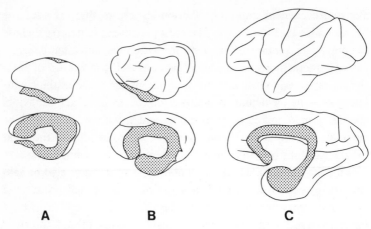

20. *The commonality of the limbic system at three levels of brain evolution: (A) rabbit, (B) cat, and (C) monkey. (From P. D. MacLean. "Studies on Limbic System, 'Visceral Brain' and Their Bearing on Psychomotor Problems," in E. D. Wittkower and R. A. Cleghorn, eds.* Recent Developments in Psychosomatic Medicine. *London: Pitman Medical, 1954, pp. 101–25)*

under similar circumstances. It is referred to as separation distress. The vocalization and agitation are immediate and reflexive, apparently as a response to the activation of innate neural circuits in the limbic system. An animal's need to regain security and comfort within its family, it has been said, is stronger than even more basic bodily needs resulting from food or water deprivation.[9]

The evidence for a linkage between brain endorphins and the concept of social comfort began to emerge in 1978 from experiments by physiological psychologist Jaak Panksepp at Bowling Green State University in Ohio. When morphine was given to young puppies and guinea pigs, they became less inclined to cry when they were separated from their mothers; the symptoms of separation distress were reduced. Yet these animals were not lethargic from the morphine; they simply behaved in the same way as they had prior to their separation.[10] It was as if the opiate was acting as a pharmacological equivalent to the mother's presence. Naloxone, on the other hand, increased the incidence of separation cries. The opposite effect of naloxone implicated the role of endorphins in this critical behavior of social bonding. No other drug (including some of the prominent antipsychotic and antianxiety medications) or peptide could produce more powerful effects upon separation-distress behavior than opiates.

Panksepp showed that these opiate effects were not limited only to mammals. The opiate connection was also seen in two related behaviors in an equally well-evolved but non-mammalian species: young chicks.[11] The first behavior was the separation-distress pattern, and the changes after morphine or naloxone were similar to those observed in the earlier studies. The second behavior, unique to this species, involved the reaction of young chicks when they were held gently in the cupped hands of a human. Normally, when they were held in this way these animals would, within 30 to 40 seconds, close their eyes and peacefully fall asleep, as if in a "simulated nest" (figure 21). Injections of morphine caused this reaction to be observed more quickly (about 9 to 12 seconds); injections of naloxone had the reverse effect, lengthening the interval to about 76 to 124 seconds. Again, the opiates were interpreted as having acted to provide a kind of social comfort in the face of maternal separation. When Panksepp and his associates injected the major forms of endorphins into the ventricles of the chick's brain, all of the endorphins produced the same effect on separation distress as morphine.[12]

The influence of endorphins on social behavior can be seen to run along the entire range of social development. It seems to begin practically from the time of birth. Endocrinologists have found that endorphins increase the mother's level of prolactin, the hormone that controls the production of milk; it is possible that endorphins may be released during suckling.[13] There is, in fact, a recently discovered endorphin in milk itself, called casomorphin (so named as a reference to the milk protein casein), that might further reinforce the bonding of mother to infant during feeding.[14]

Panksepp also found an endorphin connection in the behavior of social play. When injected with low doses of morphine, pairs of rats engaged in a greater frequency of chasing, jostling, and "pinning," the rodent version of play. Naloxone caused the frequency to decrease.[15] According to Panksepp, the effect of endorphins on social play is one of a series of influences that play a critical role in the

21. A simulated "nest" for a young chick. Close physical contact produces a closing of the eyes. (Courtesy Dr. Jaak Panksepp, Bowling Green State University, Ohio)

social aspects of an animal's development. In his view, the endorphins have evolved in the limbic system in order to make it possible to feel the safety and comfort within the mammalian family.

It is not simply a coincidence, Panksepp has theorized, that there should be such a parallel between social comfort and separation distress, on the one hand, and opiate-induced comfort and narcotic-withdrawal distress, on the other. The two phenomena appear to share the same neurochemical substrate in the mammalian brain. When endorphin levels are low, in his view, there is an innate tendency to seek social stimulation. These social stimuli then lead to a release of endorphins that not only reduces the separation distress but also produces reinforcement or reward for the behaviors of social interaction.[16] "The imprint of this evolutionary progression remains imbedded within human and animal language," he has said. "The semantics of social loss are the semantics of pain. It hurts to lose a loved one and we cry. Social separation makes young animals more sensitive to pain and they cry."[17]

For the human species, the experience of social attachment and comfort becomes inevitably bound up with the euphoria of human affection, intimacy, and love (figure 22). There is also a behavioral dependency that becomes built into our relationships with people we care about. The slogan "Hugs are better than drugs" may be something you find on a car bumper, but it tells a basic truth of our evolution. You can feel the release of an opiate system through the acts of social comfort and love or by exogenous opiates from the outside. This comparability can be viewed as a consequence of a momentous evolutionary event, the development of the limbic system, that many millions of years ago turned the organism away from the negative stress of raw survival and toward the joyful emotions and positive stress that would serve to reinforce behaviors characteristic of a social being.

Many of our everyday experiences bear witness to the effectiveness of these reinforcing systems. We take pleasure in our feeling that we are part of a larger entity than ourselves. We feel secure in our ties to family and a sense of connection to groups defined along social, political, and cultural lines. We are able to feel love from others and give it in return. For most of us, the evolutionary mechanism for

22. *Four young monkeys, raised without mothers, huddle against one another during their early months. At one year of age they are normal. (Harlow Primate Laboratory, University of Wisconsin)*

social reinforcement has worked well, guided by the hypothesized balance of endorphin systems in the brain. For some of us, however, this balance has been upset, and the resulting aberrant behaviors represent an organism steering away from the course of its mammalian evolution. As we will see, an analysis of endorphin functioning can shed light upon these disorders.

ENDORPHINS AND AUTISTIC BEHAVIOR

There is a strange and striking parallel between behaviors associated with a high level of opiate activity in the brain and symptoms associated with childhood autism. Autistic behaviors, for example, include a general lack of crying, a failure of the infant to cling to the parents, and an overall deficiency in generating emotional responses to social relationships. At a later age, the autistic child appears to be unable to appreciate fully the impact of physical pain, tends to have little desire for social companionship, and shows an extreme persistence in repetitive behavior that seems independent of external rewards. Many of these behaviors are also observed in the adult opiate addict.

THE THEORETICAL PARALLELS BETWEEN NARCOTIC ADDICTION AND SOCIAL DEPENDENCE, ACCORDING TO JAAK PANKSEPP

Similarities between	
Narcotic Addiction	Social Dependence
Psychic dependence	Love
Tolerance (as larger doses are required)	Estrangement (as the lover's eye begins to wander)
Withdrawal distress	Loss of a loved one
Psychic pain	Loneliness
Lacrimation	Crying
Anorexia	Loss of appetite
Depression	Despondency
Insomnia	Sleeplessness
Aggressiveness	Irritability

James Kalat at North Carolina State University in 1978 and Panksepp in 1979 independently developed the idea that these similarities may not be occurring merely by chance. They proposed that childhood autism may be caused by an overactivity of the child's own brain opioid system.[18] By having an oversupply of endorphin activity to start with, according to this theory, the autistic child would not be in a position to be rewarded by social relationships in the same way as would a normal child. In other words, autistic behavior might represent the fact that there is no biochemical need to reach out to others. This viewpoint would also help to explain the dramatic shifts in mood among autistic children, from emotional detachment to intense distress, as Panksepp has put it:

If the autistic child's brain is over-opiated, then any condition which shuts down this system (i.e., separation from familiar objects) would produce symptoms like withdrawal in the narcotic addict: intense panic, crying, and an insistence to be reunited with the comfort of the familiar. In this way, some autistic children may be caught in an inexorable conflict. To sustain psychological comfort, they must sustain the constancy of environment which permits their high opiate activity to continue.[19]

Leo Kanner, the individual who first developed the concept of the autistic syndrome, has written of the Nirvana-like existence of such children, a sense of serenity rather than agitation when left alone. Autistic children would give the impression, he has said, of "fighting for their aloneness and basking in the contentment that it gave them."[20]

Assuming the theoretical linkage to excessive endorphin activity, one promising strategy for the treatment of autism would be to reduce endorphin levels through the administration of a long-term opiate antagonist like naltrexone. So far, there have been only a limited number of studies examining the potential benefits of naltrexone, but there is preliminary evidence of some positive results, particularly for those autistic children who inflict injury on themselves.[21]

ENDORPHINS AND DEPRESSION

Between 10 million and 14 million Americans have been estimated as suffering from significant depression, feelings that extend beyond the bouts of sadness, loneliness, and fatigue that all of us experience from time to time. To the hedonic, or pleasurable, side of normal human experience, depression is the other side of the coin: anhedonia, or the inability to feel pleasure.†

The recent suggestion that endorphin systems may play a role in depression relates back to the writings of the late-nineteenth-century and early-twentieth-century German psychiatrist Emil Kraepelin, the father of modern concepts of abnormal psychology, who consid-

† The late psychiatrist Nathan Kline once remarked that a patient he was treating, a bank robber, displayed severe anhedonia, a feeling of worthlessness, and preoccupation with suicide. The patient reported that the only time he could feel *anything at all* was when he was robbing a bank.[22]

ered opiates (usually laudanum) as a therapeutic aid for patients with melancholia. This approach to depression became known as the "opium cure." Kraepelin was evidently sensitive at the time to the potential for abuse of the drug: He prescribed slowly increasing and later decreasing dosages so the patients avoided becoming opium-dependent.[23] Later in the twentieth century, there appeared reports in the rehabilitation literature of detoxified opiate addicts showing signs of depression.[24]

On the basis of these observations, there has arisen the suspicion that depression could be related to a low level of brain endorphins or some inadequacy in the responsiveness of endorphins in times of social stress. According to this view, a deficiency in an endorphin system that ordinarily would support feelings of pleasure and reinforcement might lead to feelings of inadequacy and sadness. It may be the case that, far from showing increased endorphin levels and increased analgesia in stressful situations, the population of depressive individuals would be found unable to tap into normally reinforcing mechanisms in the brain, and to suffer accordingly in their perception of personal helplessness.[25] Reward would not be experienced in the same way that a normal individual would experience it. Losses and failures would be overgeneralized and exaggerated.

While the success of antidepressant drugs since the 1950s in the treatment of depression has led to the major focus of attention oriented to the neurotransmitters norepinephrine and serotonin (Chapter 3), the consideration of a connection between endorphins and depression has also produced its own lineage of therapeutic medications. The drug buprenorphine, for example, with a mixture of excitatory and inhibitory effects on opiate receptors in the brain, has been shown recently to be a promising new antidepressant medication.[26] There has, in addition, been some success in administering beta-endorphins to depressed patients.[27] It is unlikely, however, that an endorphin-oriented approach will replace traditional therapy with drugs presently in use. A treatment based upon brain endorphins may be appropriate only for those patients that do not respond well to the agents acting upon norepinephrine and serotonin systems.

ENDORPHINS AND THE LONG-DISTANCE RUNNER

Throughout our culture, we have reinforced the myth of the athletic champion who gains victory over seemingly overwhelming odds, a suffering hero who somehow has transcended pain to make it finally into the winner's circle. We speak of "the joy of victory and the agony of defeat" not only as a kind of media slogan to increase the viewing audience of a sports event, but as a phrase that we can relate to on a primitive emotional basis. We feel, at a gut level, that a physical victory can give us an experience of euphoria. The long-distance runner is the quintessence of this mythic goal; in its pure state, there is no need for special equipment (other than a good pair of running shoes), no rules, not even a need for an audience. It is a matter of pitting pure stamina against the limitations of time and space, one human body testing the boundaries of its own physiology. It is fitting that, in the modern Olympiad, the epitome of heroic athleticism would be the marathon (figure 23). It is created from the legend of the heroic messenger Pheidippides, who ran the twenty-two-mile distance to Athens from the site of the Battle of Marathon in 490 B.C. and announced the Athenian victory with his dying words, "Rejoice, we conquer."‡

Given the euphoria and exhilaration that many runners report having experienced in the course of their run, it has been tempting to relate these feelings ("the runner's high") to an increase in brain endorphins. There is circumstantial evidence that a connection might exist. Daniel Carr and his associates at the Massachusetts General Hospital in Boston, for example, found that physically untrained volunteers going through a two-month exercise program produced significantly higher levels of ACTH, beta-endorphin, and their joint precursor beta-lipotropin in their blood system.[28] In another study, for trained runners (a minimum running schedule of thirty miles per

‡ It is not widely known, however, that Pheidippides was probably already tired when he started his famous run to Athens. He had previously managed a 300-mile round-trip to Sparta to enlist aid in fighting the Persians in the first place. (The Spartan army was delayed in its journey to Marathon and arrived after the Athenians had won the battle.)

23. *A small portion of the thousands of runners in the New York City Marathon. (Barton Silverman/NYT Pictures)*

week for males and fifteen miles per week for females), beta-endorphin levels in blood plasma increased after an eight-mile race to levels 3½ times higher than levels taken immediately beforehand.[29] It is possible, however, that the endorphin increases could have been secondary to the ACTH increases (since both are normally released together) and that we might be seeing here a general response to the stress of physical exertion. Besides, it has been difficult to observe a consistent relationship between the reports of euphoria and the endorphin increase per se. A major problem may lie in the difficulty of associating a feeling that varies so greatly from individual to individual and moment to moment with a blood-sample measurement. Nevertheless, it is plausible that an endorphin system could be involved in the experience of running.

A linkage to endorphins is also suggested by the significant parallel between the behavior associated with extreme levels of exercise and behaviors normally associated with opiate addiction. Individuals, for example, who run between fifty and one hundred miles or more a week often will feel that they have to cover their minimal distance each day or else risk feeling depressed and irritable or suffering insomnia and decreased appetite—symptoms characteristic of withdrawal from addictive drugs. It is as if these runners become dependent on the effect of running, as a means for combating a significant level of anxiety and depression.

For some, running can evolve into a ritualistic attempt to achieve some control over pain itself. One researcher in this area, endocrinologist Edward Colt, as medical director for the New York City Marathon, has observed many individuals who insist upon running despite extensive stress fractures in the legs. One woman told him that she continued "because running made her feel so relaxed, and she believed the pains would disappear if she strengthened her legs with more running."[30] The champion marathon runner Alberto Salazar reportedly insisted on running more than one hundred miles a week on an unhealed stress fracture rather than break training.[31]

As one psychiatrist has put it, the self-enhancement phase of physical exercise (the attainment of the euphoric "runner's high" and the positive changes in one's physical condition and mental attitudes) has the potential for leading to a self-destructive phase—"when exercise begins to work against you."[32] It is estimated that about 10 percent of the 20 million to 30 million recreational runners in the United States proceed into the second phase and can be considered "obligatory runners."[33]

COMPULSIVE RUNNING AND ANOREXIA NERVOSA

Recent analyses have pointed to parallels between the behaviors of obligatory running among males and the compulsive self-starving behaviors of anorexia nervosa among females. Psychiatrist Alayne Yates and her associates at the University of Arizona found that, in both cases, there is a reported feeling of being "high," a bizarre preoccupation with food, and an unusual emphasis on lean body mass.[34] There is also a similar underlying depression in both the obligatory runner and anorexic patient. Once again, the concept of endorphin functioning in the brain may provide a valuable clue to a possible biochemical basis for these behavioral parallels. As Yates has written:

> Both runners and ordinary dieters report that vigorous exercise will attenuate hunger and can be employed to expedite a diet. A single determi-

nant of the attenuation of [the painful sensations] of hunger in the an-orexic patient, fatigue in the long-distance runner, and the altered state of consciousness in both could be an increase in circulating endorphins, which are thought to serve as modulators of both mood and pain.[35]

As predicted by this viewpoint, emaciated anorexic women have been found to have higher endorphin levels in their cerebrospinal fluid than control patients without anorexic symptoms.[36] It has also been found that when the anorexic body weight is later restored to normal, the endorphin levels decline.[37]

It can be speculated that the undercurrent of depression in such individuals reflects a general deficiency in the way endorphin levels respond to the reinforcement of social behaviors. It may be the case that the rise in endorphins, as a result of the *bodily* stress from food deprivation and physical exertion, serves an important function in light of this deficiency. Unfortunately, without the ordinary regula-tory mechanisms in these endorphin systems, the behaviors of the anorexic individual and obligatory runner have the potential for be-coming more and more extreme and bizarre, as if no amount of self-denial appears enough. In Yates's view, there has arisen a basic insta-bility of self-concept in these people, "as if they were not able to form an enduring or absolute sense of who they are . . . perpetuated by the fear that if one stops, one will cease to exist."[38] Perhaps it is only through a reestablishment of one's self-esteem and self-identity, by the process of social reinforcement in the first place, that the vicious cycle inherent in these addictive behaviors can be broken.

ENDORPHINS AND OPIATE ADDICTION

There is no question of the magnitude of individual and commu-nity disruption that can be attributed to drug abuse. The epidemic of drug addiction in general, and opiate addiction in particular, is one of the social realities of our time. It has become a kind of Gordian knot that defies any easy solution. Some researchers in the field have viewed the present legal and societal obstacles to the availability of opiate drugs as being the primary contributor to the social problems. Edward Brecher, one of the leaders of this viewpoint, has argued that

the best strategy lies in the reexamination of the current law-enforce-
ment policies and public attitudes.[39] Others have concentrated their
efforts on identifying the important psychological factors that lead to
addictive behavior. Still others have turned to the new understanding
of the endorphin systems in the brain as a basis for explaining the
way in which opiate drugs become addicting. From this last perspective, the inclination toward opiate addiction might be seen as a natural consequence of some internal deficiency in endorphin functioning.

Avram Goldstein, often credited for the endorphin-deficiency idea,
has drawn the analogy to a diabetic who might be unable to tell that
there exists a bodily need for insulin:

> If insulin were available (perhaps in an illicit market) normal people
> would find it most unpleasant, for it would cause hypoglycemia, weak-
> ness, dizziness, etc. But diabetics would discover, at their very first "fix,"
> that they felt normal for the first time in their lives, and they would
> certainly go to any extreme to secure insulin thereafter. . . . Experimen-
> tally administered morphine [is] unpleasant to many normal subjects, in
> contrast to its euphorigenic effects in addicts.[40]

This point of view would help account for the puzzling variability
from individual to individual in the addictive power of opiate drugs.
If an endorphin deficiency exists, however, the question would still
remain as to what precipitating circumstances would lead to such a
deficiency and whether these circumstances were environmental, in-
herited genetically, or a product of both.*

The great variability in the psychological make-up of addicts in
general limits the possibility of finding a completely defined "addictive personality." Nevertheless, a few significant characteristics are
frequently identified: impulsive behavior, a tendency to desire instant
gratification, a disposition toward sensation-seeking, a feeling of social alienation, and a vulnerability to the effects of heightened

---

* Ring Lardner once made the glib observation that some people seem to be "born
two drinks under par."[41] His remark, however, touched upon the possibility that an
addiction to alcohol may have its roots in a process that sets up a need for alcohol,
based upon some metabolic or biochemical deficiency. We do not presently understand
the exact mechanism underlying alcohol addiction, but the deficiency theory remains
one alternative.

stress.[42] Some researchers have tied these characteristics to individual life experiences.[43] Lawrence Hatterer, a psychiatrist active in addiction treatment programs, has recently related the inclination toward addictive behavior to the stress of unstable interpersonal relationships:

> Every addictive adult I have treated has told either of excesses or inconsistencies or of deprivation or overindulgence in early life. There were shifts from too much to too little love, protection or discipline . . . marked swings from unrealistic praise to destructive hypercritical behavior.[44]

A prominent theorist on the concept of addiction, Stanton Peele, has argued that the compulsive behavior characteristic of any form of addiction is situationally, socially, and culturally determined. Addiction, in his view, "is a result of a dynamic social-learning process in which the person finds an experience rewarding because it ameliorates urgently felt needs, while in the long run it damages the person's capacity to cope and ability to generate stable sources of environmental gratification."[45]

With a social-reinforcement interpretation of endorphin functioning, as developed in this chapter, it is possible to offer a theoretical bridge between the analysis of addiction as a cognitive, psychological process and the analysis of addiction, in the reductionist tradition, as a biochemical process in the brain. In the research studies of Jaak Panksepp, the evidence pointed toward the role of endorphin systems in creating a feeling of belonging and social comfort. If the reinforcements from interpersonal bonds are not allowed to develop, following this line of reasoning, then individuals who feel lonely and alienated might be inclined to seek out external means for that social comfort. This perspective can then be reconciled with theories of addiction that deal exclusively with a molar, nonphysiological level of analysis. It would be consistent, for example, with the ideas expressed recently by Peele concerning the present state of our society as it pertains to the inclination toward addictive behavior:

> If addiction is a retreat from the attempt to attain a balanced set of gratifications in life, then its increase means that more people are finding their resources for coping to be insufficient relative to the benefits they

believe an active involvement in this world will yield. This chronic deficiency can be traced to a lack of practice at self-reliance, of feelings of
competence, of an ability to tolerate discomfort, and of self-confidence
combined with the absence of positive values toward achievement, toward experience, toward society and community (and, in the most extreme cases of addictiveness, toward health and toward the self).[46]

In the context of an endorphin model of addiction, we can see the
"retreat of addiction" as a failure in the normal role of endorphin
systems to provide the comfort and reinforcement from consistent
patterns of social relationships, and in turn a failure in these systems
to provide a sense of personal competence and control over the
stressors in our lives.[47] It can be argued, in the context of the triune
model, that we have achieved the competence and control over the
stress in our environment, as well as the rewards of social connec-
tiveness, by the development of anatomical systems in the protoreptilian and paleomammalian brains. The process of addiction,
whether by virtue of our own behaviors or by chemical substances,
can be viewed as a failure of that evolution.

ENDORPHINS AND OPIATE-ADDICTION TREATMENT

The endorphin-deficiency model of opiate addiction is based upon
the idea that opiate receptors are being inadequately supplied with
endogenous opioids and that the morphine, heroin, or other opiates
are being delivered to these same receptors. It is further theorized
that, as a consequence of the supply from the outside, a feedback
mechanism sets off a further reduction in the endogenous system—
the receptors become increasingly dependent upon drug intake from
the outside. As their endogenous source of supply is gradually lost,
these receptors require an increasing amount of the drug to compensate, and a tolerance effect develops. If the opiate drug is later withdrawn, the receptors are now left without a supply from any source
at all, and the symptoms of withdrawal are a consequence of this
physiological dilemma.[48] Out of this working model of opiate addiction, there has arisen a new treatment strategy for opiate addiction:
long-term maintenance on the opiate antagonist, naltrexone. The argument is that, in doing this, you would satisfy the need of these

receptors for something to occupy them, without producing the euphoric effects that external opiates would accomplish if *they* were in
the receptor sites.

Naltrexone (brand name: Trexan), the long-lasting version of the
classic opiate antagonist naloxone, would be ideal for this purpose. It
has few, if any, pharmacological effects other than to block opiate
receptors; it has virtually no significant toxic effects and has no
"street value" since it fails to produce euphoric effects in the user.
The primary advantage is that naltrexone removes the craving for
opiates; naltrexone maintenance functions then as a way of protect-
ing the addict against the impulsive use of drugs.[49] Over the long
term, however, the aim is to help these individuals begin to experience life situations as nonusers and to develop a new attitude toward
life-styles that are worth defending and maintaining. It is necessary,
in other words, to build up self-reinforcing systems in a social environment that can sustain an individual throughout his or her life-
time.†

Another important use of opiate antagonists has been in the process of detoxification. When either gradually withdrawn from maintenance levels of methadone or subject to a complete, "cold turkey"
break from heroin, the addict suffers symptoms of intense restless-
ness, cold sweats, chills, uncontrollable shaking, and a powerful
craving for the drug that is being withdrawn. The procedure often
spans a week or more. By giving naloxone injections, however, it has
been possible to reduce the period of detoxification to a day or so,
enabling patients to make the transition from opiate dependency to
naltrexone maintenance within forty-eight hours after their last opiate dose.[51] With an opiate antagonist, the symptoms of withdrawal
are unfortunately still present, but the period of time during which
these symptoms are suffered is greatly reduced. Indeed, the symptoms of withdrawal themselves can be now dealt with, thanks to the
recent development of a nonopioid drug called clonidine.[52]

† Aside from their application in rehabilitation programs, opiate antagonists have
been found to be immensely useful in emergency situations. Naloxone (brand name:
Narcan), for example, has become a now-standard treatment for comatose patients
after a heroin overdose. It is also effective in reversing the drop in blood pressure after
blood loss or a depression of breathing after severe alcohol or barbiturate intoxication.[50]

The application of clonidine (brand name: Catapres) in reducing opiate-withdrawal symptoms is a direct result of a growing understanding of how opioid peptides interact with a host of other biochemical systems in the brain. In this case, a small region of the pons, the locus ceruleus (literally the "blue spot," since early anatomists noticed that it had a bluish color), has a high concentration of receptors sensitive to both endorphins and norepinephrine. Researchers have found, in animal studies, that either electrical or chemical stimulation of neurons in the locus ceruleus produces fear and anxiety that are virtually identical to symptoms produced by the withdrawal from opiate drugs.[53] Since opiates inhibit noradrenergic neurons (those sensitive to norepinephrine), the locus ceruleus is quiescent while the individual is addicted to opiates.[54] When the drugs are taken away, the noradrenergic neurons now rebound to a hyperactive state, a level that produces the symptoms of withdrawal. Clonidine and other similar drugs are able to inhibit these hyperactive cells and reduce the intensity of the symptoms.[55] Thus, with a combined use of clonidine and either naloxone or naltrexone, it has been possible to provide a relatively rapid, safe, and effective treatment for withdrawal from these drugs.[56] Beyond that, however, the prognosis depends heavily upon the individual. Within a cognitive model, as Peele has eloquently expressed it, the road back from addiction is a return to a life of social reinforcement.

> The best antidotes to addiction are joy and competence—joy as the capacity to take pleasure in the people, activities, and things that are available to us; competence as the ability to master relevant parts of the environment and the confidence that our actions make a difference for ourselves and others.[57]

Within the model of addiction developed here, a break from opiate dependency requires a movement back to the normal functioning of endorphin processes in the brain.

8

Third Step Toward Paradise

THE QUEST FOR COHERENCE AND CERTAINTY

Nothing is more wondrous about the fifteen billion neurons in the human brain than their ability to convert thoughts, hopes, ideas, and attitudes into chemical substances. Everything begins, therefore, with belief. What we believe is the most powerful option of all.

NORMAN COUSINS, *Human Options*, 1981

What a piece of work is man! how noble in reason! how infinite in faculty!

WILLIAM SHAKESPEARE, *Hamlet*, 1602

To a newborn human infant, the world is a long way from being coherent and predictable, but it is also equally far from what William James, the nineteenth-century American psychologist, called "one great blooming, buzzing confusion."[1] We now know that newborns have a much better-developed perceptual system than we have ever realized. Facial expressions, for example, can be imitated by infants as young as two to three weeks old.[2] A black triangle in an infant's visual field produces a fixation of gaze on one of its corners for several seconds, as if the triangular shape is being methodically analyzed, angle by angle.[3] It is true that an infant may, in James's words, "belong less to himself than to every object which happens to catch his notice,"[4] but there is also a rapidly growing sense of priority and attentiveness. Out of this accumulating sense of perceptual coherence comes a sense of competence and a sense of self.

The extraordinary power of human information processing can be seen as a product of the third great thrust of neural development that Paul MacLean has called the "neomammalian brain"—culminating in the structure of the human neocortex. The quest for coherence in the world, the search for a pattern to sequential events, is a reflection upon a long series of evolutionary changes in brain organization and complexity. These changes have brought us to the point where we can study in others, and admire in ourselves, a level of thinking far beyond anything that can be achieved in even the closest of our nonhuman relatives.

Yet, at what seems to be the pinnacle of brain evolution, the human brain remains tied to its biological past in several fundamental ways. We still see in our behavior, for example, the influence of a protoreptilian drive toward territoriality, as well as the paleomammalian drive toward the comfort and sustenance of a family unit. It can be argued that these influences affect our intellectual judgments and beliefs on a largely unconscious level, in a language that has little to do with our present means of communication. As MacLean has pointed out, it is as though "we are continually tried by a jury that cannot read or write."[5] If endorphins have played central roles in these past existences, then the next question is what role they play in the present one.

OPIATE RECEPTORS AND SENSORY CODING IN THE NEOCORTEX

Neurophysiologist Vernon Mountcastle once remarked that "each of us lives within the universe—the prison—of his own brain."[6] He was referring to the fact that our personal knowledge of the world is a product largely of our own making. We are lucky to possess specially adapted receptors that can sample certain forms of energy from our environment—heat, light, vibrations of air molecules, gravitational force—but that is all we ever know of the world directly. Everything else is a matter of logical inference. The world arrives at the various thresholds of our nervous system in a raw state; we have to make it coherent by subsequent stages of information processing.

The processing of a visual stimulus, like all of the forms of sensation, begins from a point of simplicity and builds stage by stage to an increasing level of complexity. Starting at the cells of the retina, about a million nerve fibers from each eye carry the initial information along the optic nerve to the brain. Most of these fibers eventually extend to the neocortex.*

The primary destination for visual information at the cortical level lies in the back portion, the occipital lobe. It is here that the organization of visual images begins. Some of the neurons in this region are uniquely sensitive to projections of straight lines onto the retina; others react to moving edges; still others, to corners.[7] These reactions can be thought of as the ingredients to be later combined into a perception of objects. Further processing beyond the occipital lobe is a result of activity in the bottom portion of each cortical side, an area called the inferotemporal cortex (since it is located in the inferior, or lower, end of each temporal lobe). We know that monkeys, after experimental lesions in this area, can no longer discriminate one object from another on a visual basis, even in those cases where the

* In the human case, about 80 percent of optic nerve fibers travel to the neocortex. The other 20 percent extend to the midbrain and synapse in a primitive system for vision that is associated with the brains of fish, birds, and reptiles. As you go back in evolutionary history, a greater and greater proportion of optic nerve fibers can be traced to this midbrain system.

objects themselves are simple ones.[8] There are single neurons in the monkey inferotemporal cortex that are "tuned" so specifically that they can, on an individual basis, "recognize" highly complex objects. These cells can be shown to fire more and more vigorously as objects are presented that increasingly resemble the object to which the neuron is apparently tuned, as in a child's game of "hot and cold."

It is impossible to predict ahead of time the precise features of the stimulus to which a given neuron in this area might be sensitive; the neuron you are recording might be sensitive to a horizontal line and you would not know it if all you presented was vertical-line images. It is unfortunately a long, arduous procedure of trial and error, and success is often a matter of considerable luck. A good case in point is the experience of a team of researchers, headed by Charles G. Gross of Princeton University, who were studying in 1972 a particularly "stubborn" inferotemporal neuron in a monkey. At first, it seemed hopeless to identify any consistent response, no matter what stimulus was attempted. Finally, in desperation, one of the researchers began to wave his hand in front of the monkey's eyes. The reluctant neuron instantly responded with an excited burst of firing. Something had obviously happened that corresponded to this neuron's special sensitivity. It took twelve hours of testing one silhouette after another—five-pointed stars, leaf patterns, cutouts of the human hand—before they finally found the answer. The neuron was sensitive to an image of the monkey's own paw. It was that stimulus that evoked the most vigorous response.[9] Gross and his associates had identified one of probably many neurons in the inferotemporal cortex that were specifically tuned in this way (figure 24). In a subsequent study in the same laboratory, a group of neurons in the superior (top) portion of the monkey's temporal lobe was found to be sensitive to the presentation of faces.[10]

While we cannot manage to survey the millions and millions of neurons in this region of the brain to get a complete idea of the perceptual world of this animal, it is clear that the world is being made into some kind of coherent whole through neural processing of visual information in the inferotemporal cortex. We ourselves function in much the same way. Who is to say that there does not exist in this region of our own brains what neurophysiologists like to call the

24. *The stimuli in the "monkey paw" experiment. Numbers underneath each figure show the relative response rates of a single cortical neuron, increasing as the stimulus more closely resembles a monkey's paw. (From C. G. Gross, C. E. Rocha-Miranda, and D. B. Bender. "Visual Properties of Neurons in Inferotemporal Cortex of the Macaque,"* Journal of Neurophysiology, *1972, 35:104, Figure 6.)*

"grandmother cell"—a neuron that has the special capability of responding to visual images of grandmother herself?

When Michael E. Lewis and Mortimer Mishkin, along with other associates at the National Institute of Mental Health (NIMH) laboratories, set out to measure the distribution of two types of opiate receptors in the monkey neocortex, they were trying to explore what role, if any, endorphins played in the process of perception.[11] Opiate-receptor mapping in all parts of the brain had been going on ever since the discovery of these receptors in 1973, but this was the first time that the mapping was specific enough to identify individual areas *within the neocortex.*[12] It was also the first time that separate distributions could be identified for each of the two principal types of opiate receptors: the mu-type and delta-type.

As may be recalled from Chapter 5, there are three (and perhaps more) categories of opiate receptors in the nervous system. In the Lewis and Mishkin study, the distribution of mu-receptors was tested by measuring the binding to naloxone, since naloxone will not bind well to the delta-receptor unless the dose is very high.[13] The distribution of delta-receptors was tested by measuring the binding to a modified form of leucine-enkephalin, known to be selectively sensitive to this subtype. Their results were startling. Lewis and Mishkin found an increasing density of cortical mu-receptors as they progressed from the occipital region, which coded the visual stimulus in a primitive manner, to the inferotemporal region, which was responsible for more complex coding. The highest-density readings of all were obtained in the amygdala of the limbic system, situated just underneath the inferotemporal cortex. No differences, however, were found in the density of delta-type receptors; there was a relatively even distribution throughout the neocortex and the density was no higher in the amygdala.†

Lewis, Mishkin, and their associates had discovered, in effect, a plausible biochemical mechanism that linked the world of information processing with the world of emotions.[14] In the case of vision, through a system of mu-type opiate receptors originating in the amygdala, extending to the inferotemporal cortex, then "backward" to the occipital lobe, it would be possible for endorphins to influence the particular visual stimuli that were selected for attention or how the stimuli might be interpreted. A similar system would exist for auditory perception. In both cases an "amygdala-to-neocortex" system would perform a vital function. The emotional response of an animal to its environment would set the priorities for information processing, and, in doing so, increase the chances for survival. In short, the paleomammalian brain (through the amygdala) would be setting the parameters through which the neomammalian brain would operate.

What particular endorphin substance might be involved in this filtering process remains unknown, but we do know that the mu-type opiate receptors are at the heart of it. Just as we had seen (in Chapter 6) the ways in which an endorphin system in the midbrain and medulla acted downward upon a pain pathway to filter out pain, here is another endorphin system, with the amygdala acting upward upon the neocortex to direct the processing of information related to vision and hearing. It turns out, however, that the influence of an endorphin system in the amygdala does not stop there. We can also identify a degree of influence at an even higher level of cortical information processing: the processing of language.

---

† The same pattern held true in the cortical regions associated with auditory processing as well: mu-receptors were more concentrated as the level of auditory processing became more advanced, while delta-receptor concentrations stayed the same.

THE NEUROANATOMY OF LANGUAGE

One of the striking features about the neocortex is that there is an inherent "two-ness" about it: a left hemisphere and a right hemisphere in seeming opposition to each other. From even the most cursory inspection of a dissected brain there is the unmistakable appearance of two brains linked together as one (figure 25). In 1726 political satirist Jonathan Swift seized upon this fact as he suggested in *Gulliver's Travels* a novel way of settling political disputes. Two political leaders who took opposing views, he wrote, would have their brains split apart and each of the brains would receive the hemisphere from the brain of the other. "The two half-brains being left to debate the matter between themselves within the space of one skull" would presumably produce a degree of political moderation.[15] The implication still remains today that somehow the two hemispheres are set up to work together in some kind of integrative mission.

The cortical organization of vision can be imagined as one large, crossed X. All of the information from the left visual field is initially delivered to the right hemisphere and all of the information from the right visual field is initially delivered to the left hemisphere. And yet we do not live in a "split-screen" world; what we see is a continuity of vision from our extreme left to our extreme right. The reason is that the two halves of the brain, while not physically joined to each other, are nevertheless joined functionally via a set of nerve fiber tracts, called commissures, that carry information from one side to the other. One of these fiber systems, the posterior commissure, links areas of the midbrain. Another system, the anterior commissure, links the two sides of the limbic system and the temporal lobes. The rest of the neocortex (besides the temporal lobes) is linked together by the largest commissure of the three, a massive system of 200 million nerve fibers called the corpus callosum.

These commissures are the routes for information to travel from left hemisphere to right hemisphere and vice versa. It is due essentially to the functioning of the anterior commissure and corpus callosum that we develop an integrative mind.[16] The importance of

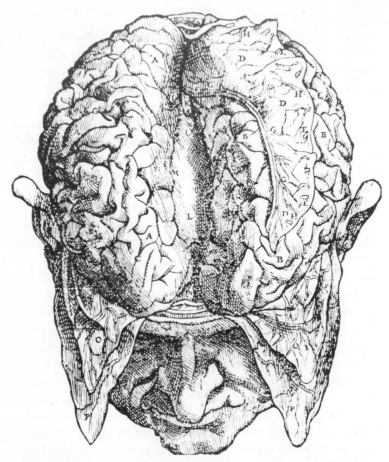

25. An illustration from Vesalius' De Humani Corporis Fabrica (On the Fabric of the Human Body), *published in 1543, showing the separation of the cortical hemispheres and the corpus callosum (marked by "L"). Executioners supplied Vesalius with the heads of decapitated criminals, and the dissections were made with the brains still warm. (From C. Blakemore.* Mechanics of the Mind. *New York: Cambridge University Press, 1977, p. 157)*

these systems cannot be overemphasized. "The perceptually seamless nature" of the anatomically divided right and left visual fields, neurophysiologist Robert Doty has said, "bears continual testimony to the profound role of the . . . commissures in creating a unified experience from the disparate and potentially divisible mental lives of the two cerebral hemispheres."[17] When these communicating fibers are severed, however, we are able to witness behavior that sheds light not only on the cognitive make-up of a human being, but also on the ways in which the interplay of emotions and language influence our daily lives.

For at least a hundred years, the implications of having a disconnected pair of cortical hemispheres have intrigued psychologists and philosophers alike. Would the unity of consciousness, as some of them proposed, be so dependent upon a continuity of brain tissue that any surgical division would produce essentially a duplication of the human being? One British psychologist, William McDougall (1871–1938), argued against this idea and even reportedly volunteered to have his corpus callosum cut (providing he had an incurable disease; he was no fool) to prove that his consciousness would remain unitary.[18] In the early 1960s a medical rationale for this kind of surgery emerged. Two California neurosurgeons, Philip Vogel and Joseph Bogen, found that a sectioning of corpus callosum and anterior commissure was successful in reducing seizure activity in intractable epileptic patients, individuals for whom no medication or other treatment had been previously effective. It was admittedly a drastic step to take; but these patients, as it turned out, benefited enormously. It was as if a brush fire (the abnormal neuronal activity) in a forest (the neocortex) could be controlled by physically isolating the activity to one and only one hemisphere. Yet, in at least partial vindication of McDougall, these patients' personality, intelligence, and behavior in general remained unchanged.‡ Only when they were tested under special laboratory conditions was there any discernible alteration in the way they responded to the world.[20]

One of the primary deficits in these patients was in their ability to

‡ Often the immediate effect of the surgery was an improvement in the patient's mood. One patient, less than two days afterward, was heard to quip that he suddenly had "a splitting headache."[19]

respond equivalently to information flashed briefly in their left or right visual field. If a patient, for example, was asked to look directly at a small dot in the center of a screen and suddenly a picture of a cup appeared to the right of the dot, the response would be "cup." If another picture, say a spoon, was flashed to the left of the dot, either the response would be "nothing" or the patient would simply make a wild guess. The image of the spoon had been projected to the right hemisphere alone and, without the commissures to transmit the information to the other side, this was where the information remained. The left hemisphere was capable of a verbal response ("cup") and the output of language; the right hemisphere was not.

The left hemisphere, conversely, was totally ignorant of the presentation of a spoon on the screen, since this information had been delivered exclusively to the right hemisphere. Nevertheless, the idea of "spoon" could be communicated in other ways. If the patient was asked to reach under a screen with the left hand and select (by touch only) the object that had been just presented, the spoon would be selected. If asked about what unseen object the patient was holding, the response would be "pencil" or another wild guess.[21] Evidently, the right hemisphere could communicate the idea of "spoon" only in a nonverbal way, through its control over the left hand. Meanwhile, the verbally adept left hemisphere would be ignorant of what the right hemisphere knew, so that when a verbal response was required, its answer of "pencil" was essentially random.

There had been a quiet but decided split in human consciousness. As one of the early and still-primary researchers in this field, Michael Gazzaniga, has remembered it, these studies were nothing short of revolutionary:

> No one was prepared for the riveting experience of observing a split-brain patient generating integrated activities with the mute right hemisphere that the language-dominant left hemisphere was unable to describe or comprehend. That was the sweetest afternoon. . . . For the first time in the history of brain science, the specialized functions of each hemisphere could be positively demonstrated as a function of which hemisphere was asked to respond.[22]

When emotionality entered into the picture, the right hemisphere appeared to be fully capable of a response, even though no verbal justification could be made. In one instance in the study of these patients, a woman was flashed a picture of a nude female in the left visual field (and hence to the right hemisphere). The woman blushed and started to giggle, covering her mouth with her hand. When asked what she saw, she replied, "Nothing, just a flash of light." When asked why she was laughing, she replied, "I don't know . . . nothing . . . oh—that funny machine."[23] The left hemisphere was obviously puzzled by the behavior and could offer only a lame rationalization for the fact that some bodily reactions were occurring. In this woman's brain, her right hemisphere could respond to the emotional content of the stimulus without being able to process it verbally.

We cannot be sure of the way in which the coding of "emotional tone" in our experience is accomplished; but it is plausible that a neural mechanism for this kind of coding lies in the mutual interaction of limbic system structures, particularly the amygdala, with the neocortex.[24] Drawing upon the results of the study by Lewis and Mishkin in 1981, it is equally plausible that a biochemical mechanism would involve mu-type opiate receptors. Through some kind of endorphin system, a visual stimulus could be encoded along a nonverbal, emotional dimension quite independently of its verbal characteristics. For individuals that had undergone a surgical separation of the cortical hemispheres, the emotional coding of events and stimuli taken in through the left visual field would be trapped in the right hemisphere, a neural system that would be essentially mute in its ability to express itself linguistically. For a time it appeared that the nonverbal, emotional world of the right hemisphere might never be fully open for exploration. A rare exception to this general rule, however, was identified in 1977; and researchers for the first time were able to gain entry into the previously inaccessible right-hemispheric mind.

EMOTIONALITY AND THE REMARKABLE CASE
OF PAUL S.

The individual, code-named P.S., was different from the earlier "split-brain" patients in several important ways. First of all, he was considerably younger than the rest. The surgery was performed when P.S. was fifteen years old. He had had recurring epileptic seizures since he was eighteen months of age and had sustained, early in his life, damage to his left hemisphere. The surgery itself was different as well. Unlike that of the patients of Bogen and Vogel in California, the surgery of P.S. had been performed by Donald H. Wilson of the Dartmouth Medical School, whose practice it had been to section the corpus callosum but leave the anterior commissure intact.[25] Consequently, there remained in the brain of P.S. some means (the anterior commissure) of transferring information from one hemisphere to the other. The kinds of transferable information, however, tended to be associated with an emotional, as opposed to verbal, mode of communication. He could transfer information about odors, for example, by verbally identifying a familiar smell presented to the right nostril (and right hemisphere).[26] The left hemisphere in this case was able to respond with the correct odor after receiving information from the right hemisphere, an accomplishment not possible in those patients that had had their anterior commissure sectioned.*

Most of all, P.S. was capable of a degree of right-hemispheric communication of language beyond anything yet observed with this patient population. It is likely that since P.S. had suffered some disturbance in his left hemisphere early in his life, the customary dominance of this hemisphere for the development of language had been arrested, leaving an opportunity for the right hemisphere to develop

---

* There is a strong suspicion that the anterior commissure is an older neural structure, from an evolutionary point of view, than the corpus callosum. In prenatal development, the anterior commissure in the human brain is formed during the third month of gestation, approximately two weeks before the corpus callosum.[27] Generally, we can gauge the relative antiquity of a structure in evolutionary history by how early it appears in prenatal development.

language capabilities of its own. His right hemisphere was not able actually to speak in verbal terms, but words could be formed by arranging Scrabble letters with his left hand.

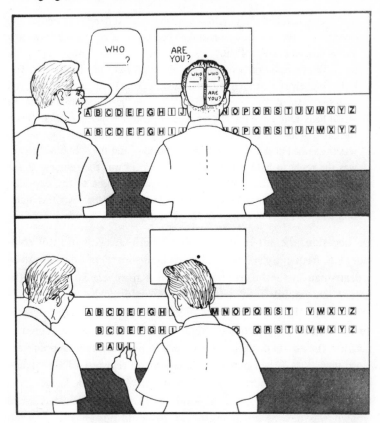

26. *The study of Paul S., where instructions to the right hemisphere could be executed by movements of the left hand. (From M. S. Gazzaniga and J. E. LeDoux.* The Integrated Mind. *New York: Plenum Press, 1978, p. 144)*

The illustration (figure 26) shows how the procedure for communication was carried out. When the question "who———" was asked, the words "are you" were flashed to the left visual field. Consequently, only the right hemisphere was in a position to know the complete question. One of the reports of this case by Joseph LeDoux, along with Gazzaniga and Wilson, captures the emotions surrounding what followed:

> As his eyes scanned the 52 letters available, his left hand reached out and selected the "P," set it down and then proceeded to collect the remaining letters needed to spell "Paul." . . . Overflowing with excitement, having just communicated on a personal level with a right hemisphere, we collected ourselves, and then initiated the next trial by saying, "Would you spell the name of your favorite 'blank?' " Then "girl" appeared in the left visual field. Out came the left hand again, and this time it spelled "Liz," the name of his girlfriend at the time. On the next two trials, the question was the same but the key words were "person" and then "hobby." "Car" was the reply to hobby, and "Henry Wi Fozi" was the response to his favorite person (Henry Winkler is the real-life name of the television character, Fonzie, that P.S., a 15-year-old boy, idolizes). Another question was "What is tomorrow?" He correctly spelled "Sunday."[28]

On occasion, the left- and right-hemispheric answers did not coincide. P.S. frequently spoke (via his left hemisphere) of his desire to be a draftsman in the future, but his right hemisphere spelled out the letters "automobile race" as the job he would pick!

Strangely, the left hemisphere of P.S. often appeared to experience an emotion in the absence of cognition. When he was instructed to perform the action described by a word in his left visual field and the word was "kiss," the impact of the command registered immediately in his right hemisphere. The left hemisphere responded, "Hey, no way, no way. You've got to be kidding." Yet, when P.S. was asked what it was he was not going to do, he could not answer. The left hemisphere had caught the emotional impact of the word without knowing the word itself. When "kiss" was presented to the left hemisphere, the verbal expression of the emotional implications was very similar. Thus, the emotional dimension of a word could be registered directly in the left hemisphere or transferred over from the right.[29] Presumably, the route of transfer in the case of P.S. was the anterior commissure.

The fact that the anterior commissure links the limbic systems of the left and right brainstem, as well as the temporal lobes of the left and right hemisphere, leads to the intriguing possibility that an emotional coding of a stimulus could be accomplished by several interacting systems that includes the amygdala and the right hemisphere of the neocortex. The "translation" of this emotionality into verbal terms could be accomplished either by the 200 million nerve fibers of the corpus callosum (if this system is intact) or, as in the case of P.S., via the 3 million nerve fibers of the anterior commissure. It is also possible that the mu-type opiate receptors are instrumental in the establishment and later transfer of the emotional tone in a stimulus, since these receptors have been identified to be so plentiful in the amygdala and in those areas of the temporal lobes that are responsible for the highest levels of perception.

The implications of this idea are far-reaching as applied to the dynamics of emotion in our language. Just as the left hemisphere of P.S. understood the emotional dimension of something processed in his right hemisphere, our own left hemisphere might register a mood state that has been generated in the right hemisphere without always being aware of its origin and later have to concoct a post hoc explanation in verbal terms to account for its presence. LeDoux and his associates have put it in the following way:

> The environment has ways of planting hooks in our minds, and while the verbal system may not know the why or what of it all, part of its job is to make sense out of the emotional and other mental systems and in so doing allow man, with his mental complexity, the illusion of a unified self.[30]

The position being taken here is that the mu-type opiate receptors are involved in generating the content of this emotional system at the level of the amygdala and later the right hemisphere. It would be interesting to find out if there are higher densities of this opiate-receptor subtype in the right hemisphere when compared against the left.†

---

† While there has been considerable progress very recently in mapping mu-type opiate receptors in the human brain,[31] no one has yet identified any difference between receptor densities in the two cortical hemispheres.

THE RIGHT HEMISPHERE AND THE IMPACT
OF PROSODY IN OUR LANGUAGE

A great deal is often made of the left hemisphere's ability to generate the words of speech that constitute the bulk of human communication. We certainly see the devastating effects that can result from
left hemispheric-damage (through lesions or stroke) on the production of verbal behavior. We refer to these verbal deficits in general as
aphasias, of which two forms are best known. The first, called
Broca's aphasia, is named for the French physician who in 1861 first
showed that a language disorder could be linked to a specific cortical
lesion. It is a deficit in the *expression* of words and writing, after
damage to an area of the (usually left) frontal lobe. The second,
called Wernicke's aphasia, is named for a German neurologist who
first described in 1873 how damage to an area of the (usually left)
temporal lobe produced a deficit in the *comprehension,* though not
the expression, of speech and writing. We seldom consider, however,
the fact that it is not only *what* we say that conveys meaningful
information to others but *how* we say it. Neuropsychologists include
the emotional coloring, melody, and cadence of speech under a category called prosody. Together with bodily gestures, prosody makes a
major contribution to the richness and complexity of human communication. It is in these aspects of language that the right (not the left)
hemisphere is firmly in control, playing a critical role in the verbal
expression of attitudes and emotions.[32]

Over the last ten years, neuropsychologists have begun to recognize that patients who have suffered right-hemispheric damage display a varying degree of emotional "flatness" that has become known
as the syndrome of aprosodia (literally, "an absence of prosody"). In
some cases called motor aprosodia, the deficit involves the output
aspect of prosody, where the individual still feels the emotion but
fails to convey it in terms of speech. In other cases called sensory
aprosodia, the deficit involves the input aspect of prosody, where the
individual's speech can be spontaneously modulated to reflect various emotional levels but cannot imitate the emotional tone of others
or cannot comprehend the emotion being conveyed by them. A good

example of the first type is the case of a thirty-five-year-old school-teacher who found herself without the slightest ability to express her feelings in a verbal manner after a stroke in her right hemisphere.[33] Even after she had recovered from the paralysis brought on by her stroke and was able to return to her career, the prosodic deficiency remained. She found herself unable to maintain classroom discipline through the emotional quality of her speech. At home, she tried to circumvent her deficiency by attaching parenthetical statements, like "God damn it, I mean it," or "I am angry and mean it," though her expressions, even in these instances, were made in a completely monotone voice. There was also an inability to cry and laugh, even though she stated that she still was experiencing emotion, only the expression of it was lost.

The various types of aprosodia and their association with physical disorders of the right hemisphere underscore the necessity for an intermingling of emotion and language in order for individuals to communicate appropriately with each other. Our normal sensitivity to the tone of one's own voice and that of others can be seen to link us to a heritage of communication that predates our recent development of linguistic behavior. Early in our lives, we respond to the world through the modulations of the human voice, prior to arriving at the point where we can comprehend the linguistic aspects of that message. Parents know, early on, the effect of sternness in their voices to exert discipline or the effect of softness in comforting a child. Even after we have acquired the ability to process the information of language, we can sometimes lose ourselves in the flooding experience of rhetoric and oratory, where we no longer hear the words as much as we are swept up in the power of cadence and phrasing. It is at these times that we are conquered by the power of a speech as it is being delivered. Later, if we read the speech in written form, we may wonder why we were so strongly affected.

EMOTIONALITY AND TEMPORAL-LOBE EPILEPSY

The feelings of sadness and happiness that we attach to and integrate into our verbal lives can be considered as a further demonstration of the functioning of an amygdala-cortical system in the brain, with the operation of mu-type opiate receptors providing the critical mechanism for processing this kind of information. In the cases of individuals with aprosodia, we see the enormous impact that being deprived of prosody can have upon one's social, professional, and domestic relationships.[34] In the most extreme cases, when the actual circuitry between neocortex and limbic system becomes disturbed, there is the potential for profound changes in one's personality. This phenomenon can be observed in cases of individuals with temporal-lobe epilepsy, a condition where an abnormal firing of neurons in either the left or right or both sides of the temporal lobes results in often bizarre episodes of behavior. Sometimes the seizures them-selves produce abnormal thoughts and feelings, anxiety coupled with a déjà vu sensation that they have been in this situation before. There may be a perceived depersonalization, as if they feel like strangers in their bodies. There can be distortions in visual images as well as objects heard, smelled, or tasted. The motor behavior during a seizure shows equally unusual features. Automatic movements are often observed: chewing, swallowing, lip smacking. Some, but not all, of these occasions are also marked by violent behavior toward others that have been perceived by the patient as being an earlier source of frustration.[35]

During the intervals of time between the seizures of a temporal-lobe epileptic, serious emotional abnormalities continue. Patients as-sume a social posture of humorlessness and sobriety; sexual interests are absent. They may develop an unusual degree of religious fervor and begin to write voluminous notes and diaries.‡ Neuropsychologist David Bear has expressed well the dynamic interaction of these per-sonality changes; as he describes it, the principal theme lies in the enhanced emotional associations that are made in temporal-lobe epi-lepsy to previously neutral stimuli, events, or concepts:[36]

> Objects and events shot through with affective coloration may be incor-porated into a mystical or religious view of the world. As immediate

‡ The excessive output of writings in these patients usually has little literary merit. A notable exception, however, is the great Russian novelist Fyodor Dostoevsky, who suffered many of the behavioral symptoms described here of temporal-lobe epilepsy. In particular, his novel *The Idiot*, written in 1868, drew upon the author's experiences and contains vivid descriptions of the personal feelings associated with this disorder.

actions and thoughts are similarly charged with emotion, the patient experiences a heightened sense of personal destiny. Events discussed by others are perceived as affectively relevant, allowing for paranoid interpretations or the conviction that the patient is a pawn in the hands of powerful forces which structure his experiences. Feeling fervently about rules and laws may lead him to a punitive type of hypermoralism. . . . Since details bear the imprimatur of affective significance, many will be mentioned in lengthy, circumstantial speech or writing.[37]

In the cases of unilateral (one-sided) temporal-lobe epilepsy, these symptoms diverge as a function of which hemisphere contains the abnormal excitatory activity. As might be expected, the right-temporal patient shows a preponderance of *emotional* reactivity: anger and aggressiveness, depression, and a moralistic or religious fervor. The left-temporal patient shows a greater tendency toward *verbal* behavior: a sense of personal destiny, extensive explorations into philosophical issues, and a sober sense of intellectual and moral self-scrutiny.[38] In other words, the new interpretations of the self in the context of society are altered along the lines of hemispheric specialization—verbal on the left, nonverbal on the right.

The disturbed integration of emotion and human communication in temporal-lobe epilepsy can be viewed as instances in which the limbic system and neocortex have clearly failed to function normally. Yet the symptoms are only extreme degrees of less serious, but nonetheless troublesome, circumstances where feelings of personal identity and self-worth become embroiled in the ways we remember and interpret events and relationships, as well as in the ways we construct our beliefs about the world. In general, we have every right to feel uncomfortable about the fact that it may be impossible to shake loose the ties to emotional systems so deeply rooted in the evolution of our brains, particularly when we consider the behavior of language. "It is one thing," MacLean has remarked, "to have the anciently derived limbic system to assure us of the authenticity of such things as food or a mate, but where do we stand if we must depend on the mental emanations of this same system for belief in our ideas, concepts, and theories?"[39] The fact remains that we never seem to be far from the influences of the limbic brain, nor perhaps from the endorphin influences that are associated with it.

ENDORPHINS AND THE THRILL
OF MUSICAL EXPERIENCE

In 1980 Avram Goldstein surveyed eighty-eight students at Stanford University as to what personal experience gave them most often a moment of emotional pleasure commonly referred to as a thrill.[40] At the top of this list were "musical passages" (96 percent) and "a scene in a movie, play, ballet, or book" (92 percent). About one half of the group reported feeling a tingling sensation during these experiences, and invariably there were reports of a sudden change in mood. "Often, subjects told me," Goldstein has noted, "what makes a certain musical passage able to elicit thrills is some association with an emotionally charged event or a particular person in the subject's past, as though the music had become a conditional stimulus for the emotional response."[41]

In order to probe the possible role of endorphins in this phenomenon, Goldstein compared the intensity of the thrill experience, before and after subjects had been administered injections of either naloxone or a placebo control (saline) substance. Neither the subjects nor the experimenter knew which injection had been given. Goldstein showed that, at least for some individuals, the presence of an opioid antagonist had a significant suppressant effect upon the emotional reception of a piece of music.[42] Here was a verification in a laboratory setting of something we have long believed on an intuitive level: the fundamental relationship between the images of music (and the arts in general) and the physiology of emotionality. One writer has expressed it this way:

> Music can move us to tears or to dance, to fight or to make love. It can inspire our most exalted religious feelings and ease our anxious and lonely moments. Its pleasures are many, but it can also be alien, irksome, almost maddening. It is created by people to affect and communicate with other people. In one sense, it's no surprise that music grabs us—it's supposed to.[43]

It is also not surprising that at this juncture of our experience we should see evidence of the participation of an endorphin system in the brain. It is reasonable to speculate that the euphoria we feel at those special moments in musical experience is due to an increased functioning of endorphins. Against the backdrop of a mammalian heritage that has fostered the importance of socialization and family, we can appreciate the emotional "high" we obtain from musical accomplishment as a way of reinforcing our collective sense of cultural belonging. Music seems to bring us together, in a primitive and inescapable way.

Within the span of our lives, music and sounds serve as powerful sources of emotional support, practically from the very start of our existence. It has been the vocalization of mother and offspring that has formed, at least in part, the mammalian elements of our behavior. The social bonding process could not have been accomplished without it, nor could the development of social reinforcement. Early in our lives, music and the gentle rhythm of the human voice allow us to feel content and at peace. Endorphins may be the source of these feelings.

A NOTE ON AUTISM AND THE NEOMAMMALIAN BRAIN

In the last chapter, a theoretical position was described that relates the symptoms of autism to an excessive level of endorphin activity in the limbic system. It might not be surprising that autistic individuals would also show unusual characteristics that relate to the development of the neocortex as well, specifically in the relative dominance of left and right hemispheres. As psychologists Sally Springer and Georg Deutsch have viewed it, "The most salient characteristic of autism is the failure of these children to acquire language. Intelligence per se does not seem to be a factor, since even severely retarded (but not autistic) children learn to speak without special training. This suggests that some special, left-hemisphere problem may be present in autistic children."[44]

It is intriguing that an increased tendency toward right-hemispheric (and left-handed) dominance can be observed in this population. One study has shown 65 percent of observed autistic children to be left-handed or ambidextrous in contrast to a much lower propor-

27. *A drawing by an extraordinary autistic child, completed at the age of five and a half. (From L. Selfe.* Nadia: A Case of Extraordinary Drawing Ability in an Autistic Child. *New York: Academic Press, 1977, p. 33, drawing No. 24)*

tion (10 to 15 percent) in the general population.[45] Other studies show other evidence that the right hemisphere may be functioning at a higher level than the left in the autistic brain.[46] One consequence of this phenomenon would be the occasional observations of artistic or musical inclinations of patients with autism, despite the profound deficits in their language skills (figures 27 and 28).[47] It is possible that the overactivity of endorphin processes in subcortical regions of the brain, as theorized by James Kalat and Jaak Panksepp, might carry over to a comparable overactivity in the amygdala–right-hemisphere circuitry, suggested earlier as functioning to provide the emotional context of language. Here, it would be speculated that excessive endorphin levels in autism would suppress the normal development of language in the left hemisphere, leading to the disturbance in normal language-oriented behavior.

ENDORPHINS AND THE CHEMISTRY OF DOUBT

We have all experienced the gnawing doubt in our minds when we think to ourselves, Did I turn off the stove? Did I lock the door? Did I really set that alarm clock? To an individual suffering from an obsessive-compulsive disorder, these questions never end and, most significantly, these questions never seem to get resolved. We all have to some degree the need, and feel at times the compulsion, to go back to that stove, door, or alarm clock to check to see if we have completed these tasks (particularly if we are anxious at the time); but when the checking and rechecking continue on and on, it is obvious that something is seriously wrong. Consider the case of a fifty-seven-year-old retail sales executive whose career had suffered from obsessional and compulsive behavior at work: an inclination toward continual doubt and compulsive checking that had been a part of his life since the age of eighteen. As he would describe himself and his symptoms, usually it was a trivial question that he was not able to resolve: "Is the picture straight on the wall? I need to check 20, maybe 30 times until I get it right. Then I'll start to worry about something else."[48]

If there is a reward system in the brain that handles the feeling of satisfaction when a nagging doubt has been resolved, then such a

28. Another drawing by the same child, at the age of four. (From L. Selfe. Nadia: A Case of Extraordinary Drawing Ability in an Autistic Child. New York: Academic Press, 1977, p. 28, drawing No. 20)

system in these patients is clearly defective. NIMH psychiatrists Thomas Insel and David Pickar reasoned that the deficit in reaching a satisfactory level of certainty may be due to a deficiency in an endorphin-based reward system. If that were the case, then an antagonist like naloxone should exacerbate the obsessional and compulsive symptoms. Their predictions were borne out. In one patient, sixty minutes after an injection of naloxone, symptoms self-rated as occurring 20 percent of the time were occurring 70 percent of the time. Administration of a placebo produced no change at all, even though the identification of the injections was kept secret. The data suggested that the symptoms of this disorder were at least in part due to a deficiency in brain endorphins.[49]

Until recently, there has been little or no understanding of any biochemical basis for the obsessive-compulsive disorder. In the 1970s, however, there emerged a new drug called chlorimipramine (marketed under the brand name Anafranil) that was found to help relieve individuals of their obsessional or compulsive symptoms.[50] Biochemically, chlorimipramine increases levels of brain serotonin and also (not coincidentally) helps to increase the analgesic effects of morphine. Therefore, it is entirely possible that the therapeutic effects of this drug lie in the ability to raise *both* serotonin and endorphin levels in the brain. This linkage of serotonin and endorphins would not be unprecedented. In Chapter 6 we saw how the effects of serotonin and endorphin pathways are interrelated in the control of pain at the level of the brainstem and spinal cord. Here, in the case of obsessive-compulsive behavior, we would be seeing the same linkage at a more recently evolved level of brain functioning and behavior. It would be predicted from this point of view that unmedicated obsessive-compulsive patients would have a significantly lower level of endorphin functioning. No data, however, have yet been reported on this question.

Perhaps it is good from a behavioral standpoint that we feel compelled to check that stove; we may have left it on. The concept of doubt, in that sense, may function in an important way to head off the potentially undesirable consequences of our often faulty memories. But in the banishment of doubt, there is a powerful emotional experience as well. It certainly does feel good to "put our doubts to rest," good to know when we have finally reached a resolution to a problem. There is a satisfaction, even a degree of euphoria, when we put that last piece into the jigsaw puzzle, or finish a task that has occupied our thoughts for a length of time. We feel a wonderful sense of relief when we finally remember the name of that long-ago acquaintance, and until that happens there is a feeling of discomfort that is hard to shake off.

It is quite possible that an endorphin system in the brain is providing that feeling of relief, and sometimes euphoria, when we manage to turn uncertainty into certainty, incoherence into coherence. Once

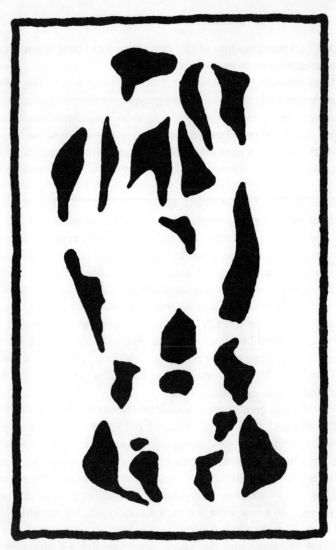

29. *An example of a figure with components that make no sense at all to us, but which in its totality produces a recognizable image. An example of Gestalt closure. (From R. Leeper. "A Study of a Neglected Portion of the Field of Learning—the Development of Sensory Organization,"* Journal of Genetic Psychology, *1935, 46:41–75. Reprinted with permission of the Helen Dwight Reid Educational Foundation, published by Heldref Publications, © 1935)*

more, we can see a linkage to our biological heritage. Even though the quest for a connectedness among ideas may be a uniquely human trait, the idea of connectedness has been a theme throughout our evolutionary history. At earlier stages of our development, neural systems have been established to assure us a connectedness to place and a connectedness to people. And, in each one of these points in brain evolution, we have seen the importance of endorphin functioning.

30. Relativity *by M. C. Escher, completed in 1953. (Collection: The Museum of Modern Art, New York)*

The power of incompletion, uncertainty, or incoherence is part of our daily experience, in ways that we do not often recognize. When we see a visual image that is incomplete, we complete it (figure 29);

when we see a picture such as a work by the Dutch artist Maurits Escher (figure 30) we feel the tension of its illogical organization and try to make sense of it. In perhaps no other area of the human condition, however, does the need to reduce uncertainty manifest itself more strongly than in the sciences, a subject of discussion in the next chapter. In describing the intense quality of scientific curiosity, Nobel laureate Sir Peter Medawar once put it this way: "You must feel in yourself an exploratory impulsion—an *acute discomfort* at incomprehension."[51] The period of struggling with a persistent question that needs an answer can indeed be a torment. St. John of the Cross called it "the dark night of the soul."[52] Fortunately for most of us, scientist and nonscientist alike, the presence of doubt is a continuing challenge to our inventiveness and creativity, rather than a cloud over our lives. We might imagine that a functional endorphin system has seen to that—just as it has helped to bring coherence and predictability to so many aspects of our experience.

9

A Glimpse of Paradise

CREATIVITY AND LAUGHTER

No one can predict how the endorphin story will turn out in the end, for it is only at its beginning. At the present stage, it might go any-where, mean anything.

LEWIS THOMAS, *The Youngest Science,* 1983

Clearly, brain opioids attract speculation as readily as honey attracts a child.

JAAK PANKSEPP, "Brain opioids—A neurochemical substrate for narcotic and social dependence," 1980

To a scientist, the road to understanding is a road that ideally never ends. It is ironic that science is in the business of reducing the uncertainty of nature, yet uncertainty is something that few scientists would ever really want completely to conquer. They like traveling a route on which something new lurks around the next curve; when the scenery starts getting predictable, the fun is gone.

Consider the dilemma of modern-day physics where the latest attempt to provide a unifying model of the universe looks as if it may finally succeed. Based upon a revolutionary concept called superstrings and a hypothesized ten-dimensional universe, this new model is being touted (with the playful humor characteristic of theoretical physics) as the Theory of Everything, or T.O.E.[1] In one writer's words, it would account for nothing short of the entirety of the universe, "All matter and energy, all forces, all people, planets, stars, cats and dogs, quasars, atoms, automobiles and everything else, from the instant of the Big Bang to the end of time."[2]

It is not hard to imagine why physicists would be entranced by the sweetness of the problem; a successful T.O.E. would be the ultimate intellectual prize. Yet it could also be an intellectual nightmare. As Robert Crease and Charles Mann, authors of *The Second Creation,* have recently put it, "A complete unified theory would mean the end of physics. . . . Science would continue, but all of the fundamental questions that physics can pose would have been answered."[3] When we experience an ambivalence toward its full realization, we are reminded of the poetic advice "Ah, but a man's reach should exceed his grasp,/Or what's a heaven for?"[4]

Many physicists will argue that theoretical physics will never stop being fun, despite the T.O.E.s that come along. Certainly, in the field of the neurosciences a comparable T.O.E. is only a distant dream, and presently researchers have the luxury of not having to grapple with the dilemma of having to embrace such a possibility. Nonetheless, the subject matters of the two disciplines have an odd parallel. The physicist considers how the universe works, while the neuroscientist considers how *our* universe works, the private experience of the mind within the context of the human brain. It is so immensely difficult an undertaking that, so far, we have been well satisfied with the occasional T.O.S.—Theory of Something.

It has been said that the supreme irony of neuroscience research is that we are using our brains, as best we can, in order to understand how our brains work. In the course of inquiring about the working of the brain, we are making use of that which is being inquired about.[5] In the study of brain endorphins, there is the possibility of an even more striking twist. In this particular field, the fuel for the process of discovery may be identical to the subject matter itself. In Chapter 8, an argument was developed that the pleasure we feel in the satisfying of our curiosity, in the resolution of doubt and uncertainty, was a result of an increase of endorphins in the brain. It was speculated that this function of endorphin release was essentially the latest of three major contributions that endorphin systems have made in the evolutionary development of the triune brain, from its protoreptilian ancestry to the present-day neomammalian form. In that sense, we can view the excitement of endorphin research as arising from the functioning of endorphins themselves. No other area of scientific endeavor can claim such a curious circularity.

One of the major motivators in a scientist's drive for professional success lies in the need to achieve a significant level of respect among one's professional peers. It is a dream that pervades the entire scientific community. Yet there is no question that the process of discovery elicits powerful *intrinsic* rewards of their own, feelings of satisfaction and pleasure. Psychologist Mihaly Czikszentmihalyi has termed this phenomenon the "flow experience."[6] Many of the scientific advances that have been made in the understanding of our world can be traced to individuals seeking these intrinsic rewards. "It is likely," Czikszentmihalyi has written, "that the evolution of mankind to its present precarious mastery of the planet was helped by the fact that, in the human mind, meeting difficult challenges became genetically linked with a form of pleasure. Just as we have learned to enjoy what is necessary to survive and to preserve the species, like eating and sex, so we might have learned to enjoy the flow experience, which spurs us to master increasingly complex challenges. This *cor irrequietus,* this Faustian engine, could be the source of what we count as human progress."[7] It is not unreasonable to suppose that the flow experience is linked to endorphin systems in the brain.

One of the most vivid accounts of a flow experience in a scientist's life was expressed in 1934 through a novel, *The Search* by scientist-novelist C. P. Snow. Here is how one of his characters reflected upon the moment of his particular insight:

> Then I was carried beyond pleasure. . . . My own triumph and delight and success were there, but they seemed insignificant beside this tranquil ecstasy. It was as though I had looked for a truth outside myself, and finding it had become for a moment a part of the truth I sought; as though all the world, the atoms and the stars, were wonderfully clear and close to me, and I to them, so that we were part of a lucidity more tremendous than any mystery.
>
> I had never known that such a moment could exist. . . . Since then I have never quite regained it. But one effect will stay with me as long as I live; once, when I was young, I used to sneer at the mystics who have described the experience of being at one with God and part of the unity of things. After that afternoon, I did not want to laugh again; for though I should have interpreted the experience differently, I thought I knew what they meant.[8]

The words of neuroscientists Candace Pert and Huda Akil, as related earlier in this book, echo these feelings of triumph and satisfaction, in their own ways, when they describe their personal connections to the early days of endorphin research.

There is an essential commonality between the process of discovery in the sciences and the creative experience in other human endeavors. One connecting thread seems to be what psychologist Jerome Bruner once called the phenomenon of "effective surprise." In 1962 he proposed that this element was the hallmark of the creative enterprise, no matter where or when it occurs:

> The content of the surprise can be as various as the enterprises in which men are engaged. . . . I could not care less about the person's intention, whether or not he intended to create. The road to banality is paved with creative intentions. . . . It is the unexpected that strikes one with wonder or astonishment. What is curious about effective surprise is that it need not be rare or infrequent or bizarre and is often none of these things. Effective surprises . . . seem rather to have the quality of obviousness about them when they occur, producing a shock of recognition following which there is no longer astonishment.[9]

Through effective surprise, there is a new placement, perhaps merely a rearrangement, that yields in the end a new perspective, so that we can be transported beyond the everyday ways of experiencing the world. As a result, the world is changed, never to be quite the same again.*

In exploring the experience of flow itself, however, we are tapping not only into the *creative* enterprise but into any activity for which there is a sensation of total involvement. We could be speaking as much to the intensity of concentration in an artist molding a sculpture of clay as to that of a business executive resolving a corporate crisis. The places where a flow experience occurs can be humble or exalted; the circumstances can be relaxed or highly stressed. The overriding criterion lies in the intensity of the emotionality at the time, not necessarily in the content of the activity.

Csikszentmihalyi has pointed out, in his analysis of the phenomenon, that it is during these moments that there is typically a temporary loss of ego. These are intervals when we seem to ignore the needs of our body; we go without sleep, without food and drink, as we get caught up in a private euphoria that we sometimes wish would never end. It is a kind of Paradise of our own internal making, and we discover that time seems to have stood still. A composer once expressed it in this way:

> You yourself are in an ecstatic state to such a point that you feel as though you almost don't exist. I've experienced this time and time again. My hand seems devoid of myself, and I have nothing to do with what is happening. I just sit there watching it in a state of awe and wonderment. And it just flows out by itself.[10]

Or as a world-class chess player put the feeling:

> Time passes a hundred times faster. In this sense, it resembles the dream state. A whole story can unfold in seconds, it seems.[11]

Above all, the essential ingredient of the flow experience is that it appears to need no goals or rewards external to itself. The passion

---

* All too often, when we experience the finished product, a dance or a painting, we forget that what makes a performance look or sound so easy, so effortless, is the application of talent and technique that we do not ourselves possess.

toward doing what one feels has to be done can override the hope of material success, the pain that may have to be undergone in the process, or the danger that might exist. In effect, a mountain is climbed because it is there, a dancer dances, and a writer writes—it is as simple as that. In Csikszentmihalyi's words, "Climbers do not climb to get to the top but get to the top so that they can climb; chess players do not play to win but try to win so that they can play."[12]

There is more than just an air of addictiveness about it all. The sensations of rapture and euphoria produce a significant amount of dependency. They are indeed habit-forming. When a flow has ended, there is a feeling of crashing. We can relate to, if not experience ourselves, the feelings of Alexander the Great, who, according to long-standing tradition, wept at the end of his conquests because he felt there were no more worlds to conquer. It is not uncommon to sink into varying levels of depression after a period of stress, even when one's goals have been realized. There are numerous examples of this phenomenon from the lives of well-known public figures. During his political career, now retired U.S. Senator Thomas Eagleton suffered periods of depression following election campaigns that had culminated in substantial victories.[13] Edwin "Buzz" Aldrin, astronaut on the 1969 Apollo 11 mission, during which he became the second person to set foot on the moon, started to show serious depressive symptoms within a year of his return.[14] While these examples may not be typical, it is nonetheless apparent that a triumph in life can sometimes be followed by a rebound on an emotional level.

A break away from the flow experience can frequently produce a sense of discomfort and withdrawal, like being removed from the influence of a powerful drug. In one study conducted in 1975, Csikszentmihalyi focused upon the experiences of surgeons as individuals for whom the act of surgery functioned as an intense flow experience.

> One surgeon mentioned that operating was "like taking narcotics"; another, that it is like "taking heroin." A seasoned practitioner described a vacation in Mexico—the first vacation he and his wife had taken in several years. After 2 days of sightseeing, he became so restless that he volunteered his services to a local hospital and spent the rest of the holiday operating. . . . Another one confessed that the worst stress he feels is during family vacations in the Bahamas.[15]

31. St. Francis in Ecstasy *by Giovanni Bellini, 1485. (© The Frick Collection, New York)*

We can easily make the mistake of imagining the stereotypical "workaholic" in a life of torment and enslavement, but this does not take into account the powerful reward mechanisms that seem to be operating.

The similarities to drug addiction may be only suggestive and the evidence circumstantial, but nevertheless it is plausible that we are dealing in these circumstances with the functioning of brain endorphins. Just as the thrill of music was shown by Avram Goldstein in 1980 to be tied to an endorphin process, so too would we see a connection with the thrill of an activity that is so intense and self-absorbing that it could take on "a sense of personal transcendence, of merging with a reality beyond the normal bounds of individuality."[16]

32. The Ecstasy of St. Theresa *by Gianlorenzo Bernini, 1645–52. (Cornaro Chapel, Santa Maria della Vittoria, Rome. Photograph courtesy Alinari Archives, Florence)*

ENDORPHINS AND HOMO LUDENS

We are normally under an exquisitely modulated pattern of bio-chemical checks and balances that has served us well, served us long before we discovered the allures of the opium poppy or any of its derivatives. It can be argued that brain endorphins, perhaps en-kephalin, have always had a necessary suppressive effect on those noradrenergic cells in the locus ceruleus—neurons that, left to their excitatory selves, would give us terror and anxiety. It is comforting to note that, for the vast majority of us, a complex, multilayered system of enkephalins, beta-endorphin, dynorphin, and their associated opioid peptides succeeds on its own in accomplishing a great many vital services for our body and our behavior. Through these substances, as has been related in these chapters, we have achieved a measure of control over pain, over the terror of being alone, and, finally, over the anxiety of uncertainty. We can also theorize that endorphin systems in the brain have succeeded in allowing the emergence of a peculiarly human attribute: the pleasure of creating something new. In this regard, Lewis Thomas once observed that he could always tell when scientific research was on the verge of a major discovery:

> I think one way to tell when something important is going on is by *laughter.* It seems to me that whenever I have been around a laboratory at a time when something very interesting has happened, it has at first seemed to be quite funny. There's laughter connected with the surprise—it *does* look funny. And whenever you can hear laughter, and somebody saying, "But that's preposterous!" you can tell that things are going well and that something probably worth looking at has begun to happen in the lab.[17]

There is a strong sense of playfulness in these and other human endeavors. In fact, we may characterize our species more accurately as *Homo ludens* ("the one who plays": from the Latin *ludere,* "to play") than *Homo sapiens* ("the wise one").[18] This designation would be a fitting tribute to the real underlying process that has made it possible for human beings to be the dominant species on earth.

It was once said, in an analysis of human play published in 1944, that "the fun of playing resists all analysis, all logical interpretation."[19] Since that time, however, it has been possible to reexamine the biological foundation of ludic behavior, this strong inclination to play among each other and to play with ideas. There is indeed a primordial quality about the tendency toward playfulness in the wide range of mammalian species that seem to possess it. "Nature," it was once said, ". . . could just as easily have given her children all those useful functions of discharging superabundant energy, of relaxing after exertion, of training for the demands of life, of compensating for unfulfilled longings, etc., in the form of purely mechanical exercises and reactions. But no, she gave us play, with its tension, its mirth, and its fun."[20]

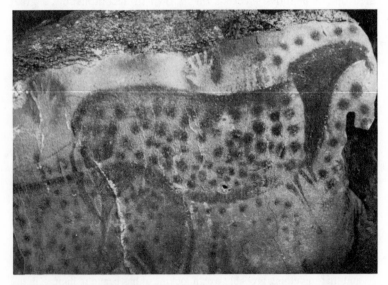

33. Cave wall paintings from Pech-Merle in France, dating from 15,000 to 17,000 years ago, the Magdalenian period. The hand prints show an unmistakable expression of human individual identity: in the words of Jacob Bronowski, "This is my mark. This is man." (© Alexander Marschack)

It may be true, as Avram Goldstein once observed, that the endorphin story is only at its beginning, but there is now reason to be optimistic that an understanding of endorphins as well as other aspects of brain chemistry will help to illuminate some of the fundamental aspects of the human condition.[21]

There is, in addition, another aspect to the benefits we may acquire from endorphin research. More than a century ago, Claude Bernard wrote, "I feel convinced that there will come a day when physiologists, poets, and philosophers will all speak the same language."[22] One candidate for the language that Bernard envisioned might turn out to be the language of endorphins. It might well be that these neurochemical processes, as we understand them and as we experience them, will allow us to break through to a common ground of communication. The physiologist, the poet, the philosopher—separated at the level of verbal communication, as well as at a more primitive level of territoriality with regard to their academic disciplines—might one day be united by a mutual appreciation of the emotional substrate that breathes life into their work. Understanding the common bond that we all share in the joys of work and play may help us to create a new dialogue. For we are not only reactors to a biological world but also potential creators of new worlds. The continuing study of brain endorphins joins together two intertwining realities: a biological past and a future of our own making. As T. S. Eliot has written:

> . . . the end of all our exploring
> will be to arrive where we started
> and know the place for the first time.[23]

Reference Notes

CHAPTER I

1. K. L. Jones, L. W. Shainberg, and C. O. Byer, *Drugs and alcohol,* 2d ed. (New York: Harper & Row, 1973).
   C. Kornetsky, *Pharmacology: Drugs affecting behavior* (New York: Wiley, 1976).
2. J. Hughes et al., Identification of two related pentapeptides from the brain with potent opiate agonist activity, *Nature* 258 (1975):577–79.
3. D. T. Courtwright, *Dark paradise: Opiate addiction in America before 1940* (Cambridge, Mass.: Harvard University Press, 1982).
4. D. Latimer and J. Goldberg, *Flowers in the blood: The story of opium* (New York: Franklin Watts, 1981).
   C. F. Levinthal, Milk of paradise/Milk of hell: The history of ideas about opium, *Perspectives in Biology and Medicine* 28 (1985):561–77.
   ———, Reply to Sapira, *Perspectives in Biology and Medicine* 29 (1986): 636–37.
   J. D. Sapira, Speculations concerning opium abuse and world history, *Perspectives in Biology and Medicine* 18 (1975):379–98.
   ———, Letter to the editor, *Perspectives in Biology and Medicine* 29 (1986):636.
5. A. Hayter, *Opium and the romantic imagination* (Berkeley: University of California Press, 1968).
   M. D. Merlin, *On the trail of the ancient opium poppy* (Cranbury, N.J.: Associated University Press, 1984).
6. R. M. Julien, *A primer of drug action,* 4th ed. (San Francisco: Freeman, 1985).
7. D. Wishart, The opium poppy: The forbidden crop, *Journal of Geography* 73 (1974):14–25.
8. Hayter, *Romantic imagination.*

9. Kornetsky, *Pharmacology.*

10. E. L. Way, History of opiate use in the Orient and the United States, in *Opioids in mental illness,* ed. K. Verebey (New York: New York Academy of Sciences, 1982).

11. J. Beeching, *The Chinese opium wars* (New York: Harcourt Brace Jovanovich, 1975).

12. D. E. Owen, *British opium policy in China and India* (New Haven, Conn.: Yale University Press, 1934).

13. P. W. Fay, *The opium war 1840–1842* (Chapel Hill, N.C.: University of North Carolina Press, 1975), p. 53.

14. Beeching, *Opium Wars,* p. 23.

15. A. Waley, *The opium war through Chinese eyes* (London: George Allen & Unwin, 1958).

16. N. Allen, *The opium trade as carried on in India and China* (Boston: Milford House, 1973 [originally published 1853]), p. 7.

17. Ibid.

18. Beeching, *Opium wars.*

19. Ibid.
    Waley, *Through Chinese eyes.*

20. Fay, *The opium war,* p. 366.

21. Beeching, *Opium wars.*

22. V. Berridge, Opiate use in England, 1800–1926, in *Opioids in mental illness.*
    T. M. Parsinnen, *Secret passions, secret remedies* (Philadelphia: Institute for the Study of Human Issues, 1983).

23. Hayter, *Romantic imagination.*

24. Ibid.

25. Berridge, Opiate use in England.

26. Ibid.

27. Fay, *The opium war,* p. 11.

28. E. M. Brecher, *Licit and illicit drugs* (Boston: Little, Brown, 1972).

29. M. H. Abrams, *The milk of paradise* (New York: Harper & Row, 1962).
    T. De Quincey, *Confessions of an English opium-eater,* ed. A. Hayter (Harmondsworth, Middlesex: Penguin, 1975 [originally published 1821]).

30. G. Lindop, *The opium eater: A life of Thomas De Quincey* (New York: Taplinger, 1982), p. 248.

31. D. F. Musto, *The American disease: Origins of narcotic control* (New Haven, Conn.: Yale University Press, 1973).

32. Hayter, *Romantic imagination,* p. 104.

33. Ibid., p. 43.

34. W. Collins, *The moonstone* (Harmondsworth, Middlesex: Penguin, 1966 [originally published 1868]), p. 443.

35. S. Siegel, Psychopharmacology and the mystery of *The Moonstone,* *American Psychologist* 40 (1985):580–81.

36. Beeching, *Opium wars.*

37. Hayter, *Romantic imagination,* p. 336.

38. Brecher, *Drugs,* p. 17.

39. E. H. Kaplan and H. Wieder, *Drugs don't take people: People take drugs* (Secaucus, N.J.: Lyle Stuart, 1974).

40. Brecher, *Drugs,* pp. 42–43.

41. A. K. Reynolds and L. O. Randall, *Morphine and allied drugs* (Toronto: University of Toronto Press, 1957).

42. D. I. Macht, The history of opium and some of its preparations and alkaloids, *Journal of the American Medical Association* 64 (1915):477–81. Quotation on p. 481.

43. Courtwright, *Dark paradise.*

44. Quoted in C. E. Terry and M. Pellens, *The opium problem* (Montclair, N.J.: Patterson Smith, 1970 [Original edition 1928]), p. 5.

45. Julien, *A primer.*

46. Courtwright, *Dark paradise,* p. 47.

47. Brecher, *Drugs.*

48. Macht, History of opium, p. 477.

49. Musto, *American disease,* p. 4.

50. Ibid., p. 253.

51. G. R. Gay and E. L. Way, Pharmacology of the opiate narcotics, in *It's so good, don't even try it once: Heroin in perspective,* ed. D. E. Smith and G. R. Gay (Englewood Cliffs, N.J.: Prentice-Hall, 1972). See also Reference Note 3 for Chapter 6.

52. Terry and Pellens, *Opium problem.*

53. Gay and Way, Opiate narcotics.

54. Musto, *American disease.*

55. Ibid.

56. Ibid., p. 4.

57. Ibid., p. 65.

58. Terry and Pellens, *Opium problem.*

59. S. H. Snyder, Opiate receptors and internal opiates, *Scientific American* 236 (3) (1977):44–56.

60. C. B. Pert and S. H. Snyder, Opiate receptor: Demonstration in nervous tissue, *Science* 179 (1973):1011–14.

E. J. Simon, J. M. Hiller, and I. Edelman, Stereospecific binding of the potent narcotic analgesic [^{3}H]-etorphine to rat brain homogenate, *Proceedings of the National Academy of Sciences, USA* 70 (1973):1974–79.

L. Terenius, Characteristics of the "receptor" for narcotic analgesics in synaptic plasma membrane fraction from rat brain, *Acta Pharmacologica et Toxicologica* 32 (1973):377–84.

61. J. Hughes, Isolation of an endogenous compound from the brain with pharmacological properties similar to morphine, *Brain Research* 88 (1975):295–308.
    Hughes et al., Pentapeptides.
62. E. J. Simon, History, in *Endorphins,* ed. J. B. Malick and R. M. S. Bell (New York: Marcel Dekker, 1982), pp. 1–8.
63. H. W. Kosterlitz and J. Hughes, Some thoughts on the significance of enkephalin, the endogenous ligand, *Life Sciences* 17 (1975):91–96.
    Snyder, Opiate receptors.
64. Quoted in Macht, History of opium, p. 477.

CHAPTER 2

1. S. Rodbard, The heart as hostile witness, *Perspectives in Biology and Medicine* 18 (1975):375–78.
2. E. Clarke and C. D. O'Malley, *The human brain and spinal cord* (Berkeley: University of California Press, 1968), p. 25.
3. W. H. S. Jones, *Hippocrates,* vol. 2 (London: Heinemann, 1923). Quotation on p. 179.
4. E. S. Valenstein, History of brain stimulation: Investigations into the physiology of motivation, in *Brain stimulation and motivation,* ed. E. S. Valenstein (Glenview, Ill.: Scott, Foresman, 1973), p. 1.
5. G. Eckstein, *The body has a head* (New York: Harper & Row, 1969), p. 406.
6. C. Blakemore, *Mechanics of the mind* (Cambridge: Cambridge University Press, 1977), p. 6.
7. E. G. Boring, *The history of experimental psychology* (New York: Appleton Century Crofts, 1929), p. 57.
8. C. Sagan, *Broca's brain* (New York: Ballantine, 1980), p. 7.
9. F. Schiller, *Paul Broca: Founder of French anthropology, explorer of the brain* (Berkeley: University of California Press, 1979), p. 166.
10. P. Broca, Perte de la parole. Ramollissement chronique et destruction partielle du lobe antérieur gauche du cerveau, *Bulletin de la Société d'Anthropologie* 2 (1861):235–37.
11. P. Broca, Sur le siège de la faculté du langage articulé, *Bulletin de la Société d'Anthropologie* 6 (1865):337–93.
12. Sagan, *Broca's brain,* pp. 3–14.
    F. Schiller, personal communication, 20 December 1985.
13. J. L. Signoret et al. Rediscovery of Leborgne's brain: Anatomical description with CT-scan, *Brain and Language* 22 (1984):303–19.
14. P. D. MacLean, The triune brain, emotion, and scientific bias, in *The Neurosciences. Second study program,* ed. F. O. Schmitt (New York: Rockefeller University Press, 1970), pp. 336–49.

————, *The triune concept of the brain and behaviour* (Toronto: University of Toronto Press, 1973).

————, On the evolution of three mentalities, *Man-Environment Systems* 5 (1975):213–24. Reprinted in vol. 2 of *New dimensions in psychiatry: A world view,* ed. S. Arieti and G. Chrzanowski (New York: Wiley, 1977), pp. 305–82.

————, A mind of three minds: Educating the triune brain. *Seventy-seventh Yearbook of the National Society for the Study of Education* (Chicago: University of Chicago Press, 1978), pp. 308–42.

————, Evolutionary psychiatry and the triune brain, *Psychological Medicine* 15 (1985):219–21.

15. L. Weiskrantz, *Blindsight: A case study and implications* (Oxford: Clarendon Press, 1986).

16. H. J. Jerison, *Evolution of the brain and intelligence* (New York: Academic Press, 1973).

17. D. A. McCormick and R. F. Thompson, Cerebellum: Essential involvement in the classically conditioned eyelid response, *Science* 223 (1984):296–99.

18. P. D. MacLean, An evolutionary approach to brain research on prosematic (nonverbal) behavior, in *Reproductive behavior and evolution,* ed. J. R. Rosenblatt and B. Komisarus (New York: Plenum, 1977), pp. 137–64. Quotation on pp. 157–58.

19. MacLean, *Triune concept.*

20. H. Selye, *The stress of life,* rev. ed. (New York: McGraw Hill, 1976).

21. T. H. Bullock, *Introduction to nervous systems* (San Francisco: Freeman, 1977), p. 491.

22. C. J. Herrick, The functions of the olfactory parts of the cerebral cortex, *Proceedings of the National Academy of Sciences, USA* 19 (1933):7–14. Quotation on p. 8.

23. T. J. Teyler, *A primer of psychobiology: Brain and behavior* (San Francisco: Freeman, 1975).

24. R. M. Restak, The mind: Mirror of the brain, *Newsday,* 8 July 1986, section 3, 9.

CHAPTER 3

1. O. Loewi, *From the workshop of discoveries* (Lawrence, Kans.: University of Kansas Press, 1953).

It is interesting to note that brain chemistry is not the only area of science that can mark its beginning from a famous bed. The birthday of experimental psychology is often celebrated on October 22, 1850, to commemorate the morning that Gustav Fechner came to the inspired notion of the psychophysical law, while lying in bed.

2. S. J. Watson and H. Akil, Immunocytochemistry: Techniques, trials,

and tribulations, *Neuroscience Commentaries* 1 (1981):10–15. Quotation on p. 10.

3. B. Falck et al., Fluorescence of catechal amines and related compounds condensed with formaldehyde, *Journal of histochemistry and cytochemistry* 10 (1962):348.

4. C. F. Levinthal, *Introduction to physiological psychology,* 2d ed. (Englewood Cliffs, N.J.: Prentice-Hall, 1983).

5. J. H. Quastel and D. M. J. Quastel, *The chemistry of brain metabolism in health and disease* (Springfield, Ill.: C. C. Thomas, 1961).

6. R. F. Thompson, *The brain: An introduction to neuroscience* (San Francisco: Freeman, 1985).

7. G. Lynch, Some difficulties associated with the use of lesion techniques in the study of memory, in *Neural mechanisms of learning and memory,* ed. M. R. Rosenzweig and E. L. Bennett (Cambridge, Mass.: MIT Press, 1976), pp. 544–46.

8. F. A. Geldard, *The human senses,* 2d ed. (New York: Wiley, 1972).

9. Levinthal, *Introduction.*

10. Thompson, *The brain.*

11. E. S. Valenstein, *Brain control: A critical examination of brain stimulation and psychosurgery* (New York: Wiley, 1973).

12. S. H. Snyder, *Madness and the brain* (New York: McGraw-Hill, 1974).

13. C. Kornetsky, *Pharmacology: Drugs affecting behavior* (New York: Wiley, 1976), p. 82.

14. R. C. Duvoisin, *Parkinson's disease: A guide for patient and family,* 2d ed. (New York: Raven Press, 1984).

15. Duvoisin, *Parkinson's.*

16. O. Hornykiewicz, Die topische lokalisation und vehalten von Noradrenalin und Dopamin (3-hydroxytyramin) in der Substantia Nigra des Normalin und Parkinsonkranken, *Wiener Klinische Wochenschrift* 75 (1963):309–12.

17. ———, The mechanisms of action of L-dopamine in Parkinson's disease, *Life Sciences* 15 (1974):1249–59.

18. Famous lady's indomitable fight, *Life,* 22 June 1959, 101–9.
    M. Bourke-White, *Portrait of myself* (New York: Simon & Schuster, 1963).

19. Duvoisin, *Parkinson's.*

20. Levinthal, *Introduction.*
    S. H. Snyder, *The biological aspects of mental disorder* (New York: Oxford University Press, 1981).

21. Levinthal, *Introduction.*

22. R. R. Bootzin and J. R. Acocella, *Abnormal Psychology,* 4th ed. (New York: Random House, 1984), p. 215.

23. Ibid.

24. Kornetsky, *Pharmacology,* p. 103.
25. Kornetsky, *Pharmacology.*
26. Levinthal, *Introduction.*
27. J. W. Maas, Biogenic amines of depression, *Archives of general psychiatry* 32 (1975):1357–61.
28. M. Stanley, J. Virgilio, and S. Gershon, Tritiated imipramine binding sites are decreased in the frontal cortex of suicides, *Science* 216 (1982):1337–39.
29. J. Greenberg, Suicide linked to brain chemical deficit, *Science News* 121 (1982):355.
30. D. J. Greenblatt and R. I. Shader, Pharmacotherapy of anxiety with benzodiazepines and beta-adrenergic blockers, in *Psychopharmacology: A generation of progress,* ed. M. A. Lipton, A. DiMascio, and K. F. Williams (New York: Raven Press, 1978), pp. 1381–90.
31. H. Möhler and T. Okada, Benzodiazepine receptor: Demonstration in the central nervous system, *Science* 198 (1977):849–51.

    R. F. Squires and C. Braestrup, Benzodiazepine receptors in rat brain, *Nature* 266 (1977):732–34.
32. A. Guidotti et al., Isolation, characterization and purification to homogeneity of a rat brain protein (GABA-modulin), *Proceedings of the National Academy of Sciences, USA* 79 (1982):6084–88.

    J. F. Tallman and D. W. Gallagher, The GABA-ergic system: A locus of benzodiazepine action, *Annual Review of Neuroscience* 8 (1985):21–44.
33. P. Taulbee, Solving the mystery of anxiety, *Science News* 124 (1983):44–45. Quotation on p. 44.
34. W. Herbert, Schizophrenia: From adolescent insanity to dopamine disease, *Science News* 121 (1982):173–75. Quotation on p. 175.
35. Herbert, Schizophrenia, p. 175.
36. E. Edelson, The neuropeptide explosion, *Mosaic* 12 (May–June 1981):15–18. Quotation on p. 15.

CHAPTER 4

1. N. Wade, *The Nobel duel* (Garden City, N.Y.: Doubleday, 1981), p. ix.
2. H. F. Judson, *The eighth day of creation: Makers of the revolution in biology* (New York: Simon & Schuster, 1979), p. 182.
3. J. D. Watson, *The double helix: A personal account of the discovery of the structure of DNA* (New York: Atheneum, 1968), p. 7.
4. Judson, *Eighth day,* pp. 24–25.
5. Ibid., p. 194.
6. P. Gwynne, review of *The Nobel Duel,* New York *Times Book Review,* 20 December 1981, pp. 8, 21.
7. Wade, *Duel,* p. 283.

8. A. Goldstein, L. Aronow, and S. M. Kalman, *Principles of drug action: The basis of pharmacology* (New York: Harper & Row, 1968), p. 133.

9. A. Goldstein, L. I. Lowney, and B. K. Pal, Stereospecific and nonspecific interactions of the morphine congener levorphanol in subcellular fractions of mouse brain, *Proceedings of the National Academy of Sciences, USA* 68 (1971):1742–47.

10. A. H. Beckett and A. F. Casy, Synthetic analgesics: Stereochemical considerations, *Journal of Pharmacy and Pharmacology* 6 (1954):986–1001.

11. D. Grady, Candace Pert: Addicted to research, *Discover* (December 1981), 54–60. Quotation on p. 54.

12. Grady, Pert, p. 60.

13. C. Pert, taped interview by author, Cincinnati, 9 November 1980.

14. Ibid.

15. S. H. Snyder, taped interview by author, New York, 5 November 1984.

16. Cuatrecasas is presently senior vice-president for research and development at Glaxo, Inc., Research Triangle Park, North Carolina.

17. Snyder, interview, 1984.

18. Pert, interview, 1980.

19. Snyder, interview, 1984.

20. C. Pert, Type 1 and type 2 opiate receptor distribution in brain—What does it tell us? in *Neurosecretion and brain peptides,* ed. J. B. Martin, S. Reichlin, and K. L. Bick (New York: Raven Press, 1981), pp. 117–31.

21. C. Pert, transcript of *The Keys of Paradise,* "Nova" series, WGBH Educational Foundation, Boston, 1979.

22. L. Thomas, *The youngest science: Notes of a medicine-watcher* (New York, Viking, 1983), pp. 146–47.

23. E. J. Simon and D. Von Praag, Studies on the intracellular distribution and tissue binding of dihydromorphine-7, 8-³H in the rat, *Proceedings of the Society for Experimental Biology and Medicine* 122 (1966):6–11.

24. E. J. Simon, taped interview by author, New York, 19 May 1981.

25. C. B. Pert and S. H. Snyder, Opiate receptor: Demonstration in nervous tissue, *Science* 179 (1973):1011–14.
   E. J. Simon, J. M. Hiller, and I. Edelman, Stereospecific binding of the potent narcotic analgesic [³H]-etorphine to rat brain homogenate, *Proceedings of the National Academy of Sciences, USA* 70 (1973):1974–79.
   L. Terenius, Characteristics of the "receptor" for narcotic analgesics in synaptic plasma membrane fraction from rat brain, *Acta Pharmacologica et Toxicologica* 32 (1973):377–84.

26. L. Terenius, personal communication, 16 September 1985.

27. Ibid.

28. S. H. Snyder, Opiate receptors and internal opiates, *Scientific American* 236 (3) (1977):44–56.

29. G. Epps, The relentless quest of Candace Pert, *LI Magazine, Newsday,* 6 January 1980, 42.

CHAPTER 5

1. J. C. Liebeskind, taped interview by author, New York, 1 May 1985.
2. D. V. Reynolds, Surgery in the rat during electrical analgesia induced by focal brain stimulation, *Science* 164 (1969): 444–45.
3. J. Olds and P. M. Milner, Positive reinforcement produced by electrical stimulation of septal area and other regions of rat brain, *Journal of Comparative and Physiological Psychology* 47 (1954):419–27.
4. J. Olds, Self-stimulation of the brain, *Science* 127 (1958):315–24.
5. J. Olds, Pleasure centers in the brain, *Scientific American* 193 (4) (1956):105–16.
6. J. Olds, The central nervous system and the reinforcement of behavior, *American Psychologist* 24 (1969):114–32.
   ———, Commentary, in *Brain stimulation and motivation,* ed. E. S. Valenstein (Glenview, Ill.: Scott, Foresman, 1973), pp. 81–99.
7. D. J. Mayer, taped interview by author, New York, 1 May 1985.
8. D. J. Mayer et al., Analgesia from electrical stimulation in the brain stem of the rat, *Science* 174 (1971):1351–54. Quotation on p. 1352.
9. Mayer, interview, 1985.
10. Liebeskind, interview, 1985.
11. J. M. Liebman, D. J. Mayer, and J. C. Liebeskind, Mesencephalic central gray lesions and fear-motivated behavior in rats, *Brain Research* 23 (1970):353–70.
12. H. Akil, D. J. Mayer, and J. C. Liebeskind, Comparaison chez le rat entre l'analgesie induite par stimulation de la substance grise peri-aqueducale et l'analgesie morphinique, *Comptes Rendus de la Société de Biologie* (1972):3603–5.
13. H. Akil, transcript of *The Keys of Paradise,* "Nova" series, WGBH Educational Foundation, Boston, 1979.
14. Akil et al., Comparaison.
15. H. Akil, taped interview by author, New York, 1 May 1985.
16. H. W. Kosterlitz, The best laid schemes o' mice an' men gang aft a-gley, *Annual Review of Pharmacology and Toxicology* 19 (1979):1–12. (Title originates from a poem of Robert Burns, roughly translated as "The best-laid plans of mice and men often go awry.")
    A. T. McKnight, H. W. Kosterlitz: A thumbnail sketch, in *Opioids: Past, Present and Future,* ed. J. Hughes et al. (London: Taylor & Francis, 1984), pp. x–xii.
17. Kosterlitz, Best laid schemes.
18. E. A. Gyang, H. W. Kosterlitz, and G. M. Lees, The inhibition of autonomic neuro-effector transmission by morphine-like drugs and its use as a screening test for narcotic analgesic drugs, *Naunyn-*

Schmiedeberg's Archiv für experimentelle Pathologie und Pharmaka-logie 248 (1964):231–46.

19. G. M. Lees, Introduction, in *Opioids,* pp. 1–8.

20. J. Hughes, Reflections on opioid peptides, in *Opioids,* pp. 9–19.

21. G. Henderson, J. Hughes, and H. W. Kosterlitz, A new example of a morphine-sensitive neuroeffector junction: Adrenergic transmission in the mouse vas deferens, *British Journal of Pharmacology* 46 (1972):764–66.

22. H. F. Judson, *Search for solutions* (New York: Holt, Rinehart & Winston, 1980), p. 99.
    N. Wade, *The Nobel duel* (Garden City, N.Y.: Doubleday, 1981), p. III.

23. Hughes, Reflections, p. II.

24. Ibid.

25. Akil, interview, 1985.

26. C. Pert, taped interview by author, Cincinnati, 9 November 1980.

27. J. Hughes, Search for the endogenous ligand for the opiate receptor, in *Opiate receptor mechanisms (NRP Workshop Session, May 1974): Neurosciences Research Program Bulletin. vol. 13,* ed. S. H. Snyder and S. Matthysse (Cambridge, Mass.: MIT Press, 1977), pp. 55–58.

28. L. Terenius, Narcotic receptors in guinea pig ileum and rat brain, in *Opiate receptor mechanisms,* pp. 39–42.
    L. Terenius and A. Wahlström, Inhibitor(s) of narcotic receptor binding in brain abstracts and cerebrospinal fluid, *Acta Pharmacologica et Toxicologica* 35 (Supplement 1) (1974):55 (abstract).

29. Akil, interview, 1985.

30. B. Villet, Opiates of the mind, *Atlantic Monthly,* June 1978, 82–89. Quotation on p. 86.

31. Akil, interview, 1985.

32. J. Hughes, Isolation of an endogenous compound from the brain with pharmacological properties similar to morphine, *Brain Research* 88 (1975):295–308.

33. L. Terenius and A. Wahlström, Morphine-like ligand for opiate receptors in human CSF, *Life Sciences* 16 (1975):1759–64.
    G. W. Pasternak, R. Goodman, and S. H. Snyder, An endogenous morphine-like factor in mammalian brain, *Life Sciences* 16 (1975):1765–69.

34. J. Hughes et al., Identification of two related pentapeptides from the brain with potent opiate agonist activity, *Nature* 258 (1975):577–79.

35. C. H. Li, Lipotropin: A new active peptide from pituitary glands, *Nature* 201 (1964):924.

36. C. H. Li, J. S. Dixon, and D. Chung, The structure of bovine corticotropin, *Journal of the American Chemical Society* 80 (1958):2587.
    C. H. Li, The chemistry of human pituitary growth hormone, in *Growth*

hormone, ed. A. Pecile and E. E. Muller (Amsterdam: Excerpta Medica Foundation, 1968), pp. 3–28.

37. C. Kahn, The man who discovered the happiness hormone, *Family Health,* December 1978, 48–51.

38. Villet, Opiates of the mind.

39. Kahn, Happiness hormone, p. 48.

40. Ibid.

41. Kosterlitz, Best laid schemes.

42. Villet, Opiates of the mind, p. 86.

43. Hughes et al., Pentapeptides.

44. E. J. Simon, History, in *Endorphins: Chemistry, physiology, pharmacology and clinical relevance,* ed. J. B. Malick and R. M. S. Bell (New York: Mercel Dekker, 1982), pp. 1–8.

45. M. W. Adler, Minireview: Opioid peptides, *Life Sciences* 26 (1980):497–510.

A. Goldstein, personal communication, 1986.

46. D. G. Smyth, transcript of *The Keys to Paradise,* "Nova" series, WGBH Educational Foundation, Boston, 1979.

47. Ibid.

48. A. F. Bradbury et al., C-Fragment of lipotropin has high affinity for brain opiate receptors, *Nature* 260 (1976):793–95.

49. C. H. Li and D. Chung, Isolation and structure of an untriakontapeptide with opiate activity from camel pituitary glands, *Proceedings of the National Academy of Sciences, USA* 73 (1976):1145–48.

50. B. M. Cox, A. Goldstein, and C. H. Li, Opioid activity of a peptide beta-lipotropin (61–91) derived from beta-lipotropin, *Proceedings of the National Academy of Sciences, USA* 73 (1976):1821–23.

H. Teschemacher et al., A peptide-like substance from pituitary that acts like morphine: 1. Isolation, *Life Sciences* 16 (1975):1771–75.

51. B. M. Cox et al., A peptide-like substance from pituitary that acts like morphine: 2. Purification and properties, *Life Sciences* 16 (1975):1777–82.

52. A. Goldstein et al., Dynorphin-(1–13), an extraordinarily potent opioid peptide, *Proceedings of the National Academy of Sciences, USA* 76 (1979):6666–70.

53. N. Ling, R. Burgus, and R. Guillemin, Isolation, primary structure and synthesis of alpha-endorphin and gamma-endorphin, two peptides of hypothalamic-hypophysial origin with morphinomimetic activities, *Proceedings of the National Academy of Sciences, USA* 73 (1976):3942–46.

54. A. Goldstein et al., Porcine pituitary dynorphin: Complete amino acid sequence of the biologically active heptadecapeptide, *Proceedings of the National Academy of Sciences, USA* 78 (1981):7219–23.

55. E. Weber, C. J. Evans, and J. D. Barchas, Predominance of the ami-noterminal heptapeptide fragment of dynorphin in rat brain, *Nature* 199 (1982):77–79.

56. H. Akil et al., Endogenous opioids: Biology and function, *Annual Review of Neuroscience* 7 (1984):223–55.

57. W. R. Martin et al., The effects of morphine and nalorphine-like drugs in non-dependent and morphine dependent chronic spinal dog, *Journal of Pharmacology and Experimental Therapeutics* 197 (1976):517–32.

58. J. A. H. Lord et al., Endogenous opioid peptides: Multiple agonists and receptors, *Nature* 267 (1977):495.

59. Akil et al., Endogenous opioids.

60. G. W. Pasternak, S. R. Childers, and S. H. Snyder, Naloxazone, a long-acting opiate antagonist: Effect on analgesia in intact animals and on opiate receptor binding *in vitro, Journal of Pharmacology and Experimental Therapeutics,* 214 (1980):455–462.

61. R. E. Mains, B. A. Eipper, and N. Ling, Common precursor to corticotropins and endorphins, *Proceedings of the National Academy of Sciences, USA* 74 (1977):3014–18.

62. R. Guillemin et al., Beta-endorphin and adrenocorticotropin are secreted concomitantly by the pituitary gland, *Science* 197 (1977):1367–69.

63. J. M. Hiller, J. Pearson, and E. J. Simon, Distribution of stereospecific binding of the potent narcotic analgesic etorphine in the human brain: Predominance in the limbic system, *Research Communications in Chemical Pathology and Pharmacology* 6 (1973):1052–61.

    C. Pert, D. Aposhian, and S. H. Snyder, Phylogenetic distribution of opiate receptor binding, *Brain Research* 75 (1974):356–61.

64. G. B. Stephano, R. M. Kream, and R. S. Zukin, Demonstration of stereospecific opiate binding in the nervous tissue of the marine mollusc *Mytilus edulis, Brain Research* 181 (1980):440–45.

65. J. L. Marx, Lasker award stirs controversy, *Science* 203 (1979):341.

66. G. Epps, The relentless quest of Candace Pert, *LI Magazine, Newsday,* 6 January 1980.

67. J. Arehart-Treichel, Winning and losing: The medical awards game, *Science News* 115 (1979):120, 126.

68. Epps, Relentless quest.

69. Ibid., pp. 39–40.

70. Arehart-Treichel, Winning and losing, p. 120.

71. W. Pollin, Letter to the editor, *Science News* 115 (1979):179.

72. T. H. Maren, Letter to the editor, *Science* 203 (1979):834.

73. R. Kanigel, *Apprentice to genius: The making of a scientific dynasty* (New York: Macmillan, 1986).

74. Akil et al., Endogenous opioids.

CHAPTER 6

1. R. Melzack, *The puzzle of pain* (New York: Basic Books, 1974), p. 15.

2. D. T. Courtwright, *Dark paradise: Opiate addiction in America before 1940* (Cambridge, Mass.: Harvard University Press, 1982).

3. G. Marks and W. K. Beatty, *The medical garden illustrated* (New York: Scribners, 1971).

   In 1918 the Sterling Products Incorporated (now Sterling Drug, Inc.) bought the trademark rights to the name aspirin, from confiscated property belonging to the Bayer Company of New York. Later, a federal judge ruled that the name was common enough to be treated generically, a practice that continues today. Nevertheless, Sterling still markets its aspirin product as "Bayer aspirin."

4. M. S. Fanselow, Conditioned fear-induced opiate analgesia: A competing motivational state theory of stress analgesia, in *Stress-induced analgesia,* ed. D. Kelly (New York: New York Academy of Sciences, 1985), pp. 40–54.

   American Psychological Association, Distinguished scientific awards for an early career contribution to psychology, 1985, Michael S. Fanselow, *American Psychologist* 41 (1986):363–73.

5. M. S. Fanselow, Naloxone attenuates rats' preference for signaled shock, *Physiological Psychology* 7 (1979):70–74.

6. M. S. Fanselow and R. C. Bolles, Triggering of the endorphin analgesic reaction by a cue previously associated with shock: Reversal by naloxone, *Bulletin of the Psychonomic Society* 14 (1979):88–90.

   A. J. MacLennan, R. L. Jackson, and S. F. Maier, Conditioned analgesia in the rat, *Bulletin of the Psychonomic Society* 15 (1980):387–90.

7. M. S. Fanselow, Odors released by stressed rats produce opioid analgesia in unstressed rats, *Behavioral Neuroscience* 99 (1985):589–92.

8. L. S. Lester and M. S. Fanselow, Exposure to a cat produces opioid analgesia in rats, *Behavioral Neuroscience* 99 (1985):756–59.

9. Fanselow, Conditioned fear-induced opiate analgesia.

   There is also increasing evidence for a link between endorphin functioning and the immune system.

   N. P. Plotnikoff et al., eds., *Enkephalins and endorphins: Stress and the immune system* (New York: Plenum, 1986).

   R. J. Weber and C. B. Pert, Opiatergic modulation of the immune system, in *Central and peripheral endorphins: Basic and clinical aspects,* ed. E. E. Muller and A. R. Genazzani (New York: Raven Press, 1984), pp. 35–42.

10. R. E. Mains, B. A. Eipper, and N. Ling, Common precursor to corticotropins and endorphins, *Proceedings of the National Academy of Sciences, USA* 74 (1977):3014–18.

11. S. Nakanishi et al., Nucleotide sequence of cloned cDNA for bovine corticotropin-beta-lipotropin precursor, *Nature* 278 (1979):423–27.

   J. L. Roberts et al., Corticotropin and beta-endorphin: Construction and analysis of recombinant DNA complementary to mRNA, *Proceedings of the National Academy of Sciences, USA* 76 (1979):2153–57.

12. R. Guillemin et al., Beta-endorphin and adrenocorticotropin are secreted concomitantly by the pituitary gland, *Science* 197 (1977):1367–69.

13. P. D. MacLean, *The triune concept of the brain and behaviour* (Toronto: University of Toronto Press, 1973).

14. R. Broom, *The mammal-like reptiles of South Africa and the origin of mammals* (London: Witherby, 1932).

15. P. D. MacLean, A triangular brief on the evolution of brain and law, *Journal of Social and Biological Structures* 5 (1982):369–79.

16. MacLean, *Triune concept.*

17. MacLean, A triangular brief, p. 375.

18. Ibid., p. 376.

19. MacLean, *Triune concept,* p. 7.

20. H. Selye, *The stress of life,* rev. ed. (New York: McGraw-Hill, 1976).

21. Ibid., p. 64.

22. C. F. Levinthal, *Introduction to physiological psychology,* 2d ed. (Englewood Cliffs, N.J.: Prentice-Hall, 1983).
   Selye, *Stress of Life.*

23. Quoted in A. Yuwiler, Stress, in *Handbook of Neurochemistry,* Vol. 6, ed. A. Lajtha (New York: Plenum, 1971), pp. 103–71. Quotation on p. 143.

24. W. B. Cannon, "Voodoo" death, *Psychosomatic Medicine* 19 (1957):182–90.

   S. Wolf, The end of the rope: The role of the brain in cardiac death, *Journal of the Canadian Medical Association* 97 (1967):1022–25.

25. N. E. Gross, *Living with stress* (New York: McGraw-Hill, 1958).

26. J. M. Weiss, Effects of coping behavior with and without a feedback signal on stress pathology in rats, *Journal of Comparative and Physiological Psychology* 77 (1971):22–30.

27. J. B. Overmier and M. E. P. Seligman, Effects of inescapable shock upon subsequent escape and avoidance learning, *Journal of Comparative and Physiological Psychology* 63 (1967):28–33.

   S. F. Maier and M. E. P. Seligman, Learned helplessness: Theory and evidence, *Journal of Experimental Psychology: General* 105 (1976):3–46.

28. S. B. Klein, *Motivation: Biosocial approaches* (New York: McGraw-Hill, 1982).

29. S. F. Maier, Stress controllability and stress-induced analgesia, in *Stress-induced analgesia,* ed. D. Kelly (New York: New York Academy of Sciences, 1985), pp. 55–72.

30. J. M. Ivancevich, M. T. Matteson, and C. Preston, Occupational stress, Type A behavior, and physical well-being, *Academy of Management* 25 (1982):373–91.

31. D. Naber et al., Episodic secretion of opioid activity in human plasma and monkey CSF: Evidence for a diurnal rhythm, *Life Sciences* 28 (1981):931–35.

32. J. W. Lewis, J. T. Cannon, and J. C. Liebeskind, Opioid and nonopioid mechanisms of stress analgesia, *Science* 208 (1980):623–25.

33. H. Akil et al., Endogenous opioids: Biology and function, *Annual Review of Neuroscience* 7 (1984):223–55.

S. F. Maier, R. C. Drugan, and J. W. Grau, Controllability, coping behavior, and stress-induced analgesia in the rat, *Pain* 12 (1976):47–56.

34. L. R. Watkins and D. J. Mayer, Organization of endogenous opiate and nonopiate pain control systems, *Science* 216 (1982):1185–92.

35. Ibid.

36. Ibid.

37. Ibid.

38. G. W. Terman et al., Intrinsic mechanisms of pain inhibition: Activation by stress, *Science* 226 (1984):1270–77.

39. Levinthal, *Introduction.*

40. A. I. Basbaum and A. L. Fields, Endogenous pain control systems: Brainstem spinal pathways and endorphin circuitry, *Annual Review of Neuroscience* 7 (1984):309–38.

41. H. Akil, D. J. Mayer, and J. C. Liebeskind, Antagonism of a stimulation-produced analgesia by naloxone, a narcotic antagonist, *Science* 191 (1976):961–62.

42. D. J. Mayer and R. L. Hayes, Stimulation produced analgesia: Development of tolerance and cross-tolerance to morphine, *Science* 188 (1975):941–43.

43. Y. Hosobuchi, J. E. Adams, and R. Linchitz, Pain relief by electrical stimulation of the central gray matter in humans and its reversal by naloxone, *Science* 197 (1977):183–86.

44. H. Akil et al., Enkephalin-like material elevated in ventricular cerebrospinal fluid of pain patients after analgetic focal stimulation, *Science* 201 (1978):463–65.

45. Y. Hosobuchi et al., Stimulation of human periaqueductal gray for pain relief increases immunoreactive beta-endorphin in ventricular fluid, *Science* 203 (1979):279–81.

46. Akil et al., Enkephalin-like material.
47. B. Almay et al., Endorphins in chronic pain: Differences in CSF endorphin levels between organic and psychogenic pain syndromes, *Pain* 5 (1978):153–62.
48. J. Kangilaski, Beta-endorphin levels lower in arthritic patients, *Journal of the American Medical Association* 246 (1981):203.
49. D. J. Mayer, Pain inhibition by electrical brain stimulation: Comparison to morphine, *Neurosciences Research Program Bulletin* 13 (1975):94–100.
50. B. H. Pomeranz and D. Chiu, Naloxone blockade of acupuncture analgesia: Endorphins implicated, *Life Sciences* 19 (1976):1757–62.
51. R. S. S. Cheng and B. H. Pomeranz, Electroacupuncture analgesia could be mediated by at least two pain-relieving mechanisms: Endorphin and non-endorphin systems, *Life Sciences* 25 (1979):1957–62.
52. M. Fitzgerald, Monoamines and descending control of nociception, *Trends in Neurosciences* 9 (1986):51–52.
53. A. R. Gintzler, Endorphin-mediated increases in pain during pregnancy, *Science* 210 (1980):193–95.
54. B. V. R. Sastry et al., Occurrence of methionine enkephalin in human placental villus, *Biochemical Pharmacology* 29 (1980):475–78.
55. H. Akil, Transcript of *The Keys of Paradise,* "Nova" series, WGBH Educational Foundation, Boston, 1979.
56. C. A. Cahill and H. Akil, Plasma beta-endorphin-like immunoreactivity, self reported pain perception and anxiety levels in women during pregnancy and labor, *Life Sciences* 31 (1982):1871–73.
57. P. D. MacLean, Brain evolution relating to family, play, and the separation call, *Archives of General Psychiatry* 42 (1985):405–17. Quotation on p. 407.

CHAPTER 7

1. C. Pert, Transcript of *The Keys of Paradise,* "Nova" series, WGBH Educational Foundation, Boston, 1979.
2. P. D. MacLean, Brain evolution relating to family, play, and the separation call, *Archives of General Psychiatry* 42 (1985):405–17. Quotation on p. 411.
3. Ibid.
4. Ibid.
5. P. Broca, Anatomie comparée des circonvolutions cérébrales: Le grande lobe limbique et la scissure limbique dans la série des mammifères, *Revue d'Anthropologie* 1 (1878):385–498.
6. MacLean, Brain evolution.
7. R. L. Isaacson, *The limbic system* (New York: Plenum, 1974).
8. MacLean, Brain evolution, p. 415.

9. J. Panksepp et al., Endogenous opioids and social behavior, *Neuroscience and Biobehavioral Reviews* 4 (1980):473–87.

10. Ibid.

11. J. Panksepp et al., Opioid blockade and social comfort in chicks, *Pharmacology, Biochemistry and Behavior* 13 (1980):673–83.

12. J. Panksepp et al., Reduction of distress vocalization in chicks by opiate-like peptide, *Brain Research Bulletin* 3 (1978):663–67.

13. M. Gold et al., Increase in serum prolactin by exogenous and endogenous opiate: Evidence for antidopamine and anti-psychotic effects, *American Journal of Psychiatry* 135 (1978):1415–16.

    L. Grandison and A. Guidotti, Regulation of prolactin release by endogenous opiates, *Nature* 270 (1977):357–59.

14. V. Brantl and H. Teschemacher, A material with opioid activity in bovine milk and milk products, *Life Sciences* 28 (1981):1903–9.

    P. Kehoe and E. M. Blass, Behaviorally functional opioid in infant rats: I. Evidence for olfactory and gustatory classical conditioning, *Behavioral Neuroscience* 100 (1986):359–67.

    J. Panksepp et al., Casomorphins reduce separation distress in chicks, *Peptides* 5 (1984):829–31.

15. J. Panksepp et al., Opiates and play dominance in juvenile rats, *Behavioral Neuroscience* 99 (1985):441–53.

    J. Panksepp S. Siviy, and L. Normansell, The psychobiology of play: Theoretical and methodological perspectives, *Neuroscience and Biobehavioral Reviews* 8 (1984):465–92.

16. J. Panksepp, Brain opioids—a neurochemical substrate for narcotic and social dependence, in *Theory in psychopharmacology,* Vol. 1, ed. S. J. Cooper (London: Academic Press, 1981).

17. Panksepp, Brain opioids, p. 171.

18. J. W. Kalat, Letter to the editor: Speculations on similarities between autism and opiate addiction, *Journal of Autism and Childhood Schizophrenia* 8 (1978):477–79.

    J. Panksepp, Point of view: A neurochemical theory of autism. *Trends in Neurosciences* 2 (1979):174–77.

19. Panksepp, Point of view, p. 176.

20. L. Kanner, Follow-up study of eleven autistic children originally reported in 1943, *Journal of Autism and Childhood Schizophrenia* 1 (1971):119–45. Quotation on p. 145.

21. B. H. Herman et al., Role of opioid peptides in autism: Effects of acute administration of naltrexone (Paper presented at the meeting of the Society for Neuroscience, Washington, November 1986).

22. N. Kline, Introductory remarks, in *Opioids in mental illness,* ed. K. Verebey (New York: New York Academy of Sciences, 1982), p. 433.

23. E. Kraepelin, *Einführung in die psychiatrische Klinik* (Leipzig: Joh. Ambrosius Barth-Verlag, 1901).

———, *Psychiatrie I* (Leipzig: Joh. Ambrosius Barth-Verlag, 1927).

24. M. S. Gold et al., Rapid opiate detoxification: Clinical evidence of antidepressant and antipanic effects of opiates, *American Journal of Psychiatry* 136 (1979):982-83.

25. K. A. Miczek, M. L. Thompson, and L. Shuster, Opioid-like analgesia in defeated mice, *Science* 215 (1981):1520-22.

26. H. M. Einrich, P. Vogt, and A. Herz, Possible antidepressive effects of opioids: Action of buprenorphine, in *Opioids in mental illness*, pp. 108-12.

27. R. H. Gerner et al., Beta-endorphin: Intravenous infusion causes behavioral change in psychiatric patients, *Archives of General Psychiatry* 37 (1980):642-47.

D. Pickar et al., Behavioral and biological effects of acute beta-endorphin injection in schizophrenic and depressed patients, *American Journal of Psychiatry* 138 (1981):160-66.

28. D. B. Carr et al., Physical conditioning facilitates the exercise-induced secretion of beta-endorphin and beta-lipotropin in women, *New England Journal of Medicine* 305 (1981):560-63.

29. E. W. D. Colt, S. L. Wardlaw, and A. G. Frantz, The effect of running on plasma beta-endorphin, *Life Sciences* 28 (1981):1632-40.

30. B. Hathaway, Running to run, *Psychology Today*, July 1984, 14-15. Quotation on p. 14.

31. A. Yates, K. Leehey, and C. M. Shisslak, Running: An analogue of anorexia, *New England Journal of Medicine* 308 (1983):251-55.

32. A psychiatrist's theory of exercise phases: From casual fun to obsession, *Newsday*, 27 October 1980, 8-9.

33. Hathaway, Running.

34. Yates, Leehey, and Shisslak, Running: An analogue.

35. Ibid., p. 254.

36. W. H. Kaye et al., Cerebrospinal fluid opioid activity in anorexia nervosa, *American Journal of Psychiatry* 139 (1982):643-45.

37. D. Pickar et al., Clinical studies of the endogenous opioid system, *Biological Psychiatry* 17 (1982):1243-76.

38. Yates, Leehey, and Shisslak, Running: An analogue, p. 255.

39. E. M. Brecher, *Licit and illicit drugs* (Boston: Little, Brown, 1972).

40. J. Fincher, Natural opiates in the brain, *Human Behavior* 2 (1979):28-32. Quotation on p. 30.

41. Ibid.

42. B. Nelson, The addictive personality: Common traits are found, New York *Times*, 18 January 1983, C1, C8.

43. D. F. Duncan, Life stress as a precursor to adolescent drug dependence, *International Journal of the Addictions* 12 (1977):1047-56.

44. Nelson, Addictive personality, p. C8.

45. S. Peele, *The meaning of addiction: Compulsive experience and its interpretation* (Lexington, Mass.: Lexington Books, 1984), p. 97.

46. Ibid., p. 157.

47. Panksepp, Point of view.
    Panksepp, Brain opioids.

48. H. W. Kosterlitz and J. Hughes, Some thoughts on the significance of enkephalin, the endogenous ligand, *Life Sciences* 17 (1975):91-96.
    S. H. Snyder, Opiate receptors and internal opiates, *Scientific American* 236 (3) (1977):44-56.

49. A. Goldstein, Naltrexone in the management of heroin addiction: Critique of the rationale, in *Narcotic antagonists: Naltrexone progress report, NIDA research monographs, no. 9,* ed. D. Julius and P. Renault (Washington, D.C.: U.S. Department of Health, Education, and Welfare, 1976).

50. A. I. Faden and J. W. Holaday, Opiate antagonists: A role in the treatment of hypovolemic shock, *Science* 205 (1979):317-18.
    D. B. Jefferys, R. J. Flanagan, and G. N. Volans, Reversal of ethanol-induced coma with naloxone, *Lancet* 14 (1980):308-9.
    R. A. Moore et al., Naloxone: Underdosage after narcotic poisoning, *American Journal of Disabilities in Childhood* 134 (1980):156-57.
    S. C. Sorenson and K. Mattison, Naloxone as an antagonist in severe alcohol intoxication, *Lancet* 12 (1978):688-89.

51. R. B. Resnick et al., Naloxone-precipitated withdrawal: A method for rapid induction onto naltrexone, *Clinical Pharmacology and Therapeutics* 214 (1977):408-13.

52. M. S. Gold et al., Clonidine in acute opiate withdrawal, *New England Journal of Medicine* 302 (1980):1421-22.

53. D. E. Redmond and J. H. Krystal, Multiple mechanisms of withdrawal from opioid drugs, *Annual Review of Neuroscience* 7 (1984):443-78.

54. C. M. Pepper and G. Henderson, Opiates and opioid peptides hyperpolarize locus coeruleus neurons in vitro, *Science* 209 (1980):394-96.

55. C. Llorens et al., Hypersensitivity to noradrenaline in cortex after chronic morphine: Relevance to tolerance and dependence, *Nature* 274 (1978):603-5.

56. D. S. Charney et al., Clonidine and naltrexone: A safe, effective, and rapid treatment of abrupt withdrawal from methadone therapy, *Archives of General Psychiatry* 39 (1982):1327-32.
    C. E. Riordan and H. D. Kleber, Rapid opiate detoxification with clonidine and naloxone, *Lancet* 14 (1980):1079-80.

57. Peele, *Meaning of addiction,* p. 157.

CHAPTER 8

1. W. James, *Principles of Psychology* (New York: Holt, 1890), p. 488.
2. A. N. Meltzoff and M. K. Moore, Imitation of facial and manual gestures by human neonates, *Science* 198 (1977):75–78.
3. W. Kessen, Sucking and looking: Two organized congenital patterns of behavior in the human newborn, in *Early behavior: Comparative and developmental approaches,* ed. H. W. Stevenson, E. H. Hess, and H. L. Rheingold (New York: Wiley, 1967), pp. 149–179.
4. W. James, *Psychology: A briefer course* (New York: Fawcett, 1963), p. 203 (original edition 1892).
5. P. D. MacLean, Ictal symptoms relating to the nature of affects and their cerebral substrate, in *Biological foundations of emotion,* vol. 3 of *Emotions: Theory, research and experience,* ed. R. Plutchik (New York: Academic Press, 1986), pp. 61–90. Quotation on p. 87.
6. V. B. Mountcastle, The view from within: Pathways to the study of perception, *Johns Hopkins Medical Journal* 136 (1975):109–31. Quotation on p. 131.
7. D. H. Hubel and T. N. Wiesel, Receptive fields, binocular interaction and functional architecture in the cat's visual cortex, *Journal of Physiology* 160 (1962):106–54.
———, Receptive fields and functional architecture in two nonstriate visual areas (18 and 19) of the cat, *Journal of Neurophysiology* 28 (1965):229–89.
8. K. H. Pribram and M. Mishkin, Simultaneous and successive visual discrimination by monkeys with inferotemporal lesions, *Journal of Comparative and Physiological Psychology* 48 (1955):198–202.
9. A. S. Gilinsky, *Mind and brain: Principles of neuropsychology* (New York: Praeger, 1984), pp. 151–52.
C. G. Gross, C. E. Rocha-Miranda, and D. B. Bender, Visual properties of neurons in inferotemporal cortex of the macaque, *Journal of Neurophysiology* 35 (1972):96–111.
10. C. Bruce, R. Desimone, and C. G. Gross, Visual properties of neurons in a polysensory area in superior temporal sulcus of the macaque, *Journal of Neurophysiology* 46 (1981):369–84.
11. M. E. Lewis et al., Opiate receptor gradients in monkey cerebral cortex: Correspondence with sensory processing hierarchies, *Science* 211 (1981):1166–69.
12. J. M. Hiller, J. Pearson, and E. J. Simon, Distribution of stereospecific binding of the potent narcotic analgesic etorphine in the human brain: Predominance in the limbic system, *Research Communications in Chemical Pathology and Pharmacology* 6 (1973):1052–61.
M. H. Kuhar, C. B. Pert, and S. H. Snyder, Regional distribution of

opiate receptor binding in monkey and human brain, *Nature* 245 (1973): 447-50.

C. C. LaMotte et al., Opiate receptor binding in rhesus monkey brain: Association in limbic structures, *Brain Research* 155 (1978):374-79.

13. H. Akil et al., Endogenous opioids: Biology and function, *Annual Review of Neuroscience* 7 (1984):223-55.

14. M. Mishkin and J. Aggleton, Multiple functional contributions of the amygdala in the monkey, in *The Amygdaloid Complex,* ed. Y. BenAri (Amsterdam: Elsevier Press, 1981), pp. 409-20.

15. Quoted in G. Eckstein, *The body has a head* (New York: Harper & Row, 1970), p. 569.

16. M. S. Gazzaniga and J. E. LeDoux, *The integrated mind* (New York: Plenum, 1978).

17. R. W. Doty, J. L. Ringo, and J. D. Lewine, Forebrain commissures and visual memory: A new approach (unpublished manuscript).

18. S. P. Springer and G. Deutsch, *Left brain, right brain,* rev. ed. (New York: Freeman, 1985).

19. M. S. Gazzaniga, The split brain in man, *Scientific American* 217(2) (1967):24-29.

20. Springer and Deutsch, *Left brain, right brain.*

21. Ibid.

22. M. S. Gazzaniga and J. Y. Lettvin, 1981 Nobel Prize for physiology or medicine, *Science* 214 (1981):517-20. Quotation on p. 517.

23. Gazzaniga, Split brain. Quotation is on p. 29.

24. M.-M. Mesulam et al., Limbic and sensory connections of the interior parietal lobule (area PG) in the rhesus monkey: A study with a new method for horseradish peroxidase histochemistry, *Brain Research* 136 (1977):393-414.
Mishkin and Aggleton, Multiple functional contributions.
S. P. Wise and M. Herkenham, Opiate receptor distribution in the cerebral cortex of the rhesus monkey, *Science* 218 (1982):387-89.

25. This surgical approach to the treatment of epilepsy is understandably limited to a small population of patients, forty in all, as of 1983. Of these, eleven patients were treated by Bogen and Vogel and twenty-eight by Wilson. In addition, one case has been associated with Dr. Mark Rayport of the Medical College of Ohio. Some of these patients have not been studied in the published literature in this area. For example, in a review by Jay Myers in 1984, only twenty of the twenty-eight Wilson patients have appeared in publication form. Of these, thirteen patients (like P.S.) underwent a severing of the corpus callosum but a sparing of the anterior commissure.
M. S. Gazzaniga, Right hemisphere language following brain bisection: A 20-year perspective, *American Psychologist* 38 (1983):525-37.

J. Levy, Language, cognition, and the right hemisphere: A response to Gazzaniga, *American Psychologist* 38 (1983):538–41.

J. J. Myers, Right hemisphere language: Science or fiction, *American Psychologist* 39 (1984):315–20.

E. Zaidel, A response to Gazzaniga: Language in the right hemisphere, convergent perspectives, *American Psychologist* 38 (1983):512–46.

26. G. L. Risse et al., The anterior commissure in man: Functional variation in a multisensory system, *Neuropsychologia* 16 (1977):23–31.

27. C. Chiarello, Congenital absence of the corpus callosum: Neurobehavioral functioning (Paper presented at the meeting of the American Psychological Association, 1984).

28. J. E. LeDoux, D. H. Wilson, and M. S. Gazzaniga, Beyond commissurotomy: Clues to consciousness, in *Neuropsychology,* Vol. 2 of *Handbook of behavioral neurobiology,* ed. M. S. Gazzaniga (New York: Plenum, 1978), pp. 543–54. Quotation on pp. 544–45.

29. Gazzaniga, Right hemisphere language.

M. S. Gazzaniga, *The social brain: Discovering the networks of the mind* (New York: Basic Books, 1985).

30. LeDoux, Wilson, and Gazzaniga, Beyond commissurotomy, p. 553.

31. J. J. Frost et al., Imaging opiate receptors in the human brain by positron tomography, *Journal of Computer Assisted Tomography* 9 (1985):231–36.

32. E. D. Ross, The aprosodias: Functional-anatomic organization of the affective components of language in the right hemisphere, *Archives of Neurology* 38 (1981):561–69.

———, Right hemisphere's role in language, affective behavior and emotion, *Trends in Neurosciences* 7 (1984):342–46.

E. D. Ross and M.-M. Mesulam, Dominant language functions of the right hemisphere? Prosody and emotional gesturing, *Archives of Neurology* 36 (1979):144–48.

33. Ross and Mesulam, Dominant language functions.

34. E. D. Ross, Modulation of affect and nonverbal communication by the right hemisphere, in *Principles of behavioral neurology,* ed. M.-M. Mesulam (Philadelphia: F. A. Davis Company, 1985), pp. 239–57.

35. S. H. Snyder, *Biological aspects of mental disorder* (New York: Oxford University Press, 1980).

36. D. M. Bear, The temporal lobes: An approach to the study of organic behavioral changes, in *Neuropsychology,* ed. Gazzaniga, pp. 75–95.

37. Bear, Temporal lobes, pp. 87–88.

38. Ibid.

39. MacLean, Ictal symptoms, p. 87.

40. A. Goldstein, Thrills in response to music and other stimuli, *Physiological Psychology* 8 (1980):126–29.

41. A. H. Rosenfeld, Music: The beautiful disturber, *Psychology Today*, December 1985, 48–56. Quotation on p. 56.

42. Goldstein, Thrills.

43. Rosenfeld, Music, p. 48.

44. Springer and Deutsch, *Left brain, right brain*, p. 255.

45. K. Colby and C. Parkinson, Handedness in autistic children, *Journal of Autism and Childhood Schizophrenia* 7 (1977):3–9.
    E. G. Blackstone, Cerebral asymmetry and the development of early infantile autism, *Journal of Autism and Childhood Schizophrenia* 88 (1978):339–53.

46. G. Dawson, S. Warrenburg, and P. Fuller, Cerebral lateralization in individuals diagnosed as autistic in early childhood, *Brain and Language* 15 (1982):353–68.

47. L. Selfe, *Nadia: A case of extraordinary drawing ability in an autistic child* (New York: Academic Press, 1977).

48. T. R. Insel and D. Pickar, Naloxone administration in obsessive-compulsive disorder: Report of two cases, *American Journal of Psychiatry* 140 (1983):1219–20. Quotation on p. 1219.

49. Ibid.

50. T. R. Insel and D. L. Murphy, The psychopharmacological treatment of obsessive compulsive disorder: A review, *Journal of Clinical Psychopharmacology* 1 (1981):304–11.
    J. A. Yaryura-Tobias and F. A. Neziroglu, *Obsessive-compulsive disorder: Pathogenesis, diagnosis, treatment* (New York: Marcel Dekker, 1984).

51. H. F. Judson, *The search for solutions* (New York: Holt, Rinehart & Winston, 1980), p. 5.

52. Ibid., p. 6.

CHAPTER 9

1. M. B. Green, Superstrings, *Scientific American* 255 (3) (1986):48–60.
   M. Kaku and J. Trainer, *Beyond Einstein* (New York: Bantam, 1987).

2. G. Taubes, Everything's now tied to strings, *Discover*, December 1986, 34–56. Quotation on p. 34.

3. Quoted in J. Maddox, review of *The second creation* by R. P. Crease and C. C. Mann, New York *Times Book Review*, 29 June 1986, 9.

4. R. Browning, Andrea Del Sarto, 1855, *The complete poetical works of Robert Browning*, Cambridge edition (Boston: Houghton-Mifflin, 1895), pp. 346–48. Quotation on p. 346.

5. C. F. Levinthal, *Introduction to physiological psychology*, 2d ed. (Englewood Cliffs, N.J.: Prentice-Hall, 1983).

6. M. Czikszentmihalyi, Reflections on enjoyment, *Perspectives in Biology and Medicine* 28 (1985):489–97.

7. Ibid., p. 496.

8. C. P. Snow, *The Search* (London: Victor Gollancz, 1934). Quoted in H. F. Judson, *The search for solutions* (New York: Holt, Rinehart & Winston, 1980), p. 8.

9. J. Bruner, The conditions of creativity, in *Consciousness: Brain, states of awareness and mysticism,* ed. D. Goleman and R. J. Davidson (New York: Harper & Row, 1979), pp. 58–62. Quotation on p. 58.

10. M. Czikszentmihalyi, The flow experience, in *Consciousness,* p. 65.

11. Ibid.

12. Csikszentmihalyi, Reflections, p. 494.

13. Eagleton's own odyssey, *Time,* 7 August 1972, 14–15.
    Eagleton: After the fall, *Time,* 14 August 1972, 20–21.

14. E. E. Aldrin and W. Warga, *Return to earth* (New York: Random House, 1973).

15. Csikszentmihalyi, Reflections, p. 495.

16. Ibid., p. 491.

17. Quoted in H. F. Judson, *Search for solutions,* p. 69.

18. H. Pagels, *Perfect symmetry* (New York: Simon & Schuster, 1985).

19. J. Huizinga, *Homo ludens: A study of the play-element in culture* (Boston: Beacon Press, 1950), p. 3. Translation from the original German edition, published in 1944.

20. Huizinga, p. 3.

21. A. Goldstein, Endorphins, *The Sciences* 21 (1981):14–19.

22. Quoted in N. Cousins, *Human options* (New York: Norton, 1981), p. 220.

23. T. S. Eliot, Little Gidding, *Collected Poems, 1909–1962* (New York: Harcourt, 1963). Quotation on p. 208.

Index